The Critical Shaw

on

Religion

Edited by

Michel Pharand

Contents

General Editor's Preface

Bernard Shaw is not the household name he once was, but in the 1920s and 1930s he was certainly the world's most famous English-language playwright, and arguably one of the most famous people in the world. His plays were internationally performed and acclaimed, his views on matters great and small were relentlessly solicited by the media, he was pursued by paparazzi long before the word was even invented, the biggest names in politics, the arts, entertainment, even sports—Gandhi, Nehru, Churchill, Rodin, Twain, Wells, Lawrence of Arabia, Elgar, Einstein, Garbo, Chaplin, Stalin, Tunney and many more—welcomed his company, and his correspondents in the tens of thousands of letters he wrote during his long lifetime constitute a veritable who's who of world culture and politics. And Shaw remains the only person ever to have been awarded both a Nobel Prize and an Oscar.

Shaw's reputation rests securely not just on his plays, a dozen or so of which have come to be recognized as classics—*Man and Superman, Major Barbara, Pygmalion,* and *Saint Joan* perhaps now the most familiar of them—but also on his early work as a music, art, literary, and theater critic, and on his lifelong political activism. After he moved to London from his native Dublin in 1876, and after completing five novels, he established himself as one of London's most controversial, feared, and admired critics, and while he eventually retired from earning his living as a critic in order to focus on playwriting, he continued to lecture and write about cultural and other issues—religion, for example—with scorching in-telligence. As for politics, his early commitment to Socialism, and his later expressed admiration for Communism and con-tempt for Capitalism, meant that while his views were relent-lessly refuted by the establishment press they could rarely be ignored—hardly surprising given the logic and passion that underpinned them.

Winston Churchill once declared Shaw to be "the greatest living master of letters in the English-speaking world," and the selections from Shaw's reviews, essays, speeches, and cor-respondence contained in the five volumes of this Critical Shaw series provide abundant evidence to validate Churchill's high regard. Shaw wrote—and spoke—volumi-nously, and his complete works on the topics covered by this series—Literature, Music, Religion, Theater, and Poli-tics—would fill many more than five volumes. The topics reflect Shaw's deepest interests and they inspired some of his most brilliant nondramatic writing. The selections in each volume give a comprehensive and representative survey of his thinking, and show him to be not just the great rhetori-cian that Churchill and others acknowledged, but also one of the great public intellectuals of the twentieth century.

Leonard Conolly
Robinson College, Cambridge
December 2015

Introduction

"As my religious convictions and scientific views cannot at present be more specifically defined than as those of a believer in Creative Evolution I desire that no public monument or work of art or inscription or sermon or ritual service commemorating me shall suggest that I accepted the tenets peculiar to any established Church or denomination nor take the form of a cross or any other instrument of torture or symbol of blood sacrifice."

—Paragraph 4 of Shaw's Last Will and Testament, dated 12 June 1950, quoted in Michael Holroyd, *The Last Laugh* [1992], 101.

Although it would be presumptuous to place Shaw alongside Thomas Aquinas or Martin Luther or Emanuel Swedenborg as a "religious thinker," let alone a theologian, there is no aspect of religious ideology and belief that Shaw, over the course of a very long life, did not question and critique. In his speeches, lectures, essays, prefaces and plays, he commented—often vociferously—on every conceivable facet of "religion" in its broadest sense: on Christianity and the Church, Protestantism and Catholicism, Mormonism and Quakerism, Christian Science and Fundamentalism, Calvinism and Lutheranism, Hinduism and Buddhism, Judaism and Islam, ritualism and idolatry, atheism and agnosticism, atonement and salvation, sin and punishment, the crucifixion and the resurrection, transubstantiation, the Holy Trinity and the Immaculate Conception, prayer, baptism, Saint Paul ("very unchristlike" (page 147)), the Bible, the Ten Commandments ("unsuited and inadequate to modern needs" (page 206)), the *Book of Common Prayer* ("saturated with blood sacrifice beyond all possible revision" (page 224)), the Thirty-nine Articles of the Anglican Church, and the Athanasian Creed. In speech after essay after preface, Shaw relentlessly scrutinizes doctrines and dogma, only to find most of them in need of reform—or scrapping altogether.

Though some "religions and their sects" held his respect—"I am not so bigoted as to dismiss their experience as the inventions of liars and the fancies of noodles" (page 303)—he found it impossible to wholeheartedly accept most of their teachings and precepts. For all of his wide-ranging knowledge of systems of beliefs and their sacred texts, Shaw, in the end, found little in them that satisfied his personal quest for a meaning to life. "At present there is not a single credible established religion in the world," he wrote in his 1906 preface to *Major Barbara* (1905), one of many *bons mots* collected at Positive Atheism's Big List of George Bernard Shaw Quotations. That Shaw has been co-opted as the archetypal atheist is no surprise: he has a great deal to say about atheism, and agnosticism, in many of the thirty-seven selections collected here. "Better atheist than agnostic," he stated in 1911, as "an agnostic is only an atheist without the courage of his opinions" (page 45).

"I preferred to call myself an Atheist," Shaw recalled in 1949, the year before his death at age ninety-four, "because belief in God then meant belief in the old tribal idol called Jehovah" (page 233). That barbarous, tribal and violent aspect of religion is at the very root of Shaw's atheism; so is his abhorrence of the easy rationalization that "the vengeance of a terribly angry god can be bought off by a vicarious and hideously cruel blood sacrifice [that] persists even through the New Testament" (page 206). Shaw denounces on several occasions "the old doctrine of the Atonement, the old idea that in some way or other you could always get rid of your guilt and your responsibility by seizing on some innocent victim and destroying it—sacrificing it, as it was said. Whether that victim was a goat, as in the sacrifice which Abraham substituted for the sacrifice of his own son, or whether, as it afterwards came to be, it was the sacrifice of a man [Christ], still the idea was the same—the notion that in some way or other you could get rid of your guilt or your sin by shifting it on to innocent shoulders" (page 71). This idea of atonement through sacrifice, so fundamental to so many religions, was for Shaw an "abominable doctrine" (page 57) and an unacceptable abrogation of personal responsibility.

Thus, believing that "it is very important we should have a religion of some kind" (page 28), and that "there is not a single creed of an established church on earth at present that I can subscribe to" (page 114), Shaw duly invented a religion and creed of his own. He called his personal credo the Life Force: "a miracle and a mystery, ...an evolutionary appetite for power and knowledge" (page 230) that "proceeds by trial and error and creates the problem of evil by its unsuccessful experiments and its mistakes" (page 238), and what we call "evil is nothing but imperfection" (page 63). The Life Force "has got into the minds of men as what they call their will. Thus we see people who clearly are carrying out a will not exclusively their own" (page 48). Shaw, of course, considered himself one of those people. "There is no God as yet achieved, but there is that force at work making God, struggling through us to become an actual organized existence," he told an audience in 1907, enjoining them to "stand up and say, 'I am God and here is God, not as yet completed, but still advancing towards completion, just in so much as I am working for the purpose of the universe, working for the good of the whole of society and the whole world, instead of merely looking after my personal ends.' In that way... we begin to perceive that the evil of the world is a thing that will finally be evolved out of the world, that it was not brought into the world by malice and cruelty, but by an entirely benevolent designer that had not as yet discovered how to carry out its benevolent intention. In that way I think we may turn towards the future with greater hope" (page 39). In short, "We are experiments in the direction of making God" (page 50), specifically "an omnipotent and benevolent God" (page 64).

This optimistic (if flawed) Life Force, then, which instills in us "courage, self-respect, dignity, and purpose" (page 106), is Shaw's personal alternative to the teachings of the Bible, which nonetheless contains "the best examples in ancient Jewish literature of natural and political history, of poetry, morality, theology, and rhapsody" (page 201). Shaw's remarkably thorough knowledge of the Bible is evidenced by the abundance of quotations and allusions in his speeches and writings. But he was not blind to the shortcomings of its tenets, which he often discounted or disparaged. "The English Bible," he wrote in 1944, "though a masterpiece of literary art in its readable parts, ...is yet a jumble of savage superstitions, obsolete cosmology, and a theology which... recoils into sceptical disillusioned atheistical Pessimism... reverts to blood sacrifice... and finally explodes in a mystical opium dream of an impossible apocalypse" (page 222). How could anyone, he argued, use such a book, with all of its cruelties and mystifications and impossibilities, to guide one's life? For Shaw, writes Warren Sylvester Smith, "Religion must be practical. It must concern itself with justice and economics and the social order and the divine value of life (*Bishop of Everywhere*, p. 53). Expounding at length on that idea in the selections that follow, Shaw links religion to every dimension of life, from political systems (such as Communism) and scientific discoveries (such as natural selection) to marriage, divorce and the education of children.

In addition to his comments on religion and related matters scattered throughout his writings, Shaw wrote a number of full-length works dealing with religious themes. Although too lengthy to be included here, they dramatize many of Shaw's fundamental "religious" ideas and beliefs: *Passion*

Play: A Dramatic Fragment (1878), *Major Barbara* (1905), *The Shewing-up of Blanco Posnet* (1909), *Androcles and the Lion* (1912)—with its 37,000-word "Preface on the Prospects of Christianity" that includes sections on each of the four Gospels—*Saint Joan* (1924), *The Adventures of the Black Girl in Her Search for God* (1932) and *On the Rocks* (1933), which includes a dialogue between Pilate and Jesus. Clearly, a compendium of Shaw's writings on religion—at the platform, in print and onstage—would take up many volumes. In fact Shaw himself had once planned a volume entitled *Religion and Religions*, to be included in an edition of his Collected Works (Laurence *Bibliography* I: 30). Although Shaw abandoned the project, perhaps this Rosetta collection will prove an adequate substitute.

The following selections of Shaw's pronouncements and writings on religion are divided by genre: speeches and lectures, essays and journalism, and prefaces to the plays. Inevitably, context often shapes content. For instance, when at the lectern—or, rather, in the pulpit—Shaw is at his most expansive, often speaking extemporaneously or from only a few notes. But whether speaking to a live audience or writing for a vast readership, Shaw returns time and again to a favorite anecdote—William Blake's "Nobodaddy" and Percy Shelley denouncing God as an "almighty fiend," or Shaw taking out his watch and challenging God to strike him dead in five minutes—or to a favorite biblical passage (Elisha and the bears, Jonah and the whale), and invokes his favorite, like-minded authorities, among them Henri Bergson, Samuel Butler, John Bunyan, Charles Bradlaugh, Charles Darwin, Shelley, Henrik Ibsen, Karl Marx, Voltaire—and of course Shakespeare.

Although Shaw was fond of calling himself an atheist, he nonetheless recognized the necessity and importance of religion. For "without religion men are political time-servers and cowards," he stated in a message to the Shaw Society of

America on the occasion of its foundation on 26 July 1950, his ninety-fourth birthday (quoted in Allan Chappelow, *Shaw the Villager and Human Being* [1961], 334). Neither was Shaw devoid of belief. Take this remarkable passage (published only once before) written in 1922: "Nothing must come between me and the spirit that moves within me; and though I do not walk by the inner light alone, but by all the light I can get, from without or within, yet I must interpret what I see for myself. And if that is not the quintessence of Quakerism, and indeed of genuine Quakerism, I do not know what Quakerism means" (page 164). That "spirit," in which Shaw believed with unshakable certainty, is his own quintessence: the Life Force.

On 27 August 1895, Shaw wrote to bookseller Frederick H. Evans: "I want to write a big book of devotion for modern people, bringing in all the truths latent in the old religious dogmas into contact with real life—a gospel of Shawianity" (*Collected Letters* I:551). Something of a Gospel According to GBS can be found in the following pages.

Bernard Shaw and His Times: A Chronology

[This chronology is common to all five volumes in the Critical Shaw series, and reflects the topics of the series: Politics, Theater, Literature, Music, and Religion. For a comprehensive and detailed chronology of Shaw's life and works, see A. M. Gibbs, A Bernard Shaw Chronology (Basingstoke: Palgrave, 2001).]

1856 Shaw born in Dublin (26 July).

1859 Charles Darwin publishes *On the Origin of Species by Means of Natural Selection.*

1864 Herbert Spencer publishes *Principles of Biology* (and coins the phrase "survival of the fittest").

1865 The Salvation Army is founded by Methodist preacher William Booth.

1870 The doctrine of papal infallibility is defined as dogma at the First Vatican Council.

1876 Shaw moves from Dublin to London. He begins ghostwriting music reviews for Vandeleur Lee for *The Hornet.*

1879 Shaw begins writing music reviews for *The Saturday Musical Review, The Court Journal,* and other publications. He writes his first novel, *Immaturity,* quickly followed by four others: *The Irrational Knot* (1880), *Love Among the Artists* (1881), *Cashel Byron's Profession* (1882), and *An Unsocial Socialist* (1883).

1883   Shaw reads Karl Marx's *Das Kapital* (in a French translation) in the British Museum Reading Room.

1884   The Fabian Society is founded; Shaw joins in the same year. He publishes his first book review in *The Christian Scientist*.

1885   Shaw begins publishing book reviews regularly in *The Pall Mall Gazette*.

1886   Eleanor Marx, daughter of Karl Marx, organizes a reading of Ibsen's *A Doll's House*; Shaw reads the part of Krogstad.

1889   Having written music reviews for over a decade, Shaw becomes a full-time critic for *The Star*, and then (in 1890) *The World*.

1891   Shaw publishes *The Quintessence of Ibsenism* (revised and updated in 1922).

1892   Shaw's first play, *Widowers' Houses*, is performed.

1893   Founding of the Independent Labour Party, a socialist advocacy group.

1894   Shaw resigns from *The World* and henceforth writes only occasional music reviews. *Arms and the Man* is first performed. Shaw becomes acquainted with aspiring theatre critic Reginald Golding Bright.

1895   Shaw becomes full-time drama critic for *The Saturday Review*. He publishes a lengthy review column almost every week for the next two and a half years.

1897   Shaw is elected a member of the Vestry of the Parish of St Pancras (until 1903).

1898 Shaw marries Charlotte Payne-Townshend and resigns as *The Saturday Review* drama critic. He publishes
The Perfect Wagnerite and *Plays: Pleasant and Unpleasant*. One of the "unpleasant" plays, *Mrs Warren's Profession*, is refused a performance licence by the Lord
Chamberlain; the ban will stay in effect until 1924.

1901 *Caesar and Cleopatra* is first performed, with music
written by Shaw. Queen Victoria dies.

1904 J. E. Vedrenne and Harley Granville Barker begin their
management of the Court Theatre (until 1907), with
Shaw as a principal playwright. Eleven Shaw plays are
performed in three seasons.

1905 *Man and Superman* is first performed. Albert Einstein
publishes his theory of relativity.

1906 Founding of the Labour Party. *Major Barbara* and *The
Doctor's Dilemma* are first performed.

1908 *Der tapfere Soldat*, an unauthorized operetta loosely
based on *Arms and the Man*, with music by Oscar
Straus and libretto by Rudolf Bernauer and Leopold
Jacobson, is first performed in Vienna. It is later staged
(1910) in translation as *The Chocolate Soldier*.

1909 *The Shewing-up of Blanco Posnet* is refused a licence by
the Lord Chamberlain. W. B. Yeats and Lady Gregory
stage it at the Abbey Theatre in Dublin. Shaw appears
as a witness before the Joint Select Committee of the
House of Lords and the House of Commons on Stage
Plays (Censorship).

1911 Shaw joins the managing council of the Royal Academy of Dramatic Art. His strong support of RADA's programs will include bequeathing RADA a third of his royalties. Shaw writes an introduction for the Waverley edition of Dickens's *Hard Times*.

1913 *Pygmalion* is first performed.

1914 Beginning of the First World War. Shaw publishes *Common Sense About the War*.

1916 Easter Rising in Dublin against British rule of Ireland.

1917 The Russian Revolution overthrows the imperialist government and installs a communist government under Vladimir Ilyich Lenin. The United States joins the war against Germany. On 17 July Czar Nicholas II and his family are executed.

1918 Representation of the People Act gives the vote to all men over twenty-one, and to women over thirty if they meet certain qualifications (e.g., property owners, university graduates). End of the First World War.

1920 *Heartbreak House* is first performed. Shaw completes *Back to Methuselah*, a five-play cycle on evolutionary themes. League of Nations formed.

1921 The Irish Free State gains independence from Britain. Shaw writes the preface to *Immaturity*.

1922 Joseph Stalin becomes general secretary of the Communist Party Central Committee. Benito Mussolini becomes Italian prime minister.

1923 *Saint Joan* is first performed, with music written by Shaw.

1924 Ramsay MacDonald becomes the first Labour prime minister, in a Labour-Liberal coalition government.

1925 Adolf Hitler publishes *Mein Kampf* [*My Struggle*].

1926 General strike in Great Britain, 4–13 May. Shaw is awarded the 1925 Nobel Prize for Literature.

1928 Representation of the People (Equal Franchise) Act gives the vote to all women over twenty-one. Shaw publishes *The Intelligent Woman's Guide to Socialism and Capitalism*. *The Apple Cart* is first performed.

1929 The Wall Street Crash, 28–29 October, which signalled the beginning of the Great Depression. Shaw speaks as a delegate to the third International Congress of the World League for Sexual Reform. Sir Barry Jackson establishes the Malvern Festival, dedicated to Shaw's plays.

1931 Shaw visits Russia. He celebrates his seventy-fifth birthday on 26 July in Moscow's Concert Hall of Nobles with two thousand guests. He meets Stalin on 29 July.

1932 Unemployment reaches 3.5 million in Great Britain. South Wales and the industrial north experience mass unemployment and poverty. *Too True to Be Good* receives its English première at the Malvern Festival.

1933 Shaw makes his first visit to the United States. He speaks to an audience of thirty-five hundred at the Metropolitan Opera House (11 April). Hitler becomes German chancellor.

1934 *The Six of Calais* is first performed.

1936 Shaw makes his second (and last) visit to the United States. *The Millionairess* is first performed.

1938 *Geneva* is first performed. Shaw rejects a proposal from producer Gabriel Pascal for a musical version of *Pygmalion*.

1939 Beginning of the Second World War.

1941 The United States enters the Second World War.

1943 Charlotte Shaw dies.

1944 Shaw publishes *Everybody's Political What's What?*

1945 End of the Second World War. United Nations formed. The UK Labour Party wins its first majority government. Clement Attlee becomes prime minister. His government implements an extensive nationalization program of British industry and services.

1947 Discovery of the Dead Sea Scrolls in Qumran Caves, West Bank.

1948 World Council of Churches founded in Amsterdam.

1950 Shaw publishes his last book review in *The Observer* (26 March). He dies in Ayot St Lawrence, Hertfordshire (2 November).

A Note on the Text

Sources for the selections of Shaw's writings on religion are given in the heading for each selection. Full bibliographical details for the sources, when not included in the heading, are provided in Sources and Further Reading, where secondary sources on Shaw's religious writings are also listed. Shaw's original spelling and punctuation have been retained. All ellipses inserted in the text are editorial. Brief explanatory notes are included in square brackets. In cases where there are multiple references to the same person or event, the note is given only for the first reference.

Part I. Speeches and Lectures

1. "The Religion of the British Empire," address at the City Temple, London, 22 November 1906. [*Religious Speeches*, pp. 1–8]

[Recorded in Christian Commonwealth *27 (29 November 1906). Revised as "Bernard Shaw's Idea of God" in* New York American *(6 January 1907). After discussing "the religious man," Shaw turns to the "evolutionary process [which] to me is God: this wonderful will of the universe, struggling and struggling." Although not named here, this is the Life Force, which Shaw believed worked through him; as he says below, "I am doing God's work in the world."]*

I begin with a remark that might go without saying, though perhaps, remembering the place in which I speak, it is as well to make it clear that nobody but myself is responsible for what I say. My first proposition is that you can't have an Empire without a religion, and my next is that if the Empire is to be a real thing at all the people in it must believe the same truth—though it does not matter what legends they accept or what imagery they use. [...]

Let me define for you a religious man as I see him: He is a very rare being, and sometimes a very dangerous one, but he is a man who has a constant sense, amounting on his part to a positive knowledge, that he is only the instrument of a power which is a universal power, the power that created the universe and brought it into being, that he is not in the world for his own narrow purposes, but that he is the instrument of that power.

Given that belief, it is of no consequence what else a man might hold; without it, a man has no religion in him. The great tragedy of human character is human cowardice. We pretend that we are brave men, but the reason why a nation will allow nothing to be said against its courage is because it knows it has none. Without fear we could not live a single day; if you were not afraid of being run over, you would be run over before you got home. What will really nerve a man, what, as history has shown over and over again, will turn a coward into a brave man, is the belief that he is the instrument of a larger and higher power. What he makes of this conviction and the power it gives depends upon his brain or conscience.

There are people who imagine that they have apologized for everything when they say, "I did my best. I acted according to my conscience." But that is not enough. The one thing you will never get in this life is any simple rule of conduct that will get you through life. From that point of view, I ventured the other day in Manchester to criticize the idea—it is the idea of the old [Jewish] Pharisees [who preached strict observance of religious practices and adherence to written law]—of those people who think they have done everything when they have kept the Ten Commandments, I insisted that that did not get them a bit further in the direction of refinement. That is the specially Christian point of view, no discovery of mine, and yet when I uttered this old commonplace of Christianity, [Edmund Knox (1847–1937)] the Bishop of Manchester [1903–21] almost went into fits, denounced me in unmeasured terms for having ventured to deny that you can make the keeping of the commandments, and so on, a quite sufficient rule of life: whereas I was perfectly easily able to show, as I could show you tonight, that almost all the commandments, with perhaps two exceptions, are commandments which we ought very frequently to break as a simple matter of public and private duty.

One of the difficulties of really able and earnest ministers of religion in this country is that they cannot get their own congregations to understand how little difference there is between them and other persons who belong to other sects and congregations. I have never had any difficulty whatever in getting on with religious people; it is the irreligious people that I can't get on with. If I write a play, and critics begin to rave about my mocking at religion and my bad taste, you will find that the notice does not breathe the spirit of religion, and that the writer, though he may be a very clever and honest man, has not the slightest idea of what religion means. Furthermore, he represents a very widespread feeling in this country that any man who makes an attempt to apply religion to the actual affairs of life ought to be suppressed.

The average man of today knows and admits that he has religious duties, and knows that if they are taken seriously they conflict very seriously with his daily practice in business. Therefore he says, "I can't always be bothering with religion, I have certain religious duties, but I can't always be attending to them, and therefore I want to have a particular day set apart to keep it holy. I will do all my business on the six days and all my religion on the seventh, and then they will never come into conflict. You make that arrangement, and I will come down handsome, and build your churches and pay your stipends and keep things going for you." For myself, I like to have a little religion every day of my life. I may not keep Sunday holy in such a tremendous manner as the ordinary city man does, but then I don't altogether secularize Monday and the other days. I find life goes on best when I spread my religion over all the week.

The religious life is a happy life. Because I do not eat meat and drink whisky, people think I am an ascetic. I am not. I am a voluptuary! I avoid eating meat because it is a nasty thing to eat; I avoid drinking whisky because it gives me unpleasant and disagreeable sensations. I want to live the pleasantest sort of life I possibly can. What I like is not what people call pleasure, which is the most dreadful and boring thing on the face of the earth, but life itself. And that of course is the genuinely religious view to take, because life is a very wonderful thing. Life is this force outside yourself that you are in the hands of. You must not forget that the ordinary man who is not religious, who does not know that he is an instrument in the hands of the higher power, is nevertheless such an instrument all the time.

While I have been describing the religious man you have been saying, "That's me!" and while I have been describing the irreligious man you have been saying "That's Jones!" But I don't want you to feel uncharitable towards Jones. Although only an agricultural laborer, Jones may be doing the work of the universe in a more efficient way than the man who has become conscious of the higher power and brought his own mind to bear upon it, but not having a first-rate mind, and being mixed up with purely rationalistic theories of the universe, he may be doing a great deal of mischief, doing something to defeat the higher power. For it is possible to defeat that power, as I shall presently show.

Any personal belief is a document, at any rate. You may think mine fantastic, even paradoxical. I have more or less swallowed all the formulas, I have been in all the churches, studied all the religions with a great deal of sympathy, and I will tell you where I have come out. Most people call this great force in the universe God. I am not very fond of this form myself, because it is a little too personal, too close to the idea of the elderly gentleman with the beard. But we won't quarrel about the term. To me the higher power is something larger than a personal force. But even the people who would agree with me there still cling to the idea that it is an almighty force, that it is a force which can directly and immediately do what it likes. But if so, why in the name of common sense did he make such creatures as you and I? If he wants his will fulfilled on earth, why did he put himself in the position of having to have that will fulfilled by our actions? Because what is done in this world has to be done by us.

We know that a lot of work lies before us. What we call civilization has landed us in horrible iniquities and injustices. We have got to get rid of them, and it has to be done by us. There is the dilemma. Why is it not done by God? I believe

God, in the popular acceptance of the word, to be completely powerless. I do not believe that God has any hands or brain of our kind. What I know he has, or rather is, is will. But will is useless without hands and brain.

Then came a process which we call evolution, I do not mean natural selection as popularized [in *On the Origin of Species* (1859)] by Charles Darwin [1809–82]. He did not discover or even popularize evolution; on the contrary, he drove evolution out of men's minds for half a century, and we have only just got it back again. The general doctrine of evolution shows how, out of a perfectly amorphous form of life, something which we picture to ourselves as a little speck of protoplasm in a wonderful way by constant effort and striving evolved higher and higher forms of life, until gradually you have a thing so comparatively wonderful as men and women. That evolutionary process to me is God: this wonderful will of the universe, struggling and struggling, bit by bit making hands and brains for himself, feeling that, having this will, he must also have material organs with which to grapple with material things. And that is the reason we have come into existence.

If you don't do his work it won't be done; if you turn away from it, if you sit down and say, "Thy will be done," you might as well be the most irreligious person on the face of the earth. But if you will stand by your God, if you will say, "My business is to do your will, my hands are your hands, my tongue is your tongue, my brain is your brain, I am here to do thy work, and I will do it," you will get rid of otherworldliness, you will get rid of all that religion which is made an excuse and a cloak for doing nothing, and you will learn not only to worship your God, but also to have a fellow feeling with him.

This conception that I am doing God's work in the world gives me a certain self-satisfaction—not with the limitations of my power and the extravagance of my brain or hand—but a certain self-respect and force in the world. People like their religion to be what they call comforting. I want my religion to give me self-respect and courage, and I can do without comfort, without happiness, without everything else. This sort of faith really overcomes the power of death.

This brings me to my last heresy. I never can really respect a religion which postulates the ordinary conception of a personal immortality. You have not overcome the fear of death until you delight in your own life, believing it to be the carrying-out of the universal purpose, until you are perfectly ready to let the life that is in your brain and hand go into another brain and hand, and no longer cling to your miserable individual life.

I do not want to try and drag you to that point tonight. I have only been trying to show you one or two landmarks as they appear to me. I do not ask you to agree. I need not ask you to be shocked. I have offered you my own living convictions for what they are worth. I only ask you to think about them, and I think you will admit that, leaving out details, the spirit of what I have said is the spirit in which perhaps all the really effective men in the Empire and in the world are working together at the present time, and in that working together we have some real hope for the future of humanity.

2. "The New Theology," address at the Kensington Town Hall, London, 16 May 1907. [*Religious Speeches*, pp. 9–19]

[*Published in* Christian Commonwealth *(23 and 30 May 1907) and, abridged, in the* Los Angeles Examiner *(21 July 1907). Members of the controversial New Theology movement questioned, among other things, the accepted origins of biblical texts. (For its leading exponent, R. J. Campbell, see page 40) Here Shaw discusses Liberal MP and militant atheist Charles Bradlaugh (1833–91), founder (in 1866) of the National Secular Society, and the impact of Darwin, who "abolished adaptation and design" and (quoting Butler) "banished mind from the universe." Shaw concludes that "the aim of the New Theology [is] to conceive of the force behind the universe as working up through imperfection and mistake to a perfect, organized being." In short, to God.]*

When I last stood on this platform, I said there was not a single established religion in the world in which an intelligent or educated man could believe. Some feeling has been shown by those who have quoted that statement that somehow or other it is my fault, and I am not altogether disposed to deny it. A person who points out a thing of which the mass of people are unconscious really does to some extent create the thing which he points out, I remember not very long ago rolling up my sleeves to the elbow in order to wash my hands, and, as I have a great deal to think about, including the New Theology, I am sometimes rather absent minded. The consequence was that I forgot to roll down my sleeves, and walked about two miles in the west of London until I met a friend, who said, "What on earth are you going about in that fashion for?" Now, as I did not know that my sleeves were rolled up, they were not rolled up so far as I was concerned until that intrusive friend came and quite unnecessarily called my attention to the fact, covering me with blushes and confusion. And so my remark here last year may have destroyed the authenticity of established religions for many persons who up to that moment had believed that those religions, being established, were all right.

I want to see whether there is any possibility of our arriving at a religion on which we can agree, because it is very important we should have a religion of some kind. I know that that is quite a fashionable opinion, but we have got out of the habit of thinking that we ought to believe in the religion we have. Hardly any person in London believes in the religion he professes. Now let us come to the New Theology. It is not my habit, nor the habit of any really judicious lecturer, to begin by definitions, and when I do, I decline to be held by them. I do not address myself to your logical faculties, but as one human mind trying to put himself in contact with other human minds. By theology I really do mean the science of godhead, and I want to examine whether we have made any advance in the science, whether there is a science of it in which we can believe and on which we can get a pretty general agreement. I shall have to go back a considerable distance, because I want to make you aware of the state of your mind on the question. I am quite certain that you do not know it, unless you are familiar with the religious history of the nineteenth century, perhaps the wickedest in all human history.

When I came to London, at about the beginning of the last quarter of the nineteenth century, I found people in a very curious state as regards their religious belief. This was illustrated by something that happened at a bachelor party I attended in Kensington not far from this hall a short time after I arrived. I found myself in the company of a number of young men who either belonged to, or were qualifying for, one of the liberal professions, and they got into a dispute about religion. At this time the late Charles Bradlaugh was very notorious for the militant campaign he was carrying on as an atheist [one who rejects belief in any deity]. One of the persons present, representing what was supposed to be the pious and religious side in the controversy, accused Bradlaugh of having publicly taken out his watch and challenged the Almighty, if he had the power and will to do so, to strike him dead in five minutes. An admirer and adherent of Bradlaugh vehemently denied that story, saying it was a gross calumny. The gentleman who made the accusation took the old-fashioned view; it had prevailed in this country for about three hundred years, that very dark period in which Christians, instead of being Christians in any reasonable sense, worshipped the Bible as a talisman. For instance, in tract shops you saw copies of the Bible exhibited with the dent of a bullet in them, and you were given to understand that the soldier who had in his pocket a testament given him by his mother had been saved from death because the book had stopped the enemy's bullet. The gentleman who told the story about Mr. Bradlaugh was a Bible worshipper, and believed, among other things, the story in the Bible [in 2 Kings 2:23–25] that when Elisha the prophet was mocked because of his bald head by some young children, God sent a couple of bears out of a wood to eat those children. And the extraordinary thing is that the gentleman worshipped the God who did that! If you or I confessed doing such a thing as that probably we should be torn to pieces. But it was a common article of belief at that time that the universe was ruled by a God who was that particular sort of person, an exceedingly spiteful person, capable of taking the most ferocious revenge.

I was very much puzzled by the impassioned way in which the gentleman who was a secularist defended Charles Bradlaugh against the imputation of having taken out his watch and made this challenge, and when my turn came to speak, or rather when I spoke—I am not always in the habit of waiting for my turn exactly—I said that if the question which Charles Bradlaugh was dealing with was whether a God of that kind existed, the reported experiment seemed to me perfectly legitimate and natural and to deny the existence of such a God appeared to me to be a far more genuine religious position than that of the people who affirmed belief in him. I say it seemed to me perfectly natural and proper, if the ruler of the universe were really the petty, spiteful criminal he was represented to be, for a man who denied his existence to take his watch out of his pocket and, instead of troubling about what happened many centuries ago, to ask him to strike him dead at the end of five minutes. I said, "Since it appears that Mr. Bradlaugh never made this experiment, I, regarding it as a perfectly legitimate one, will try it myself," and with that I took my watch out of my pocket.

I have never done anything in public or private which produced such an instantaneous and extraordinary effect. Up to that moment the company had been divided into a pious and a skeptical party, but it now appeared that there were no sceptics present at all. Every one of them felt it to be extremely probable that before the five minutes were up I should be taken at my word. One of the party appealed to us to turn the conversation to a more lively channel, and a gentleman present who had a talent for singing comic songs sat down at the piano and sang the most melancholic comic song I ever heard in my life.

The incident has its amusing side, but it also has its tragic side. It is a frightful thing that it should have been possible so recently as twenty-five years ago for a party of educated men to be in that state of superstition. I am not at all certain that I have not made some of those I address very uncomfortable by what I have just said. Well, I intend to go on making people who hold such views uncomfortable. I want to make them understand in a very vivid way that it is quite impossible at this time of day to unite the world or appeal to our highest intelligence or better natures by preaching that particular sort of God. It was the preaching of that kind of tribal idol that accounted for Charles Bradlaugh calling himself an atheist, and, disbelieving with my whole soul in such a being, I always did what Charles Bradlaugh did: made myself intelligible to those people who worship such a monster by saying that I was an atheist. And in that sense I still am an atheist, as it must seem to me every humane person must be. That kind of God is morally inconceivable. The God who would send bears to eat up little children would be a wicked God—what [Percy Bysshe] Shelley [1792–1822] called [in *Queen Mab; A Philosophical Poem: With Notes* (1813)] an Almighty Fiend. Why did not Shelley's protest produce very much impression on the people of this country? Because, believing he was an Almighty Fiend, they feared and obeyed him very largely as such and supposed that if they told him the truth to his face he would probably strike them dead for blasphemy. They saw that there was a great deal of terrible cruelty in the world, which rather confirmed the idea that the force at the back of things was wicked and cruel, and therefore the denunciation of Shelley and others of the current conception of God as immoral did not remove the presumption that he existed.

There was another reason why these people had to believe in God: Everywhere in nature they saw evidence of design. It was no use telling them the universe was the result of blind chance. They said, "If you look around, if you note all that we are told even by scientific men about the marvelous adaptation of means to end, if you consider such a miraculous thing as the human eye, it is impossible for us to believe that these things came into existence without a designer, and we cannot blind ourselves to the fact that the designer is apparently cruel. We see plague, pestilence, and famine, battle, murder, and sudden death; we see out parents dying of cancer, our children dying of diphtheria. We may not dare to say that the power that wills that is cruel; it might bring worse consequences on us. But the cruelty is no reason for our ceasing to believe in its existence." And so, neither science on the one hand, nor the moral remonstrances of Shelley and his school on the other, were able to shake the current belief in that old theology that came back to the old tribal idol, Jehovah [or Yahweh, the name of the God of Israel in the Old Testament].

I hope that I have produced a sufficiently gloomy impression upon you! The reason I have been putting the matter as I have is that I want to bring into your minds very strongly the fact that in the middle of the last century all the mind, conscience, and intelligence of the best part of mankind was in revolt against the old-fashioned conception of God, and yet at the same time finding itself intellectually unable to get away from the conception of God the Designer. They were in a dilemma. There must be what they called God, and yet they could not make him responsible for the good in the world without making him also responsible for the evil, because they never questioned one thing about him: that, being the designer of the universe, he must necessarily be omnipotent. This being the situation, it is not clear that if at that time any man had risen up and said, "All this wonderful adaptation of means to end, all this design which seems to imply a designer, is an illusion; it may have all come about by the operation of what we call blind chance," the most intelligent and best part of the human race, without stopping to criticize his argument very closely, would spring at that man and take him to their arms as their moral savior, saying, "You have lifted from our minds this horrible conception that the force that is governing us all and is managing the whole world is hideous, criminal, cruel"? That is exactly what happened when Charles Darwin appeared and the reason why he had such an enormous success that the religion of the last half of the nineteenth century became Darwinian. Many people are under the impression that Darwinism meant that the world had been converted to a belief in evolution. That is a mistake; exactly the contrary has happened. Darwin was really the man who completely turned the attention of mankind from the doctrine of evolution.

Evolution is a vital part of the New Theology, but it sprang into something like completeness as a conception at the end of the eighteenth century, when all the great evolutionists, including [physician and physiologist] Erasmus Darwin [1731–1802], grandfather of Charles Darwin, brought out their books and developed the whole system. The main thing by which they astonished the world was by attacking the old conception of creation in the Garden of Eden. The amazing conception that thought of all life on this planet as having evolved from a little speck of slime in a ditch struck the world dumb. Erasmus Darwin justified the theology of it by sating, "Is not the conception that men have been developed from a speck of protoplasm much more wonderful than that the world and everything in it was made in six days?" The conception took hold of people, and its chief exponent was the great [biologist and] philosopher [Jean-Baptiste] Lamarck [1744–1829], a Frenchman who began life as a soldier and ended it as a naturalist. In one of his books Lamarck gave an illustration of the process of evolution. He said the reason that the giraffe had a long neck is that this creature wanted to feed on the soft herbage on the top of tall trees, and by dint of generations of giraffes stretching their necks, they gradually made their necks longer, until they could reach the requisite height. Now, that means that the giraffe got a long neck because it wanted a long neck—just in the same way that you learn to ride a bicycle or to speak French because you want to do so.

Well, in the year 1830, the scientific world got tired of generalizing and, instead of forming great cosmic theories, devoted itself to the study of isolated phenomena, assisted by the microscope, and shortly after this time Charles Darwin came on the scene. I am convinced that the accusations made against Darwin of having deliberately suppressed the debt that civilization owed to his grandfather for the discovery of evolution were entirely unjust, because I don't believe that Charles Darwin knew anything about evolution, or that to the end of his life he ever understood the whole theory or what it meant. From boyhood he delighted in frogs and pigeons and was the greatest pigeon fancier that ever lived. The real thing that enabled Charles Darwin to come to different conclusions from other naturalists was that between the time of the evolutionists of 1790–1830 and Charles Darwin's discovery in his book, *The Origin of Species*, the researches of the great biologist [and geologist Charles] Lyell [1797–1875] led him to teach the world that the stratification and formation of rocks and mountains in order to be scientifically accounted for forced us to assign a much greater age to the earth than had hitherto been assigned. Our grandfathers had always been taught, on the authority of [Irish] Archbishop [of Armagh James] Ussher [(1581–1656), in his *Annales* (1650)], that the world was 6,006 years old [created in 4004 BCE], and some people had actually discovered the actual day of the month when creation began. This present of millions of years gave time for Darwin's theory of natural selection. Now let us apply this theory to the case of the giraffe. Lamarck's theory implied purpose and will, and, remember, if there is purpose and will in a microbe there must be purpose and will through the whole universe. But Darwin said, in effect, "I can explain the giraffe's long neck without implying the slightest purpose or will. What really happened was this: The number of giraffes multiplied until they began to prey on the means of subsistence—until they bit off all the leaves on the tree within their reach, and then they found themselves starving. But supposing, by one of those little accidents and variations that will always occur—we do not know how—a few giraffes happened to have necks a little longer than the others, they would be able to reach vegetation, while their less fortunate fellows starved. Consequently the longer-necked giraffes would survive while the others perished and produce a race of giraffes with necks a little longer, and this without purpose or design."

My difficulty in putting this apparently commonplace story of the giraffe before a modern audience is to make them understand the unspeakable and frightful prospect opened to the world by Darwin. He abolished adaptation and design, and, as [novelist and satirist] Samuel Butler [1835–1902] said, banished mind from the universe, which was a great relief to many Englishmen who greatly dislike anything in the shape of reflection. Considering that there are and necessarily must be a large number of consciously religious men always living, and that everyone of us has a considerable religious element in him and could not exist without it, why was it that the naked horror of Darwin's conception did not strike them? I have already given you the explanation; it is Elisha and the bears again. The world had got so horrified by the old theology, with its conception of a spiteful, narrow, wicked, personal God, who was always interfering and doing stupid things—often cruel things—that for the moment it could feel nothing but relief at having got rid of such a God altogether. It did not feel the void at first. A man with a bad toothache only thinks of getting rid of the tooth; it is not till afterwards he discovers that he must have a new tooth if he is to go on eating and keep his digestion in order. So people said, "Now that we have got rid of the old conception of religion we will believe in science and evolution." Of course, they knew nothing about evolution; they thought that natural selection, Darwin's discovery, was evolution. Darwin merely turned the attention of mankind to the effects of natural selection; he did not deal with the real problem of evolution. Samuel Butler and others were very soon able to show that it was no use denying the existence of purpose and will in the universe; they were conscious themselves of having purpose, will, design. Then came the discovery of the weak point of the natural selection theory: that it not only did away with the necessity for design and purpose, but with the necessity for consciousness. Men were able to demonstrate that, according to the theory of natural selection, it was perfectly possible that all the books in the British Museum might have been written, all the pictures in the National Gallery might have been painted, all the cathedrals of Europe might have been built, automatically, without one person concerned in the process having been conscious of what he was doing. Some of the natural selectionists used to make the demonstration themselves with a certain pride in doing so. But the common sense of mankind said, "If all the operations of the species can be accounted for without consciousness, intelligence, or design, you have still got to account for the consciousness, intelligence, and design that undoubtedly exist in man." The religious people naturally turn this argument to account, saying, "It is all very well to say that life is a mere pursuit of pleasure and gain, but many men do not live in order to get a balance of pleasure over pain; you see everywhere men doing work that does not benefit them—they call it God's work; natural selection cannot account for that. There is behind the universe an intelligent and driving force of which we ourselves are a part—a divine spark."

After the Darwins and Lyell and Samuel Butler had had their say, the difficulty presented was this: How are we to retain the notion of design without going back to the idea that the design is the work of a cruel designer? The trouble, as usual, was that we had been making the entirely gratuitous assumption that the force behind the universe is omnipresent. Now, you cannot prove that that force is at once omnipresent and benevolent. If omnipresent, why did it create us? If there are three orders of existence—man as we know him, the angels higher than man, and God higher than the angels—why did God first create something lower than himself, the angels, and then actually create something lower than the angels, man? I cannot believe in a God who would do that. If I were God, I should try to create something higher than myself, and then something higher than that, so that, beginning with a God the highest thing in creation, I should end with a God the lowest thing in creation. This is the conception you must get into your head if you are to be free from the horrible old idea that all the cruelty in the world is the work of an omnipresent God, who if he liked could have left the cruelty out of creation, who instead of creating us.... Just think about yourselves, ladies and gentlemen. I do not want to be uncomplimentary, but can you conceive God deliberately creating you if he could have created anything better?

What you have got to understand is that somehow or other there is at the back of the universe a will, a life-force. You cannot think of him as a person, you have to think of him as a great purpose, a great will, and, furthermore, you have to think of him as engaged in a continual struggle to produce something higher and higher, to create organs to carry out his purpose; as wanting hands, and saying, "I must create something with hands"; arriving at that very slowly, after innumerable experiments and innumerable mistakes, because this power must be proceeding as we proceed, because if there were any other way it would put us in that way: we know that in all the progress we make we proceed by way of trial and error and experiment. Now conceive of the force behind the universe as a bodiless, impotent force, having no executive power of its own, wanting instruments, something to carry out its will in the world, making all manner of experiments, creating reptiles, birds, animals, trying one thing after another, rising higher and higher in the scale of organism, and finally producing man, and then inspiring that man, putting his will into him, getting him to carry out his purpose, saying to him, "Remember, you are not here merely to look after yourself. I have made your hand to do my work; I have made your brain, and I want you to work with that and try to find out the purpose of the universe; and when one instrument is worn out, I will make another, and another, always more and more intelligent and effective." One difficulty is that so many of the earlier efforts of this world-force—for example, the tiger—remain, and the incompatibility between them and man exists in the human being himself as the result of early experiments, so that there are certain organs in your body which are perishing away and are of no use and actually interfere with your later organs. And here you have, it seems to me, the explanation of that great riddle which used to puzzle people—evil and pain.

Numbers of things which are at present killing and maiming us in our own organism have got to be evolved out of that organism, and the process is painful. The object of the whole evolutionary process is to realize God; that is to say, instead of the old notion that creation began with a God, a personal being, who, being perfect, created something lower than himself, the aim of the New Theology is to turn that process the other way and to conceive of the force behind the universe as working up through imperfection and mistake to a perfect, organized being, having the power of fulfilling its highest purpose. In a sense there is no God as yet achieved, but there is that force at work making God, struggling through us to become an actual organized existence, enjoying what to many of us is the greatest conceivable ecstasy, the ecstasy of a brain, an intelligence, actually conscious of the whole, and with executive force capable of guiding it to a perfectly benevolent and harmonious end. That is what we are working to. When you are asked, "Where is God? Who is God?" stand up and say, "I am God and here is God, not as yet completed, but still advancing towards completion, just in so much as I am working for the purpose of the universe, working for the good of the whole of society and the whole world, instead of merely looking after my personal ends." In that way we get rid of the old contradiction, we begin to perceive that the evil of the world is a thing that will finally be evolved out of the world, that it was not brought into the world by malice and cruelty, but by an entirely benevolent designer that had not as yet discovered how to carry out its benevolent intention. In that way I think we may turn towards the future with greater hope.

It had been my intention when I began to make the few introductory remarks which I have just delivered the first part of my lecture and then to go on applying that to existing religion, to deal with the actual [thirty-nine] articles [established in 1563 and which define the doctrine] of the [Anglican] Church of England, and to show how much of this truth that I have been teaching tonight is to be found in them. You will find a great deal of this truth in them and in your Bible and in all the religious books of the world. You will find it in the modern poets. When you once seize this you will find that this idea is no idle heresy or paradox of mine, but that it has been germinating in people's minds for a century and for much more than that in the great poets and leaders of mankind.

3. "The Ideal of Citizenship," address at the City Temple, London, 11 October 1909. [*Religious Speeches*, pp. 20–28]

[*Published as an appendix to R. J. Campbell,* The New Theology *(London: Mills & Boon, 1909). Avowed Socialist and charismatic Congregationalist pastor Reginald John Campbell (1867–1956), who had published his highly controversial New Theology in 1907, was minister (1903–15) at the City Temple, the famous Nonconformist church. When Campbell became an Anglican priest in 1915, he recanted his New Theology and repudiated much of his book. Here Shaw discusses the nature of skepticism in relation to the miracle of the raising of Lazarus from the dead.*]

Mr. Campbell, Ladies and Gentlemen: I suppose I have addressed as many hopeful progressive leagues as any man in London. I have sampled them nearly all for the last thirty years, but I think this is the first time I have addressed one in the City Temple. [...] Mr. Campbell has described you as religious people. Well, if you are really religious people, you are really dangerous people, for, after the experience that I have had of various forward movements, I have discovered that the only people who are dangerous are the religious people. [...]

I want to go back even more than thirty years during which I have been addressing progressive leagues. I want to go back to my own childhood. Also, finding myself in the City Temple, I want to yield to an irresistible temptation to tell a profane story, and it will not only be a very profane story, but it will be a true story, and it will have a certain illustrative value. Now try to imagine me, a very small boy, with my ears very wide open, in what [lay theologian and writer] Mr. Gilbert K. Chesterton [(1874–1936), author of *George Bernard Shaw* (1909)] calls my "narrow, Puritan home." Well, on the occasion which I am going to recall, there were in that narrow, Puritan home three gentlemen who were having what they believed to be a very heated discussion about religion. One was my father, another my maternal uncle, and the third a visitor of ours. The subject of the dispute was the raising of Lazarus. Only one of the parties took what would then, I think, have been called the Christian view. I shall call it the evangelical view, a less compromising term. That view was that the raising of Lazarus [in John 11:1–44] occurred exactly as it is described in the Gospels. I shouldn't object to call that the Christian view of it had not involved the opinion, very popular among religious people at that time, that the reason why you admired Jesus and followed Jesus was that he was able to raise people from the dead. Perhaps the reason why some of them always spoke very respectfully of him was a sort of feeling in their mind that a man who could raise people from the dead might possibly on sufficient provocation reverse the operation. However, one of the parties took this view. Another, the visitor, took the absolutely sceptical view; he said that such a thing had never happened—that such stories were told of all great teachers of mankind—that it was more probable that a storyteller was a liar than that a man could be raised from the dead. But the third person, my maternal uncle, took another view; he said that the miracle was what would be called in these days a put-up job, by which he meant that Jesus had made a confederate of Lazarus—had made it worth his while, or had asked him for friendship's sake, to pretend he was dead and at the proper moment to pretend to come to life. Now imagine me as a little child listening to this discussion! I listened with very great interest, and I confess to you that the view which recommended itself most to me was that of my maternal uncle. I think, on reflection, you will admit that that was the natural and healthy side for a growing boy to take, because my maternal uncle's view appealed to the sense of humor, which is a very good thing and a very human thing, whereas the other two views—one appealing to our mere credulity and the other to mere scepticism—really did not appeal to anything at all that had any genuine religious value. I therefore contend that I was right in taking what was at any rate the most amusing point of view. I think you will see that there was a certain promise of salvation in the fact that at that time one of the most popular writers on Bible subjects was [American novelist] Mark Twain [(1835–1910), author of *Christian Science* (1907)], and Mark Twain mostly made fun of them.

But now I want to come to the deeper significance of this scene. The one thing that never occurred to these three men who were urgently disputing was that they were disputing about a thing of no importance whatever. They believed they were disputing about a thing of supreme importance. The evangelical really believed that if he let the miracle of the raising of Lazarus go he was letting Christianity and religion go. The sceptic believed that to disprove the story of the raising of Lazarus was to make a clean sweep of the Bible from one end to the other, and on the whole fabric of religion. Supposing any person had come into that room and said, "Gentlemen, why are you wasting so many words about this? Suppose you take out of the Gospels the story of the raising of Lazarus, what worse are the Gospels, and what worse is Christianity? Supposing even that you add to them another half a dozen raisings from the dead, how much stronger is the position, how much happier is anybody for it?" As a matter of fact, I think such a sensible person would have admitted that my maternal uncle had the best of the situation, as he did squeeze a sort of pitiful laugh out of the controversy, which was the most that was to be got out of it. Yet that really was the tone of religious controversy at that time, and it almost always showed us the barrenness on the side of religion much more than it did on the side of scepticism.

If you come to the sort of religious controversies that are started nowadays—and started very largely by Mr. Campbell—you will find that they are a very much more enlightened kind—that the beliefs from which they start are different. For instance, a man spoke to me lately of the early Christians and of the founder of Christianity. "Well," I said, "I am not exactly an expert on these matters, but you appear to be speaking of Jesus as the founder of Christianity and of the apostles as early Christians. If I am correctly informed by an authority for whom I have very great respect—and he is the preacher at the City Temple—Jesus was not an early Christian. He was a late Christian; his enemies might almost be inclined to sneer at him as a decadent Christian." Now, if you get men thoroughly to realize that Jesus did not come at the beginning of a movement which never did begin except in the sense perhaps that the world itself began somewhere, if you get people suddenly to shift their point of view so decidedly as to see him as the summit and climax of a movement, and then begin to ask why it changed after his death, you then have something worth disputing about. You see men with their minds moved instead of their tempers. You begin to count these men as religious men, and it is the fact that such a change has really taken place that gives me some

sort of hope that something may come of your Progressive
League. [...]

4. "The Religion of the Future," address to the Heretics Society, Cambridge, 29 May 1911. [*Religious Speeches*, pp. 29–37]

[*Based on reports reprinted by the Heretics Society in a pamphlet dated 11 July 1911. Shaw expands on how natural selection banished "the God of cancer, epilepsy and war" but also "purpose or design in the universe," explaining that "the typhoid bacillus" is merely "one of the failures of the life-force that we call God," a force "trying through our brains to discover some method of destroying that malign influence."*]

A Heretic is like a man with a mechanical genius who begins tinkering with a bicycle or a motor car and makes it something different from what the manufacturer has made it. Such a man is a heretic in mechanics; he has a mind and a genius which enables him to choose for himself. If he has a bad motor car he makes a good one of it—he makes it to suit himself. The Heretic is a sort of person who, no matter what religion is supplied at the shop—by which I mean the nearest church—he will tinker at it until he makes it what he thinks it should be. The Heretic is really a man with homemade religion, and if a man can make a religion for himself at home we need not bother about him—he will make his religion to suit himself. What we want to trouble about is the great mass of people who take religion as they find it—as they get it at the shop. What the Heretics have to do is to prepare a ready-made religion for the next generation for the people who have to accept religion as it comes. It is of the most enormous importance for any community what ready-made article they are supplying in their schools and churches, as a religion, to the community. Therefore, when I am dealing with the reli-

gion of the future, remember that I am not dealing with what
the Heretics of the next generation will be talking about.
They will be discussing and criticizing whatever the religion
is, and the great mass of the people will be outside and will
have a ready-made religion and will obey laws founded on
that religion, many of them founded more or less on the idea
that certain courses of conduct are more or less displeasing to
whatever force might be moving the world—the main-spring
which at present we call God, and might call other names in
future—at any rate the driving force.

Now if we want to get any systems of this kind we must
really get some sort of God whom we can understand. It is
no use falling back on the old evasion and saying that God
is beyond our comprehension. The man who says he believes
in God and does not understand God had much better turn
a good, practical atheist at once. Better atheist than agnostic
[who believes that the divine or the supernatural cannot be
known]: an agnostic is only an atheist without the courage
of his opinions. The actual, practical use we can make of
our God is that we can establish laws and morality which we
suppose to be the will of God, and if we do not understand
God's purpose we cannot do anything of the kind. Therefore we find a large number of people in the country not
understanding God who are practically atheists. It is surprising how little we hear of the name of God outside of our
places of worship. We hardly ever hear the name of God mentioned in a court of justice, except, perhaps, when a witness
is going through the preliminary form of committing perjury,
or when the judge has put on the black cap and is sentencing
some unhappy wretch to death. In Parliament we never hear
about it at all. I do not know whether you ever hear about it in
Cambridge, but you will notice that the mention of God has
gone completely out of fashion, and that if the name of God
is mentioned it is in a perfunctory sort of way, and seems to

come as a sort of shock if the person mentioning it does so in the way of taking the current conception of God seriously.

Here in England we have no fundamental religion of our own. Western Europe, of all places in the world, you will say, is, prima facie, the place for the birthplace of a modern religion, yet we have never produced one. We use a sort of Oriental religion as the nucleus of our religion—a lot of legends that we must get rid of. The man who believes the story [in Matthew 8:28–36, Mark 5:1–20 and Luke 8:26–34] of the Gadarene swine [possessed by demons] will believe anything, and we must leave him out as a critical force. Also the man who believes the story of Elisha and the bears will worship anything. But we must not leave such people out of account as a practical fact in the universe, because these are the people for whom we want to found a religion.

Religion virtually went out with the Middle Ages. If we read through [William] Shakespeare's [1564–1616] plays we find a man of very great power and imagination, who evidently had no well-considered views of any kind, who produced a mass of plays in which he set forth his own knowledge of humanity in a very wonderful way, and practically left religion out of account. Then we strike the beginning of a commercial age, an age of people who went to church but who gradually began leaving religion more and more out of their lives and practical affairs. There are many people who are made more religious if they have a God who produces frightful calamities. If we study the proceedings of African and, I have no doubt, European kings, we shall find the same thing. In order, however, not to be personal, I shall keep to the African potentates as much as possible. In Africa they had found it generally necessary, when building their palaces, to bury several people alive and to commit a great number of cruel and horrible murders. This was to create an impression on the tribe and show their majesty and greatness.

In Mahometan religion, Mahomet [c. 570–632] found it necessary to describe the Judgment Day in most revolting and disgusting terms—to introduce intimidation into religion in order to impress the wild and warlike Arabs. The man of genius finds it difficult to make people understand him. I know this, for I am by profession a man of genius. The difference between a man of genius and the ordinary man is that the man of genius perceives the importance of things. There are a great number of people who do not understand the vital truths of religion, and so the man of genius has to amuse and frighten them with more or less dreadful things.

We have hitherto been governed by a system of idolatry. We made idols of people and resorted to some sort of stage management. Men and women capable of giving orders were taken to the head of affairs—sometimes they took themselves, and we gave them crowns or gold lace on their collars, or a certain kind of hat, and sat them on a particular kind of chair. Those people generally were a sort of second-hand idol: they said, "I am the agent of the will of another idol. I understand his will and hand it on to you." We generally had to give them such a different income from our own that their way of life would be entirely removed from that of the multitude. [...] In democracy we are trying to get human nature up to a point at which idolatry no longer appeals to us. [...]

We are gradually getting more and more rid of our idols, and in the future we shall have to put before the people religions that are practical systems, which on the whole we can perceive work out in practice, instead of resulting in flagrant contradictions as they do at present. People, however, go from one extreme to the other, and when they do so they are apt to throw out the good things with the bad ones, and so they make little progress. The old-fashioned atheist revolted against the idea of an omnipresent being being the God of cancer, epilepsy and war, as well as of the good that happened. They could not believe that a God of love could allow such things. And so they seized with avidity upon the idea of natural selection put forward by Charles Darwin. Darwin was not the originator of the idea of evolution—that was long before his time—but he made us familiar with that particular form of evolution known as natural selection. That idea was seized upon with a feeling of relief—relief that the old idea of God was banished from the world. This feeling of relief was so great that for the time it was overlooked what a horrible void had been created in the universe. Natural selection left us in a world which was very largely full of horrors, apparently accounted for by the fact that it as a whole happened by accident. But if there is no purpose or design in the universe the sooner we all cut our throats the better, for it is not much of a place to live in.

Most of the natural selection men of the nineteenth century were very brilliant, but they were cowards. We want to get back to men with some belief in the purpose of the universe, with determination to identify themselves with it and with the courage that comes from that. As for my own position, I am, and always have been, a mystic. I believe that the universe is being driven by a force that we might call the life-force. I see it as performing the miracle of creation, that it has got into the minds of men as what they call their will. Thus we see people who clearly are carrying out a will not exclusively their own.

To attempt to represent this particular will or power as God—in the former meaning of the word—is now entirely hopeless; nobody can believe that. In the old days the Christian apologists got out of the difficulty of God as the God of cancer and epilepsy, and all the worst powers that were in one, by believing in God and the devil. They said that when a man did wrong he was possessed by the devil, and when he did right that he was possessed by the grace of God. It was, in fact, the conception of "old Nick." It was a conception of enormous value, for the devil was always represented as a person who could do nothing by himself, and that he had to tempt people to do wrong. I implore you to believe that, because it helps you a great deal. People always used to assume that the only way in which the devil could carry out his will was by inspiring or tempting people to do what he wanted them to do. Temptation and inspiration mean the same thing exactly as firmness and obstinacy mean the same thing, only people use the one word when they want to be complimentary and the other when they want to be abusive. Let me therefore ask you to think of God in a somewhat similar nature, as something not possessing hands and brains such as ours, and having therefore to use ours, as having brought us into existence in order to use us, and not being able to work in any other way. If we conceive God as working in that way and having a tremendous struggle with a great, whirling mass of matter, civilization means our molding this mass to our own purposes and will, and in doing that really molding it to the will of God. If we accept that conception we can see the limitations of our God and can even pity him. In this way you can imagine that something—the life-force—through trial and error, beginning in a very blind and feeble way at first, first laboriously achieving motion, making a little bit of slime to move and then going on through the whole story of evolution, building up and up until at last man was reached.

Contrast this position with that of the Christian apologists, and their God, who has to be excused the responsibility of cancer and epilepsy, excused, too, for humanity and the present audience. You require a lot of apology as a visit to the looking glass, coupled with reflections on your life during the past week, would speedily show. The only consolation is that *up to date* God has been able to produce nothing better.

We must believe in the will to good—it is impossible to regard man as willing his own destruction. But in that striving after good that will is liable to make mistakes and to let loose instead something that is destructive. We may regard the typhoid bacillus as one of the failures of the life-force that we call God, but that same force is trying through our brains to discover some method of destroying that malign influence. If you get that conception, you will be able to give an answer to those people who ask for an explanation of the origin of evil. Evil things are things that are made with the object of their doing good, but turn out wrong, and therefore have to be destroyed. This is the most important conception for the religion of the future, because it gives us what we are at present and gives us courage and self-respect. And it is ours to work for something better, to talk less about the religion of love (love is an improper subject) and more about the religion of life, and of work, to create a world that shall know a happiness that need not be the happiness of drunkenness—a world of which we need not be ashamed. The world must consist of people who are happy and at the same time sober. At the present the happiness of the world is as the happiness of drunken people. I don't mean that everybody who is happy is like the man who is locked up for being drunk, but ordinary men or women, even in the politest society, at present are not happy and do not respect themselves and do not exult in their existence until they have had at least a cup of tea. We have all sorts of factitious aids to life. We are trying to fight off the consciousness of ourselves because we do not see the consciousness of a mission, and finally the consciousness of a magnificent destiny.

We are experiments in the direction of making God. What God is doing is making himself, getting from being a mere powerless will or force. This force has implanted into our minds the ideal of God. We are not very successful attempts at God so far, but I believe that if we can drive into the heads of men the full consciousness of moral responsibility that comes to men with the knowledge that there will never be a God unless we make one—that we are the instruments through which that ideal is trying to make itself a reality—we can work towards that ideal until we get to be supermen, and then super-supermen, and then a world of organisms who have achieved and realized God. We could then dispense with idolatry, intimidation, stimulants, and the nonsense of civilization, and be a really happy body with splendid hopes and a very general conception of the world we live in. In the meantime those of you who have exceptional, expensive educations should make it your business to give such ideals to the great mass of people. If you adopt a religion of this kind, with some future in it, I believe that you can at last get the masses to listen, because experience would never contradict it. You will not have people saying that Christianity will not work out in business; you will get a religion that will work in business, and I believe that instead of its being a lower religion than Christianity, it will be a higher one. Also it will fulfill the condition which I set out at starting: it will be a Western religion, not an Oriental one. Make the best religion you can, and no longer go about in the rags and tatters of the East, and then, when the different races of the earth have worked our their own conceptions of religions, let those religions all meet and criticize each other, and end, perhaps, in only one religion, and an inconceivably better religion than we now have any conception of.

5. "Modern Religion I," notes of an address to the New Reform Club, London, 21 March 1912. [*Religious Speeches*, pp. 38–49]

[Published in Christian Commonwealth (3 April 1912). Smith notes (p. 38): "Since Shaw did not ordinarily write out his speeches in advance, he probably relied on a reporter's notes in preparing it for publication. In 1919, he used the same title for another address on the same subject" (page 85). Here Shaw surveys a number of beliefs—the Immaculate Conception, the Holy Trinity, "the abom-

inable doctrine of the atonement"—*and counters the "pure chance" of natural selection (Darwin) with the "miracle of natural creation" (the Life Force). "When you get this conception of the universe you become religious."]*

First, I wish to justify the importance of the subject. We must have a religion if we are to do anything worth doing. If anything is to be done to get our civilization out of the horrible mess in which it now is, it must be done by men who have got a religion. One of the reasons which have induced me to take up this subject of late years very seriously is the simple observation that people who have no religion are cowards and cads. You may say, "How do you reconcile that with the recent statement of Bishop [of Birmingham (1905-11) Charles] Gore [(1853–1932), a leader of the Christian Social Union] that, when he wants to get anything done, he finds it is no use going to church people—he has to go to atheists and nonconformists, and people of that kind?" Well, an atheist is not a man who has no religion, any more than a professing Christian is necessarily a person who has a religion. Obviously, the majority of Christians today have not any religion, and they have less Christianity than of any religion on earth. What I mean by a religious person is one who conceives himself or herself to be the instrument of some purpose in the universe which is a high purpose, and is the native power of evolution—that is, of a continual ascent in organization and power and life, and extension of life. Any person who realizes that there is such a power, and that his business and joy in life is to do its work, and his pride and point of honor to identify himself with it, is religious, and the people who have not got that feeling are clearly irreligious, no matter what denomination they may belong to. We may give this feeling quite different names. One man may use religious terms and say that he is here to do the work of God. Another man, calling himself an atheist, may simply say that he has a sense of honor. But the two things are precisely the same. Any man of honor is a religious man. He holds there are certain things he must not do and certain things he must do, quite irrespective of the effect upon his personal fortunes. Such a man you may call a religious man, or you may call him a gentleman. I almost apologize for using a term which has been so very much discredited. [...]

Have you ever been asked what your religious views were? Under existing circumstances I find it almost impossible to describe myself satisfactorily. Twenty or thirty years ago, when Parliament, in a state of extreme piety, was violently assaulting Charles Bradlaugh for being an atheist and refusing to allow him to contaminate the saintly people at St. Stephens [Chapel, the chamber of the House of Commons 1547–1834], I took every opportunity of calling myself an atheist publicly. I remember being intensely disgusted with people who held the same opinions as myself and Bradlaugh and persisted in calling themselves agnostics. I said, "You know perfectly well that what is called God by the people who are throwing Bradlaugh downstairs does not exist, never did, and never will, and even if you are afraid of the term atheist, or dissatisfied because it is only a negative term, nevertheless you ought to stand up and say at least that you are on Bradlaugh's side—that you are very much nearer to his beliefs than to the superstitions of his assailants." Quite a sensation was caused at the first meeting of the Shelley Society [on 1 January 1886] when I said I was an atheist: a couple of pious ladies immediately resigned—what they supposed Shelley to have been, I do not know. I found that because I called myself an atheist, people supposed me to be a materialist. When Bradlaugh died, the National Secular Society, having some temporary disagreement with his successor, Mr. [George William] Foote [1850–1915], wanted another leader—a thoroughgoing atheist—and accordingly invited various people to address them at the Hall of Science.

Among others, they invited me—no doubt because of my utterances during Bradlaugh's conflict with Parliament. I chose
for my subject "Progress on Free Thought." As some of them
thought their secularism the final term of the human intellect, they felt that the man who, having got there, wanted
to progress still further, must be an arch-atheist of all creation. I had an exceedingly pleasant evening. I do not think
it would have been possible for Bradlaugh to have thrown
the most bigoted audience of [evangelical pacifist] Plymouth
Brethren into such transports of rage as I did the freethinkers
at the Hall of Science. I dealt with the whole mass of superstition which they called free thought: I went into their Darwinism and [the theories of German biologist Ernst Haeckel
(1834–1919)] Haeckelism, and physical science, and the rest of
it, and showed that it did not account even for bare consciousness. I warned them that if any of them fell into the
hands of a moderately intelligent Jesuit—not that I ever met
one—he could turn them inside out. I reminded them that
their former leader, [prominent women's rights activist] Mrs.
[Annie] Besant [1847–1933], the greatest orator in England,
had in an extraordinarily short time become a Theosophist [a
member of the Theosophical Society (founded 1875 in New
York City) and adherent of Theosophy, an esoteric philosophy exploring the mysteries of the universe and the nature
of divinity], and gone almost to the other pole of belief. (Curiously enough, Mrs. Besant had allowed herself to be converted by [Theosophy co-founders] Madame [Helena Petro-
vna] Blavatsky [1831–91] and [American] Colonel [Henry Steel]
Olcott [1832–1907], but had refused to be converted by me, although I had been telling her the same things for a long time.)
I then said, "Let us get at simple, scientific facts. Take the
dogmas of the Immaculate Conception [of the Virgin Mary],
which I firmly believe in, and of the Trinity [of one God in
three persons: Father, Son (Christ), Holy Spirit], which is the
most obvious common sense." Now, in the Hall of Science

the Trinity was regarded simply as an arithmetical absurdity. "Do you mean to say," they said, "that one person can be three, and three persons can be one?" I replied, "You are the father of your son and the son of your father. I am not satisfied with three persons, any more than Shelley was satisfied with three primary colors in the rainbow; he called it the million-colored bow. I am prepared to believe, not only in a trinity, but in a trillion-trinity." "Do you mean to say," they demanded, "that you believe in the Immaculate Conception of Jesus?" "Certainly," I replied, "I believe in the Immaculate Conception of Jesus's mother, and I believe in the Immaculate Conception of your mother." They simply collapsed; they had not the wit to ask me the simple question, did I believe in parthenogenesis? To that question I should have said, "No." But I should have added that parthenogenesis was not the real point of the dogma of the Immaculate Conception. You can imagine how intensely disappointed the national Secularists were with me on that occasion.

Later, when I said in public that my friend, the Rev. R. J. Campbell, had altered my opinion and made me believe that Jesus actually existed, I was described in print by one indignant secularist as having crawled to the feet of Jesus—a very curious way of putting it. Suppose the debate had not been about Jesus, but about Shakespeare, and a gentleman, after making a careful study of Danish history, came forward and showed not only that there had been a prince named Hamlet but that the particular views, the curious doubts, expressed by him in Shakespeare's play had been finding expression in Denmark for about four hundred years before, so that Shakespeare's hero, instead of being the original Hamlet, was practically the last of the Hamlets—just as Mr. Campbell has pointed out that Jesus, instead of being the first Christian was practically the last Christian, for there has hardly been one since. And suppose that, in consequence of this gentleman's researches, I had said, "Hitherto I have regarded

Hamlet as a fictitious character, attributing to Shakespeare that truth which is proper to fiction and much more important than the truth of the Post Office Directory, but I am now quite prepared to believe there actually was such a person," would any one have accused me of crawling to the feet of Hamlet?

Throughout the nineteenth century scepticism finally concentrated itself in a certain dilemma which is still puzzling people: the impossibility of reconciling the omnipotence of God with his benevolence. [Economist and historian] James Mill [1773–1836] and [his son, influential political economist and philosopher] John Stuart Mill [1806–73] and their circle used to say, "There is no God, but this is a family secret." People then did not shout it out the way they do today. The slightest sign one now makes of believing in God exposes one to suspicion, almost to the risk of imprisonment: if you preach the Sermon on the Mount [in Matthew 5–7] to soldiers, you will be promptly clapped into jail. The dilemma is this: An immense number of people in the nineteenth century became atheists or secularists because some person of whom they were very fond died in some agonizing way or contracted some agonizing disease. It was all very well to talk about a God of love, but one could not live in the world without seeing that if he was responsible for everything, he was not only the God of love, but also the God of cancer and epilepsy. It is very easy to get sentimental about a God of love, but not so easy to get sentimental about a God of cancer and epilepsy. Accordingly, you have the position taken up by Shelley, who denounced God as an Almighty Fiend. All strong natures take that line in waking up Moloch worshippers [the ancient Ammonite god is a figure of idolatry] who imagine they are Christians. On the other hand, you had certain attempts to sentimentalize God by ignoring cancer and epilepsy, and talking a lot of charming flap-doodle, and saying love is enough, and love is everything, and God is love. This sickening talk about love, love [sic] went on until you got a God who was the sort of sentimental dupe denounced so fiercely by [Norwegian playwright Henrik] Ibsen's [1828–1906] Brand [the title character in Ibsen's play of the same name, written 1865, performed 1867]. [The young priest] Brand said two rather striking things. First, he told people they were worshipping a God whom they could cheat, worshipping him because he could be cheated, and because he was sentimental and did not mean business. The second thing he said was, "Your God is an old man; my God is a young one." But even Brand did not mention the absurdity of conceiving God as a person with a sex—a male sex. Nowadays we see that it is ridiculous to keep saying, "Our Father which art in heaven." What about our Mother who art in heaven? The Roman Catholic Church may claim the glory of having seen the need for our Mother who art in heaven, and it is she who has kept it alive. Clearly, if you have a personal God, one of the first difficulties is to determine the sex of that God. The unhesitating way in which we have assumed that there is a personal God and a male God not only shows that they have not seriously tackled the problem, but that, in so far as they have tackled it, they keep up the Oriental idea that women have no souls—though Mahomet did not take that view. At any rate, here is your difficulty: You have your personal God, and he is either an Almighty Fiend, according to Shelley, or a sentimental dupe.

On this point of the dupery, let me emphasize an important aspect of popular religion. In the nineteenth century [German economist and sociologist] Karl Marx [1818–83] on the Continent, and [historian Henry Thomas] Buckle [1821–62] in this country, brought a great mass of evidence to show the immense part that is played in human institutions—in religion, politics, and everything—by the economic foundation of society. Marx may almost be said to have taken the position, "Show me the tools that men work

with, and I will tell you what are their religion and politics."
That, of course, is an exaggeration; the materialistic basis of
history can be overdone. But the curious thing is that neither Marx nor his critics, who are now beginning to abound,
have shown how extraordinarily his theory was borne out by
the particular forms of religion, of so-called Christianity, that
grew up with the spread of the capitalistic system, particularly in the eighteenth century. You have, under the name of
Methodism [which stresses the missionary spirit through social service and love of others], what is to me quite the most
abhorrent and debasing form of religion that exists—the sort
of Christianity that centers round the abominable doctrine
of the atonement [the forgiveness of human sin through the
death and resurrection of Christ] as preached by the followers of [Methodism founder John] Wesley [1703–91]. This doctrine spread tremendously among dishonest small tradesmen. If you want to know precisely the kind of man I mean,
you will find him described by one who hated him just as
much as I do, a very great man, a great spiritual force. [Baptist
preacher] John Bunyan [1628–88] wrote a book called *The Life
and Death of Mr. Badman* [1680], and Mr. Badman is the typical
small tradesman, and even the typical large tradesman. It is
astonishing how much of that book might be republished
today as being absolutely contemporary. Bunyan describes
among other things a very similar process gone through today by quite reputable people—the process of becoming rich
through successive bankruptcies. Also there is in that book
a very striking criticism of the [pro–free trade] Manchester
school [led by Radical Liberals Richard Cobden (1804–65) and
John Bright (1811–89)] and of the principle that was at the base
of the old free trader's position—that of buying in the cheapest market and selling in the dearest. Bunyan used those precise terms long before the Manchester school had come into
existence. He said Badman was one of those who would buy
in the cheapest market and sell in the dearest, and what is

this, said Bunyan, but trading without conscience? It would have saved us a lot of trouble if people would have taken that simple and sufficing statement of the case about the Manchester school. But people would not take it from persons like Bunyan, just as they would not take it from [essayist and historian Thomas] Carlyle [1795–1881], who said, "This free trade is heartbreaking nonsense"—which the Manchester doctrine certainly is.

You will see that when I speak of this capitalistic system, this commercialism, as [Socialist, craftsman, designer and writer] William Morris [1834–96] called it (people will probably in the course of the next ten years gradually begin to grasp what Morris meant by commercialism). I mean the system of society in which there is no room for a gentleman—that is to say, our present existing state of society. I may describe it very shortly in this way. [...]

Now, that, practically, is the system on which our society is founded today. All the old obligations that limited that have been driven away by free trade, by freedom of contract, and so on. All the old restrictions, which represented honor, religion, patriotism, have been got rid of as intolerable restrictions on the liberty of industry, and today you have this capitalist system in full swing. Also, you observe, it makes the middle class practically the brains of society. All the other classes are dependent on the middle class. But we, who are considering society from the religious point of view, must see with misgiving—even with horror—that the phrase that I have used a little time ago—that there is absolutely no room in the system for a gentleman—is literally true. The less the middle-class man pays to the workingman, the landlord, and the capitalist, the more he has for himself, and since the other middle-class men help him to grind down the workman while they compete with him in offering rents and dividends to the propertied classes, he flatters and bribes the man of property and sweats and oppresses the working classes. His hand is against every man except the idler. Thus middle-class men get it rooted in their brains that they must make money at other people's expense and be paid for everything they do, that the man who does anything without being paid for it is a fool, and that if any man does more than any other man without being paid extra he also is a fool. That is to say, they all become ingrained and supersaturated cads from one end of society to the other. [...]

The religion which emerges from such a system is a reflection of its cheating, its adulteration, its struggle to get as much as possible for as little as possible, and, finally, to get something for nothing. Accordingly there comes from the whole body of commercialized Christians a demand for some means by which God can be cheated into giving free admission to heaven. The old Christian conception of God was that he was a person who could not be cheated and was very much to be feared. In the Middle Ages they did not bother about the dilemma of omnipotence and benevolence. On the contrary, the old chroniclers would describe a plague of famine, reveling in its horrors, and then, instead of reproaching God, after the manner of the modern sceptic, they would exclaim that these things showed the greatness, the majesty, the power of God, and bow down before him. We are still very largely governed through our admiring contemplation of very wicked things done by persons in high places.

In those days the shopkeeper used to be told pretty roundly that if he put sand in his sugar and cheated the widow and orphan he would go to hell, and he did not like it. But he soon found out a new trick, which was to cheat and oppress and go bankrupt, and then at the end of it bathe himself in the blood of the Lamb and lay his sins at the foot of the cross. This positively gave a zest to evildoing, as the more iniquities people could bring to be washed away the prouder they were. All this was associated with a conception of God as a peculiarly short-tempered and touchy sort of person, who was constantly interfering with the affairs of the world in the most capricious way. I can remember when every atheist was supposed regularly to take his watch out of his pocket and challenge God to strike him dead in five minutes. Over thirty years ago I was in the company of a number of men, some of whom had a scientific education. They were disputing whether Bradlaugh had or had not done this particular thing. I said, "Surely, if it is alleged that God strikes people dead under such circumstances the test is a very practical one." I then took my watch out of my pocket. The whole company instantly rose up in a panic and implored me to stop. I pointed out that my mind had already sent forth the challenge and that if there was anything in the notion I might be expected to perish within the next five minutes. And they were very uncomfortable until the time was up. There you have an illustration of the absurdity and degradation to which religion had been reduced. The whole consciousness of people in the first half of the nineteenth century had got saturated with the idea of continual—I won't say miraculous interferences, because all life is more or less miraculous to every intelligent person—but interferences entirely capricious and anarchic, following no sort of natural law. This was so demoralizing that the ablest people were ready to welcome any sort of theory that would get rid of this kind of God.

You may ask, "What was the difficulty in rejecting the conception straightaway?" The main difficulty was that they could not conceive the world as they saw it, with the wonderful adaptation of organs to their purpose, as being other than a deliberate manufacture, a thing made to a design by some all-powerful designer, until they were shown a way out by Darwin through his theory of natural selection, which destroyed not only the legends of Genesis, but the original religious theory of evolution which prevailed from 1790 to 1830. To that religious theory of evolution we are now returning.

What Charles Darwin revealed was the particular method of evolution he called natural selection, by which the apparent adaptation of organs to their functions was shown to be possible without any purpose or design at all, as a result of pure chance. The hole was not made for the cannon ball, the cannon ball was made for the hole. The intelligent world immediately took Darwin in to their breasts, thankful that at last they had got rid of the old interfering deity. Then followed about half a century of absolute godlessness. As Samuel Butler put it, Darwin banished mind from the universe. That suited the commercial system extremely well. The theory of the survival of the fittest [coined by biologist and anthropologist Herbert Spencer (1820–1903) in *Principles of Biology* (1864)] made the competitive system positively scientific.

The enthusiasm for getting rid of God was, like all enthusiasms, not very critical. And the reaction against false religion was like all reactions. It emptied the baby out with the bath. Even the naturalist now sees that natural selection is no explanation of many things external to ourselves, still less of many things within ourselves. Our innermost soul may have been a good deal crushed by commercialism, but it has not been altogether killed. I don't think there is a single man or woman, however corrupt and vile, who has not occasionally done things outside his or her individual interests. Thoughtful people see that there must be design and purpose in the universe because they themselves are designers and share a mysterious purpose to make the world better and wiser, whether the change will benefit themselves or not. As far as their individual struggle for existence will allow them, they are trying to further this purpose, and when there is anything in art or religious ceremony that seems to express this, it gives them a curious sort of exaltation and joy. The simple existence of that feeling gets rid of the natural selection hypothesis of the soul. What I want to do is to make people more and more conscious of their souls and of the purpose which has evolved the soul as its special organ.

We have to face the fact that we are a very poor lot. Yet we must be the best that God can as yet do, else he would have done something better. I think there is a good deal in the old pious remarks about our being worms. Modern science shows that life began in a small, feeble, curious, blind sort of way as a speck of protoplasm, that, owing to some sort of will in this, some curious driving power, always making for higher organisms, gradually that little thing, constantly trying and wanting, having the purpose in itself being itself a product of that purpose, has by mere force of wanting and striving to something higher, gradually, curiously, miraculously, continually evolved a series of beings each of which evolved something higher than itself. What you call evil is nothing but imperfection. What Shelley called the malignity of the Almighty Fiend is only the continued activity of the early attempts which, though superseded by later achievements, have not yet been destroyed by them. Cancer is not a diabolical invention to torment mankind; it was once the highest achievement of the organizing force, just as the tiger is not purposely the enemy of man; it is an attempt to improve on the oyster. And this miracle of natural creation is constantly going on. This tremendous power is continually struggling with what we call external nature and is getting hold of external nature and organizing it. Needing eyes and hands and brain for the fulfillment of its purpose, it evolves them. We are its brains and eyes and hands. It is not an omnipotent power that can do things without us; it has created us in order that we might do its work. In fact, that is the way it does its work—through us. When you get this conception of the universe you become religious; you perceive that this thing people have always called God is something in yourself, as Jesus is reported to have said. Read the Gospel of St. John, and you will find Jesus always coming back to that point—ye are members one of another [Ephesians 4:25]—the kingdom of heaven is within you [Luke 17:21]—God is the Son of Man—and at that point they always stoned him; the Pharisees could not stand that. Your purpose in life is simply to help on the purpose of the universe. By higher and higher organization man must become superman, and superman super-superman, and so on.

And what is to be the end of it all? There need be no end. There is no reason why the process should ever stop, since it has proceeded so far. But it must achieve on its infinite way the production of some being, some person if you like, who will be strong and wise, with a mind capable of comprehending the whole universe and with powers capable of executing its entire will—in other words, an omnipotent and benevolent God.

6. "What Irish Protestants Think," address at Memorial Hall, London, 6 December 1912. [*Religious Speeches*, pp. 50–53]

[*Smith notes (p. 50) that Shaw "was one of a group of prominent Irishmen called upon to speak on Home Rule by the Irish Protestant Committee." Shaw had proposed this resolution: "That this meeting express its strong desire to see the end of racial and religious feuds in Ireland, and Irishmen of all creeds and classes working together for the common good of their native country." According to Shaw, Protestantism is "a great historic movement of reformation, aspiration, and self-assertion against spiritual tyrannies."*]

I am an Irishman. My father [George Carr Shaw (1814–85)] was an Irishman, and my mother [Lucinda Elizabeth Gurly (1830–1913)] was an Irishwoman, and my father and my mother were Protestants, who would have been described by a large section of their fellow countrymen in the ruder age when I was young as sanguinary Protestants. (*Loud laughter*) Many of the duties of my mother were shared by an Irish nurse, who was a Catholic, and she never put me to bed without sprinkling me with Holy Water. (*Loud laughter*) Now, why in the name of common decency do you laugh at that? (*Laughter*) What is there to laugh at in an Irish Catholic woman sprinkling with Holy Water—and you know what Holy Water meant to her—a little Protestant infant, whose parents grossly underpaid her? (*Laughter*) The fact that you can laugh at the underpayment of a poor Irishwoman shows how this open wound of the denial of our national rights is keeping us a hundred years behind the rest of the world on social and industrial questions. I shall make a few jokes for you presently, as you seem to expect them from me, but I beg you not to laugh at them until I come to them. To my mind this relation of mine to my old nurse is not a thing to be laughed at. It is a pathetic and sacred relation, and it disposes completely of the notion that between the Catholic and the Irish Protestant there can be any natural animosity. (*Cheers and Laughter*) [...]

I am also proud of being a Protestant, though Protestantism is to me a great historic movement of reformation, aspiration, and self-assertion against spiritual tyrannies rather than that organization of false gentility which so often takes its name in vain in Ireland. Already at this meeting pride in Protestantism as something essentially Irish has broken out again and again. I cannot describe what I feel when English Unionists are kind enough to say, "Oh, you are in danger of being persecuted by your Roman Catholic countrymen. England will protect you." (*Laughter*) I would rather be burnt at the stake by Irish Catholics than protected by Englishmen. (*Cheers*) We Protestants know perfectly well that we are quite able to take care of ourselves, thank you. (*Laughter*)

I do not want to banish religion from politics, though I want to abolish the thing miscalled religion in this controversy from the world altogether. I want to bring religion back into politics. There is nothing that revolts me in the present state of things more than the unnatural religious calm in Ireland. (*Laughter*) I do not want a peaceful Ireland in that sense. I want a turbulent Ireland. (*Applause*) All free and healthy nations are full of the turbulence of controversy—political, religious, social—all sorts of controversy. Without it you can have no progress, no life.

Well, in Ireland we Protestant Nationalists dare not utter a controversial word lest we should be misunderstood on the great question of national rights. I have much to say in criticism of Catholicism in Ireland, but I dare not say it lest I should be supposed to be speaking on behalf of Unionism. I have quite as much to say in criticism of Irish Protestantism, but that, too, I must not say lest I should discredit my Protestant colleagues against the day when they will have to claim their share in the self-government of Ireland—and let me say that it will be an important share, for our Catholics are far too amiable and indulgent to take care of public money as Protestants do. (*Applause*)

The [Irish] Local Government Act of 1898 [which ended landlord control of local government] made a revolutionary change from the most extreme form of oligarchy to the most extreme form of democracy, but we Protestants are kept out of the local councils because it is feared that the return of a Protestant would be a triumph of Unionism. The denial of Home Rule [self-government; the Irish Free State was established in 1922] corrupts every election and every division in Parliament. Consider the Land Purchase Acts [of 1885, 1891, 1896 and 1903, enabling tenants to buy land with low-interest government loans]. To some of us they are the salvation of Ireland. To me they are its damnation—the beginning of landlordism all over again on a poorer and therefore a worse and more oppressive scale. Many thought as I did, but we all had to be unanimous in support of the acts, because to oppose them would have been to go over to the enemy. We Irish Protestants are bound and gagged at every turn by the Union.

As to the persecution scare, I decline to give any guarantees. I am not going to say, "Please, kind English masters, if you give us Home Rule we will be good boys." We will persecute and be persecuted if we like, as the English do. (*Cheers and Laughter*) We are not children, we do not offer conditions of good behavior as the price of our national rights. No nation should be called upon to make such conditions. Wherever there is a church that church will persecute if it can, but the remedy for that is democracy. We Protestants will take our chance. If you come to that, think of the chances our Catholic priesthood is taking! Look at what has happened to them in free France! Look at what has happened to them in Rome itself! Many of them would be glad enough to be safe in the island of the saints. (*Applause*) I am far more anxious about the future of the unfortunate English when they lose us. (*Laughter*) What will they do without us to think for them? The English are a remarkable race, but they have no common sense. We never lose our common sense. The English people say that if we got Home Rule we should cut each other's throats. Who has a better right to cut them? (*Loud Applause*) They are very glad to get us to cut the throats of their enemies. (*Applause*) Why should we not have the same privilege among ourselves? What will prevent it? The natural resistance of the other Irishmen. (*Loud Applause*)

Mr. Chairman, what I have said must not be taken as a reasoned case for Home Rule as a good bargain for the parties. That is not what we are here for, and it is not what the question will finally turn on. I leave such special pleading to the lawyers who are ashamed to call themselves Irishmen, though they have no objection to be called Irish officials. What I have uttered is a purposely unguarded expression of real feelings and instincts of a Protestant Irishman. (*Applause*)

7. "On Christian Economics," address to the City Temple Literary and Debating Society, London, 30 October 1913. [Allan Chappelow, *Shaw—"The Chucker-Out." A Biographical Exposition and Critique* (London: George Allen and Unwin, 1969, pp. 130–61]

[*Reported in the* Christian Commonwealth (*5 November 1913*). *Shaw enjoins his audience to give up revenge and punishment and adopt the (Life Force-related) doctrine of Immanence ("God is immanent in man"), then discusses Communism, Democracy and "inequality of income."*]

Ladies and gentlemen, I must warn you at the outset that though I am going to lecture on "Christian Economics," I do not profess to be a Christian. (*Applause*) I notice that two members of the audience applaud that with restrained enthusiasm. (*Laughter*)

Now I am quite aware that this announcement is an extremely unusual one. It has always struck me as being rather a curious thing that if you stop an ordinary Englishman, say the first man you meet in the street as you go home, and say: "I beg your pardon, sir; are you a great philosopher?" he would probably say: "Oh, no." If you said: "Are you a poet?", well, he would give modest cough, and admit that he has written some little things, but he does not profess to be a great poet. If you then ask him: Is he is a very capable man of business, and he will say: "Well, I do my best." If you ask him: "Are you a good oarsman?", "Are you a good boxer?", well, he doesn't like to boast, but perhaps he would go so far as to say that on his day he is not so bad. But if, instead of those questions, you simply asked him: "Are you a Christian?" he would say: "Certainly I am a Christian. How dare you ask me such a question?" He has not the slightest hesitation in making that monstrous assertion. Although, as has already been hinted, I am not altogether lacking in a due proportion of self-conceit, I have never professed to be a Christian. That is rather too large an order for me.

There is also another thing which affects my attitude here tonight. I am by profession mainly a dramatist or playwright. Now a dramatist or playwright is in the position of the King or the Prime Minister of a great modern empire. He may not have any religion whatever, in the sectarian sense. He is face to face with a large mass of people, a small minority of whom call themselves Christians, and the others are Mohammedans and Buddhists and [Hindu priests known as] Brahmins, belonging to all manner and branches of religion. Accordingly, he has to divest his mind of any prejudice in favour of one or the other of these great sects: and get into the position which is very often described as having no religion at all. This is a position which is curiously like that, as far as one can see, of Jesus himself: who seems to have been regarded by all sects as a person of no religion, because you do not find that he expressed any very strong preference between them. In fact, the outstanding thing is that whereas they all seem to have classed each other as heretics or Gentiles generally, he was perfectly willing to talk of a Gentile and talk of a heretic. Therefore, my attitude in the matter, although perhaps an unusually impartial one, is not perhaps in theory an altogether un-Christian one. Therefore what I have to put before you tonight, I put with perhaps as much impartiality as is possible to a human being: which is not saying very much.

Now Christian economics do not really concern you until you have begin to make up your mind to introduce Christianity into the world, and into the country. You see, all our existing civilisations are elaborate organisations for the prevention of Christianity. (*Hear, hear*) Our police and our soldiers, and all the coercive forces that we have at our disposal, profess to suppress murder and theft: but they do not. They do not profess to prevent Christianity; but they do. Now I must—having made that beginning, and warned you that I am going, as a sensible man, to deal with the world as it exists at present, as a world in which Christianity, however it may be existing in the hearts of some persons, is nevertheless a thing which is not established, in fact, that the entire social order as we have it at present is anti-Christian—(Hear, hear)—deal to some extent with the question of what Christianity is.

I should like, although I am rather reluctant to do it, because our Chairman [R. J. Campbell] must be extremely tired of it, to deal for a moment with our Chairman's contribution to our consciousness of Christianity. I am not speaking as one of his congregation. I am not making allowances for a great deal that he has said on the subject that I have not heard. I want merely to deal with his contribution to the subject as it reached me, and as it has struck me in order of its importance. First, shortly, what I think he has done is, he has restored Jesus. He has rescued him from the region of fable and legend; and he has restored him to the sphere of history. He has presented him in such a way that he becomes a credible historical character; which is a very remarkable advance towards the belief that Christianity may turn out to be humanly practicable. But the other thing which he has done, which is, perhaps, a little more startling, is that he has made us conscious, in the face of our previous general conviction that Christ was the first Christian, of the fact that he is the last Christian; that Christianity was a thing that had been growing, and was finally suppressed by the Crucifixion.

I want to lay particular stress on that. I want to point out to you that the Crucifixion was a great political success. It seems to have absolutely destroyed Christianity. It was meant to do so; it was meant to do so by the Jews, with the assistance of the Romans. Probably [Roman prefect of Judea (26–36 CE)] Pontius Pilate did not mean anything very particular about it;

and did not care about it: but at any rate, with his assistance the Crucifixion took place; and Christianity thereupon practically disappeared from the world.

That is a thing which you must get very carefully into your heads; because many people are under the monstrous idea that Christianity has been flourishing ever since.

It is quite true that people since that time, after a brief interval, began to call themselves Christians. That we are all aware of, of course: but as a matter of fact, if you go to the Early Church, you discover as to the religion which called itself Christianity, as it grew up it was in no sense peculiarly Christian at all; that is to say, it dealt with beliefs which were really superstition: it embodied beliefs which are superstitions. It embodied the old doctrine of the Atonement, the old idea that in some way or other you could always get rid of your guilt and your responsibility by seizing on some innocent victim and destroying it—sacrificing it, as it was said. Whether that victim was a goat, as in the sacrifice which [biblical patriarch] Abraham substituted for the sacrifice of his own son, or whether, as it afterwards came to be, it was the sacrifice of a man, still the idea was the same—the notion that in some way or other you could get rid of your guilt or your sin by shifting it on to innocent shoulders.

That clearly is not a doctrine which is in any way specially characteristic of Christianity. I do not find anywhere, in any record of any tradition of the sayings of Jesus, that He ever turned round to the Jews and said: "You need not be concerned about your personal conduct; you must do just anything you like, and put it on Me. My shoulders are broad enough to bear it all." Mind, it is an extremely comforting belief. If you have a lot of guilt on your conscience which you find you cannot get rid of, your Atonement theory comes in very well: but I am not going to deal with that. I am not going to consider that as Christianity; because it does not seem to me to be distinctively Christian.

I go further, and say that it seems to me that we are bound to get rid of that belief, in order to make people shoulder their full share of moral responsibility. (*Hear, hear*) I want to destroy every hope, as far as I can, in every human soul, that they can possibly shift responsibility by any sacrifice whatever. (*Applause*)

Now when you come to the Middle Ages, you had a religion which also called itself Christianity. It was a very fine thing in a way: it was a very inspiring thing. It produced some of the most magnificent works of art that exist in the world. It proved, in fact, that you can only get the greatest art through religion; and as the expression of a religion of some kind. It was the religion at its best of Chivalry. It was the religion of [fictional Spanish knight] Don Quixote [the hero of the eponymous two-volume novel (1605, 1615) by Miguel de Cervantes]. It was the religion of attacking evil, fighting it and destroying it. That meant, of course, putting a certain number of the members of the human race in acute antagonism to the religion, and destroying them; and it was a little tainted, I think, by the old notion of the sacrifice. It may not have been any longer the idea that you could concentrate all the guilt of the world on one particular individual, and kill it in his person: but there was always a great deal of burning and slaughter, and making war on the Saracens, or somebody else. There was a tremendous lot of fighting about that religion. The Middle Ages was a tremendous fighting time—fighting for their religion which they called Christianity. Medieval Christianity undoubtedly did a great deal of work in the world. It accustomed men to do a great many things which they could not have done without religion; some of them very necessary and very fine things. I submit to you, however, that it was not Christianity.

One of the things that it never did was, it never overcame the fear of death. You may remember that it has been said that Death is the last enemy to be overcome. We have not quite overcome that yet. Always you have had round this early Christian religion, round this mediaeval religion, not only that great fringe of legend, stories of miracles, and so on; but you have had intimidation in the shape of a hell, and you have had a refuge from death in the shape of a heaven, promising you personal immortality. It seems to me that those things were relics of the old Atonement theory. I do not say that the religion was not a useful one and a fine one: but I submit that it was not one characteristically and peculiarly Christian. It was not the thing that separates Christianity in history from all the other faiths and religions.

Then, of course, those religions were finally wiped out by modern commerce; which destroyed all pretence even of religion. I think it is something to have come to the point at which we are at present, where even the practice is gone—when it is hardly worth people's while any longer to be hypocritical. In the old mediaeval times, you had a period when no man spoke about business, and no man spoke about politics, without constant reference to his religion, without constant reference to God as an active force in the universe. But the only place where that occurs at the present time is in the wilds of Africa, among the [Ugandan] Boganda [sic] and other people who have very recently been converted to Christianity. If you read the letters they write to the missionaries and travellers who have converted them, you find that they use the old mediaeval language. You will find that they, in almost every second or third line, refer to God as actively interfering in their affairs.

It is a rather curious reflection, because this has often occurred to me: I remember asking a very famous traveller, the late [explorer and discoverer of David Livingstone] Sir Henry Stanley [1841–1904]: "Can these people use modern firearms?" He said: "Of course they can, just as well as you can." I said: "That is a very lively thing. It is evident from the letters you have shown me that these people really believe in their reli-

gion exactly as the mediaeval Christian believed in his religion. Now," I said, "supposing they learned to use firearms,
and supposing they discovered that we do not believe in Europe in the way that they believe, may it not be possible that
they may start a Crusade with the object of wiping out practically the modern European, on the ground that he is a blasphemer, a thief, and an enemy of God?"

I just throw that out as one of the dreadful suggestions
which modern civilisation is almost always making. [...]

Since we must have a really clean slate for Christianity,
shall we attempt to begin Christianity? Shall we try to found
Christianity in this country? Is it worth doing? Is it worth un-
doing the work of the Crucifixion, after this lapse of 2,000
years, during which Christianity has been suppressed—and
suppressed by organized and armed force; and during which
all the religions calling themselves Christian will really not
bear examination from a Christian point of view? Shall we
make an attempt really to take up the traditions of Christ,
and see what we can do? [...]

I warn you that, as I believe, if you attempt to go on as
Christians with a continuation of historical Christianity,
then I think you will fail; then I think you will be beaten out
of the field by other forces, some of them intensely hostile to
Christian ideas. I think, in short, that we have to make a new
beginning.

Supposing thus you say: "Yes, we will make a beginning,
as soon as we see our way to it": what does that affirmative
answer involve? What will you stand committed to, if you
begin to be Christians? In other words, what are the characteristic doctrines of Christianity? If you reject the theory of
the Atonement, the miracles, and all the rest of it, all those
things which have so often been called Christianity, what is
the thing which I am prepared to call Christianity?

Well, I recognize three main things. In the first place, you
will have to give up revenge, and you will have to give up

punishment completely and entirely: that is to say, you will have to scrap your entire criminal and juridical system. You will have to: "Judge not, that ye be not judged." [Matthew 7:1] (*Applause*) You will have to stop putting people in prison who rob you. You will have to stop hanging people who murder you. (*Applause*) You will have to give up the whole thing. You will have to stop scolding and complaining and writing to *The Times*. (*Laughter*)

Well, I am glad you take it in such a light-hearted way. Then you will have to take, in a sense, no thought for the morrow [Matthew 6:34]: that is to say, you will have to go in for Communism. (*Hear, hear*) You will have to take no thought for the morrow as to what you shall eat or what you shall drink: and that means Communism; because there is no other way in which you could possibly place yourself in the position of not having to think of what you will eat and drink tomorrow, except through Communism. Under our present system, which as you know is the very reverse of communistic, we have brought the necessity for taking thought for the morrow as to what you shall eat and drink to such a tremendous pitch, that very few of us are able to think of anything else. (*Laughter*)

Then you will have to adopt the great Christian doctrine which has recently been called the Immanence of God [His divine presence in the material world]. You will have to begin to understand the meaning of such phrases as "The divine spark in man." You will have to understand that "the Kingdom of Heaven is within you."

That, also, is rather a difficult thing to face; because, you see, God is in rather a peculiar position. God is a person who cannot be insured. What I mean by that is that He has got to stand by His mistakes. If you make a mistake, you to some extent can get out of the consequences of that mistake by insurance. You can join, as it were, with one another. If your house is burnt, we can agree all to club together in an Insurance Company, to build your house again, with only a small sacrifice to yourself. If you have an accident, we can all agree in the same way to compensate you. All these things can be done. We can help each other over the consequences of our mistakes; but the mistakes of God cannot be insured against, if he makes mistakes, and he evidently makes a great many. Those mistakes are absolutely irremediable. Therefore, if you can see God as acting through a conscious agent, that conscious agent has on him the most terrible responsibility, which he cannot shift off to anybody else.

If you once adopt this doctrine that "God is within you," and that practically, that is what you are here for, to try and give some executive force to God, that you are the instrument through which God works, then every mistake which you make becomes practically in magnitude like a mistake of God.

I remember once being told a story by a very light-hearted gentleman; and it was a very amusing story in its way. I remember that he told it to me in a tramcar at Florence. He said: There was a very pious man who had lived very humbly all his life, sustained in a life of virtue and good works by the belief that at last when he died he would see God face to face. In the course of time he died; and he presented himself at the gate of Heaven full of expectation. He found [the most important of Christ's twelve apostles] St. Peter, who admitted him, very much pre-occupied and apparently very much troubled, and very short in his manner of conversation. St. Peter, having admitted him, evidently wanted to get rid of him; but this man clung to St. Peter, and explained what it was he was looking forward to. St. Peter remonstrated and said: "You are all right; you are in Heaven; what more do you want?"

No, this man was not satisfied. To be in Heaven was a small thing to him. He wanted to look on the face of God, and be face to face with Him, and speak to Him. Nothing that St.

Peter could say would turn him from that determination. At last St. Peter called St. Paul [Saul of Tarsus (c. 5–c. 67), famously converted near Damascus], [the prophet] Moses [to whom God gave the Ten Commandments on Mount Sinai], and [the prophet and miracle worker] Elijah; he had a consultation, and said virtually: "This man insists," and they had to agree that in some way he was within his rights. Accordingly they told him that he must be very careful. They led him to a magnificent cathedral. In that cathedral he saw a wonderful Presence: an old man sitting on a throne in the choir of that cathedral. He was about to rush forward to throw himself before the figure on his knees, when St. Peter and St. Paul held him back. They said: "You must not go; you must not say anything; and you must not tell this because it is a very awful thing, but the fact of the matter is, God has gone mad."

Now, ladies and gentlemen, that is a most instructive story; because if you can once realize what it would mean if the director of the whole universe went mad, or if, to put it another way, he went wicked, perhaps you would begin to have some sort of idea of what is the matter with the world at the present time. The matter is that God in you, and in most of us, is mad and wicked; that is just what it comes to. In some way, to reach the genuine Christian doctrine, the God that is within you will have to be a sane God, and will have to be a more intelligent God: you will have to bear all the consequences, and know that you are responsible for the consequences of all His mistakes.

If you say: "We will establish Christianity," you must say: "We will shoulder this responsibility": and I leave you simply to ponder on that, and to think what it would be. The weight and terror of it is very considerable; and it explains the tremendous reluctance of people to accept this very great and central doctrine of Christianity. If you will read St. John's gospel carefully, you will find that according to it, Jesus in his teaching was always coming back to this point. He was always coming back to the fact that the Son of Man was the Son of God; trying to make people realise that God was within them, and their own godhead.

If you read carefully, you will find that although he was allowed to teach many other things, and do many other things, the moment he got on that point, the Jews generally stoned him. It is curious to know why it was; and I can only suppose that it was some dim glimpse of what it would mean for them—the fact that it would bring every man face to face, as it were, with his own conscience. He would have had to shoulder the whole responsibility of the universe, if that were brought home to him: and I suppose that is what made the Jews take to stones, and made them finally crucify Jesus.

My subject tonight really deals with the second point of Christianity. I am not going to deal any further with the Immanence of God; although I tell you, you do commit yourself to God, if you say you will try the experiment of establishing Christianity. I do not propose to deal largely with the question of the entire disuse of revenge and punishment. I am inclined to think that the disuse of revenge and punishment would make matters rather more terrible for evil-doers: because if you ever get rid of the idea of expiation again you make people uncomfortable. At present, if you punish a man, you wipe his offence off the slate. There is no man who has ever been punished for some wrong act—who has had a malicious injury perpetrated on him purposely at the instance of society, because he did something malicious, and who has really done something malicious—who does not believe that the two wrongs cancel one another, and that two blacks make a white. If you give up punishing one another for wrong acts, and if you give up revenging yourself, wrong-doers will go round the world seeking in vain for punishment. They will go about with their guilt round their neck; and every man will know to the end of time: if I have stolen a thing once, I am a thief, and I will never be able to get out of it; but at the present time you can steal, and at the end of three months you are honest men. (*Laughter and applause*)

But my subject here tonight, of course, is the economic subject: "Take no thought for the morrow." I am now going to deal with that in a quiet sort of way, and make an unexciting middle part of my speech which will give you an opportunity of going to sleep, as most people do when economics is mentioned. It goes without saying that you are committed to Communism.

You see, one of the consequences of the Immanence of God is, once we have realized that, that we immediately recognise [that] we are members one of another; and when we are members one of another, there is no further question of personal and private property. The welfare of one becomes the welfare of all the rest. You would not have people starving, and you could not possibly have people starving, in a Christian country, unless everybody is starving. As long as there is food, the food has got to go round. [...]

One of the greatest blessings which has ever been conferred on the human race was the invention of money as an instrument of exchange. It has been turned into the root of all evil: but that is not necessarily a permanent condition of affairs. When you call money the root of all evil, if you use the expression with regard to another person, you mean that he has got too much. If you use it with regard to yourself, you mean you have got too little. But what I want is to have an income and spend that income; because in no other way can I go into the market and pay my due to the actual controller of production and say: "I want such and such a thing; and I will not pay until I get that simple thing."

Communism, in a word, is supply without demand; and when you have supply without demand, you have no control over supply. It is a mere guess in the dark as to whether you are supplying things that anybody wants. If, for instance, you had general Communism in the hands of such Governments as we have today, those Governments would produce what people wanted say 200 or 300 years ago and nothing that they wanted today. (*Applause*) Well, then, your Communism will mean that everybody will have an income; and the communistic part of it will mean that everybody will have an exactly equal income.

Also, the income will not be the price of a man. In a Christian State, a man, being a part of God, is infinitely valuable. You cannot buy him; and you cannot sell him. Once you realise, for instance, that God is immanent in man, you cannot take that little instrument of God, that little organisation in which there is a spark of God, and say: "I will have 18s. worth of God; and I will make use of that 18s. worth for my own purposes, to make myself rich without regard to anything else." There is an end of that: the thing becomes inconceivable. The value is infinite: and when you come to infinite values you are done, so far as regular incomes are concerned. It is not conceivable that you could say under those circumstances: "This particular aspect of God which you call the Duke of Somebody is worth £1,000 a day; and this other person is worth a shilling a day." All that goes completely, and it is driven out of your head. [...]

Then the last point (I am running over them rapidly) is a physiological point—the point which has been brought forward under the general name of Eugenics. We are waking up to the fact that we are a very poor lot of people: we are not good-looking; I am sorry to be personal, but we are not. We are not good-looking; we are not healthy; we are not strong. A great deal of the apparent increase in the length of life seems to me to be due to taking a great deal of extra care of lives which one is almost tempted to say were hardly worth taking much trouble about. But there is the fact that we have found ourselves out.

We talk about the superman. The mere word "superman" shows that we are realising that at present we are only the super-monkey, and rather a poor sort of monkey at that. Everybody feels instinctively that we want a better sort of man. That is all very well. We are willing, no doubt, to make any sacrifice, and make every effort, to attain that better type of man. That instinctive adoration of life which is in all of us I believe will overcome almost every objection, in so far as there is an upward path before us in the development of the evolution of the highest forms of life, if only we knew exactly how to go forward. [...]

The only thing we do know positively is, that very curiously when you walk down a street in London, and sometimes even when you come to the City Temple, you are not much impressed with the people you see. [...] Then suddenly, quite unexpectedly, in an extraordinary way, you see somebody who interests you; and if it happens here, you do not listen to the rest of Mr Campbell's sermon. In other words, you fall in love.

Now that is a solid fact. People do fall in love; and it seems to me that is the only mortal thing that you have got to trust to in the breeding of the human race. You must see, if you have any sort of logic, how remarkable is that curious instinct, that singular preference, that exception from the rule of general indifference; because nothing is more infamously false than the common and vulgar assumption that love is an indiscriminate thing. It is not an indiscriminate thing. The people to whom it is indiscriminate have been brought into a thoroughly unhealthy state. It is a most fastidious thing; it is a most discriminative thing. You may go half through your life and never fall in love. Some people do not do it at all; but when it does come, it has some meaning in it.

It is a thing which has governed marriage from the time marriage began to exist; and if it had been a destructive thing, it would have destroyed the human race before this. You are bound to believe in it. You are getting some prompting from Providence. Love is really prompting you to do the right thing; and it is the only hope for improving the human race.

Whatever these Eugenic Societies [such as the Eugenics Education Society (founded 1907), renamed the Eugenics Society in 1926] may say, there is only one way of doing it; and that is by widening what they call the "area of sexual selection" to the very widest extent. Now what is the existing state of things? I do not know how many married people there are here. Probably you are all either married or going to get married; or else you have determined that nothing whatever would induce you to get married, though let me tell you, that will not save you; but the probability is that among the many people within your reach, you have probably had the choice of two or three; and none of those two or three perhaps was absolutely your ideal. I go out into the street: I see somebody, or at least this used to occur to me before I was married. I am an imaginative person: I am a romantic person. It is my profession to be romantic. I went and saw some person who attracted me enormously. She was a duchess; so she would not look at me. I went on and saw somebody else who attracted me. She was a charwoman, and I would not look at her, in spite of my socialistic instincts. I knew perfectly well that it would be quite impossible for us to live together happily. All the world over you have the same thing.

Do not suppose you can get down to any section of the community where you do not find that you are working in a little narrow circle everywhere, instead of having what you ought to have in this country: that every young man and young woman would be able to go all over the range of society through the land, and, if they fell in love with one another, have no fear of any obstacle; that any young man might go up to any young lady in the street and say: "I beg your pardon, but are you unmarried?" If the young lady says: "I am very sorry, I am engaged," then the gentleman would say: "I am sorry, too"; and he would walk off. If not, then the gentleman might say: "Would you mind," to use the popular phrase, "walking out with me?" [...]

What stops people from doing that is inequality of income. You cannot marry a £100 a year person to a £200 a year person, or a £500 a year person to a £5,000 a year person. It is no use; it cannot be done, no matter what you think. In the few cases where it does happen, it gets into the newspapers; and is usually connected with something very unpleasant. [...]

There is no use, in face of those facts, imagining that simple Democracy is going to work out our problems for us. I tell you, as an old Socialist who has studied thoroughly, as far as it can be studied, the organisation of society and industry that will be necessary under Socialism, and as one who believes that we are coming to that, that you might have the most complete Collectivism in this country; and you might have at the same time the most completely organised tyranny, the most complete suppression of all freedoms, liberties, and aspirations that make life worth living, the most complete bar to progress, far more complete than could ever have been achieved by the tyrannies of the past, under which some small sections of kings, and small aristocracies, in spite of all their will to be tyrannical, were able to inflict injury on a very small part only of the community they came into contact with. Remember that a king can only strike people that are within reach of his hand: but every one of us is within reach of the hand of democracy.

When you have got Democracy you have the instrument of the most terrible tyranny, unless you have got enlightenment at the same time. (*Hear, hear*) A democracy without enlightenment, without religion, without those things which I have shown you are the real essence of Christianity, is a thing so terrible to contemplate, that really one has to run away from the temptation to be mechanically optimistic and try to persuade oneself that it will be all right: but it will not be all right unless we work very hard to present it. I do not know what is going to be the end of it.

I have put the case to you as strongly as I possibly can. I tell you that if you are going to realise that the Kingdom of God is within you [Luke 17:20–21], unless you set to work to make the Kingdom of God exist outside of you individually, unless you really make the whole country collectively the Kingdom of God, you will be able to do nothing whatever.

There is no hope for you in Democracy; there is no hope for you in economic reform; there is no hope for you in mere economic Socialism, or mere economic anything else. You must develop your spiritual life, and your spiritual determination. You must go ahead on that. You must put certain things that you are aspiring to first; and you must put political theories and political parties next. That is what you have got to do: and if you do not do it, it will be a very bad thing for this country; and it will be a very bad thing for you. It will mean the wrecking of another civilisation.

It may mean this, and this is my last word. We talk about the superman; and we think that perhaps by some means humanity will improve; and a better sort of man will come. You do not know whether that will be so or not.

Remember, that power that is behind evolution, this wonderful power of life, has scrapped and scrapped and discarded, as being a failure, a great many forms of life. There was a time when it seemed as if to make a black-beetle was a promising experiment; as though making the bacillus of typhoid fever was a necessary bit of the organisation of life. That had to go. The aspiration of life, the thing you call God, could not be satisfied with what black-beetles and typhoid bacilli could do: and then it went on one day and it made more wonderful things. It made reptiles; and then it made animals and mammals as we know them. It made birds, which are very beautiful things; and finally it made monkeys; and then it made men. But, remember, that when the time came that it was evident that these things were not going to achieve the great thing, were not going to achieve the Kingdom of God, were not going to realise God, they were thrown aside; and something else was made. Some new thing was made which devoted itself very largely to their destruction.

Ladies and gentlemen, it is not an impossible thing that some day or other, there may walk out of a bush somewhere a new being of which you have no conception, not a man at all, or a woman at all; something new that had never occurred before; and the work of God may be handed over to that new thing; and it may be said of us: "These people have failed; they are scrapped; they are gone." Part of the mission of the new thing would be to destroy these people as part of the mission of man was to destroy the tiger. Think of that possibility, ladies and gentlemen; and make up your minds to work pretty hard.

[The Rev. R. J. Campbell, calling Shaw's speech "a grand tonic," asked him a few questions, to which Shaw replied at length (see Chappelow, pp. 156–60), emphasizing that "...one must remember with regard to the mere willing of creative energy, that everything almost that exists is created by the mere desire that it should exist. One must remember that the mere will on the part of man to do a certain thing will finally, if he goes on trying long enough, give him the power of doing it. ...Remember that by merely willing to do something, you have actually created the cellular tissue, and you have created powers which you had not before: there is nothing else which is creative in the universe. That is what you have got to believe in."]

8. "Modern Religion II," address at the Hampstead Conservatoire, London, 13 November 1919. [*Religious Speeches*, pp. 60–80]

[Published as a supplement to the New Commonwealth *on 2 January 1920. "The first thing that any empire or any political*

organization requires is religion," says Shaw, explaining how "the religion of the future will be very largely a Marxist religion, ...in the sense that it will see that the economic question comes first." After listing Samuel Butler's objections to Darwinian natural selection, he presents the Life Force alternative: "God, as it were, is in the making."]

You are the citizens and subjects of an enormous Empire which contains several hundred millions of people. The first thing that any empire or any political organization requires is religion, and it must be a religion which can be accepted by all the persons within that political organization. That may be a simple thing when the political organization is a small one, and consists of people who have all been brought up in the same way, and attended the same place of worship, and had the same teaching, but when it is a political organization which extends over the whole of the earth, which embraces very different climates, very different religions in the sense of organized religions, very different creeds, and so on, then the matter becomes very different. The official religion of the British Empire would appear to be the religion of the Church of England, an institutional religion, but the difficulty is that the Church of England is supposed to be a Christian religion, and yet in the Empire only eleven per cent of the inhabitants are Christians. Out of every one hundred people in the Empire only eleven are Christians, and a great many of that eleven are a very queer sort of Christian. For instance, a large number of them do not even profess to believe in the Christian religion in the institutional sense, do not attend any place of worship, do not read religious books, do not listen to sermons—some come and listen to me for preference. Is there any likelihood of the principles of the Church in England becoming universally credible? Is there any likelihood of their recommending themselves to the enormous majority who have not yet adopted Christianity and do not show any sign of intending to do so? [...]

Now, [noted theologian William Ralph Inge (1860–1954)] the Dean [1911–34] of St. Paul's [Cathedral] tells us with reference to those tenets which every postulant for the post of minister or clergyman of the Church of England is required unfeignedly to embrace—that is to say, there are two creeds, there are the Thirty-nine Articles and there is the matter of accepting the Bible as being a perfectly literally true document containing a correct scientific account of the origin of species and the creation—the Dean of St. Paul's tells you that if the bishops were to refuse to ordain any postulant for the clergy who could not unfeignedly and in their plain sense accept that creed, those Thirty-nine Articles and that doctrine about the Scriptures, the clergy would consist exclusively of fools, of liars, and bigots. Those are his words, and they are not mine, and this is deliberately told you by the ablest churchman you have, in a position—that of Dean of St. Paul's—which is technically perhaps not quite so high as that of [Randall Davidson (1848–1930)] the Archbishop of Canterbury [1903–28], but really carries with it equal authority, especially when the person who holds it is perhaps rather a cleverer man than the Archbishop of Canterbury. Now, under those circumstances, not only would it appear that there is no chance of whatever genuine religion you are going to make the foundation of your Empire being the Church of England, it would appear to me that if that is true there will very soon be no Church of England at all in the old-fashioned sense of the word. You may anticipate that the church will broaden, that it will relax its tests and so on. You have no historical warrant for believing anything of the kind. Everything you know of the history of these great institutional churches in the past will tend to convince you that as the church is more and more attacked, challenged, instead of liberalizing itself, it will do exactly the other thing, it will draw its lines tighter. It will say, "Sooner than give up our old doctrines we will recruit exclusively from the fools, the liars and the bigots." You know, for instance, that the Roman Catholic Church in the nineteenth century, when it also had to sustain a tremendous attack from modern thought, instead of relaxing its doctrine immediately added to it dogmas which the Middle Ages never dreamed of, and would probably never have tolerated; it drew its lines very much tighter. And when there was a Modernist movement [begun around 1890 and condemned by Pius X in 1907] in that church it excommunicated and threw out those Modernists, with an affirmation of doctrine which even the fools, liars, and bigots, if I may quote the Dean again, would not venture to impose on the Church of England.

Consequently, I think you must thoroughly make up your minds not merely that whatever the great modern religion is which is going to be a practical religion for the Empire, it will not be the Roman Catholic Church or the Church of England, but it will not be a church at all. You will find that human nature divides itself in a particular way. You meet a kind of man whose religion consists in adhering to a church, who requires a church and requires to be led by a priest, who adopts the creed and articles of a church; he attends the services of the church, and that is his religion. Very often it does not go any further than that, but still, there is the thing for him. To him religion means adhesion to a church and observance of a ritual, and the placing of authority in spiritual matters in the hands of a special class. Now over against the natural-born churchman, there are men of another type, and these men are always really mystics. They do not believe in priests; they very often hate them, and they hate churches. They are deeply religious persons, and instead of priests they have prophets, and these prophets come, if I may say so, practically at the call of God. These men believe in the direct communion of their own spirit with whatever spirit it is that rules the universe. They believe that the inspiration of that spirit may come to anybody, and that he may become a prophet. In the strict sense you may almost say that these people are genuine Protestants; I could say so without any qualification, only unfortunately we have got what many members of the Church of England do not call it, an Anglican Catholic Church. They call it a Protestant Church. If in my native land, you called it a Protestant Church, an Anglo or an Irish Catholic Church, I don't know what would happen to you. The thing would not be tolerated for a moment. I, as a born and baptized Irish Protestant, have always maintained that a Protestant Church is a contradiction in terms, that the genuine Protestant knows no Church and knows no priest. Practically, he believes in the direct communion between himself and the spirit that rules the universe, and the man he follows is a prophet and not an ordained priest, not a man who claims an apostolic succession because a long succession of hands have been laid on heads, and so on; claims practically that apostolic succession is a direct inspiration, which may come to him and which may come to anybody.

Now that the distinction between the churchman, between the person the Dean of St. Paul's calls the institutionalist, and the genuine out-and-out Protestant mystic, will always cause a certain division, therefore any religion that is going to unite men will have to be a religion which both of these people can accept. It must have room for mystics, prophets, and for priests, and it must be a religion of such a character as will prevent the priests from stoning the prophets, as they always do. Some of you who have had a perfectly conventional religious education, that is to say an entirely unintelligent one, have been very likely left to draw conclusions for which there is no warrant. For instance, in reading the Bible—you have heard it read in churches, and you have perhaps had it imparted to you by an ordained clergyman—you have derived an impression that the prophets of whom you read were only a sort of old-fashioned clergy. You are entirely wrong in that; they were prophets who were stoned by the old-fashioned clergy. If you read them carefully you will see that they are continually complaining of the persecution which came from the church of their day. You must keep that distinction in mind. And we have to consider this point, as to whether it is possible to get any sort of common ground where you can get a religion for your Empire.

Now, some of you who are thoroughly modern, educated, and intellectual persons may say, "Why do you want a religion for your Empire at all? Why not be pragmatic?" as the modern phrase goes. These religious people are continually pursuing ideals of rightness and truth. "Well," you may say, "in the modern pragmatic way, anything that works is right; anything people believe is true. That is what constitutes truth, and that is what constitutes right." I do not deny that if you wish to be an accomplished man or woman of the world and get on nicely, easily, and sensibly in it you had better be acquainted with this peculiar view. In the ordinary intercourse of society it has its uses. But it is not any use when you come to governing a great state. There it is no use saying that the thing that works is right, because things that you know to be abominably wrong, and that you cannot pretend to be made right by any sort of working, can nevertheless be made to work politically if only you will put sufficient brute force into making them work.

Let me take two particularly atrocious examples of bad and tyrannical government in the modern world. Take, for instance, the government of Russia by the Czars. This I can only describe by saying that if you take as true the very stupidest, the most mendacious, the most outrageous, and prejudiced account that you can find in our more reactionary papers today of the regime of [Vladimir] Lenin [1870–1924] and [Leon] Trotsky [1879–1940] in Russia, you may assume quite safely that the present state of things in Russia is practically heaven compared to what it was under the Czar [Nicholas II (1868–1918; reigned 1894–1917)], and the fact that we nevertheless made an alliance with that power is a thing that ought to make you very carefully consider whether there may not be some sort of divine retribution in the heavy price we had to pay for making that alliance, and making it with our eyes open.

The other instance of atrociously bad government which has lasted for three or four centuries, I need hardly tell you, is the case of my own country, Ireland. Nevertheless, it worked. The Czar's government worked perfectly, not without a certain amount of friction, because it was made to work by the simple process of getting rid of any person who was opposed to it, putting him in prison, killing him, or otherwise persuading him to be quiet. You will see, therefore, that to suppose a country can be governed pragmatically, that any country can justify its government because it can say it works, is entirely out of the question. Six months of that would knock the pragmatism out of the most inveterate agnostic, the most inveterate shirker of fundamental moral questions you can find anywhere.

In the same way, there is no use in saying that anything the people can be induced to believe to be true is true. That is not so at all, because, just exactly as the most tyrannical state can make a government work, in the same way you will find that that same government, by means of a state church, or by means of an institution like the Holy Inquisition [the notorious judicial body of the Roman Catholic Church established to combat heresy], the [Tribunal of the] Holy Office [of the Inquisition], as it was called, can also get anything believed. If you kill all the people that don't believe it, or at any rate silence them, get hold of the education of the children, take them from their earliest years and tell them it is true, and it is very wicked to doubt it, you can immediately create such a body of belief as will pragmatically justify the most monstrous creed you can possibly put before the human mind.

Accordingly, when you come to governing a country, then there is no use in talking pragmatism. You have to come back to your old Platonic ideals [the abstract idea of perfection taught by Greek philosopher Plato (c. 428–c. 347 BCE)]. You will have to use your reason as best you can, to make up your mind that there are certain things that are right and certain things that are true. You may always have at the back of your mind the fact that you may be mistaken, but you cannot sit down and do nothing because you are not sure what you have to do. In governing a country you have to arrive at the best conclusion you can, the conclusion that certain institutions are in harmony with what we call the Platonic ideal of right and truth[,] and trust your instinct more or less to guide you, and also, of course, trust history and experience—except that if you are a politician in this country you will never know anything about history, and your experience is mostly that of trying to cheat other people. Nevertheless, in so far as our laws and creeds can be dictated by persons who have had rather a better preparation for public life than that—gentlemen like the Dean of St. Paul's, although he has certainly had the most frightful antecedents anybody can imagine; no one ever came out with intellectual distinction in the face of such disadvantages—I must interrupt myself to say that in justice. He is the son of the head of an Oxford college and a doctor of divinity. His mother was the daughter of an archdeacon, and, in spite of that he went deliberately, with his eyes open, and married a lady who was the granddaughter of a bishop and the daughter of an archdeacon. He has been an Eton schoolboy and an Eton master [at Eton College (founded 1440), the exclusive boarding school]. He has taken every possible scholarship that could be got at the University, and how it is he has come out of that with any mind whatever I do not know. It only shows what a splendid mind it is that he was able to stand all that. As I say, if you take men of that type and get them to dictate your creeds and your laws, you will find that they will have to fall back for public purposes on the good old Platonic ideals. They will have to believe in absolute ideas with regard to right and truth, absolute at least for the time. They will have to make an elaborate series of laws in order to maintain what they call right government, and in order to hold up the truth to people.

I rather think that the religion of the future will dictate our laws, particularly our industrial laws—because remember that in the future law will not be the very simple thing it has been in the past, a mere matter of preventing ordinary robbery, I do not mean robbery from which this country really suffers, which is the robbery of the poor by the rich, but what the policeman recognizes and charges you with as robbery and murder. All that is very simple, but we now know that in the future governments will have to do a great deal more of what they are already doing on a scale which fifty years ago would have seemed perfectly Utopian; that is to say, they will have to interfere in the regulation of industry, will have to dictate the rate of wages, or rather, as a matter of fact, there will not be wages at all. What governments in future will have to recognize as one of their first duties is the very thing they do not interfere with at all, and that is the distribution of the national income among the people of the country. And when you come to that you will see that the religion of the future will be very largely a Marxist religion. That will mean nothing probably to a good many people here because there will be persons who are not socialists and have not read Marx, and persons who are socialists and have only pretended to read Marx but never really have. Therefore I had better explain exactly what I mean. What I mean is that one of the things Marx impressed on the world, and he did it to a certain extent by exaggerating it, was that the economic constitution of society was practically at the bottom of everything in society. [...] Some of the gentlemen in the Natural History Museum at South Kensington will tell you, "If you bring me a single bone of an extinct antediluvian monster, I will reconstruct the entire monster from that bone," which, of course, is an easy thing to do, as nobody can possible contradict him when he has reconstructed it. Marx may be imagined as saying in the same way, "If you will bring me from any period of history, if you can dig it up, the tool a man worked with, or dig up some evidence of the conditions under which he worked, whether a cottage industry, factory industry, or what not, from that alone I will reconstruct the entire politics, religion and philosophy of that stage of civilization, whatever it was." That, of course, is an exaggeration. Nevertheless, it is enormously important, and it must be recognized in the future by any religious nexus that we may spread, it must be acknowledged that you have to begin with economics. One may illustrate that in a very simple way. Here I am addressing you on a very important subject, a very lofty subject, I am accordingly stretching my intellect as far as I possibly can to rise to the occasion. I have in action all the highest part of me, we will say, all the best bits of my brain for your benefit. Supposing you keep me here for a long time—I know you won't do that, it is extremely likely I would keep you here even when you wanted to go anyway—nevertheless, supposing you said, "We really cannot stand this fellow with his airs and intellect and philosophy and all this sort of thing, talking about his superiors, like the Dean of St. Paul's and persons of that kind, and daring to criticize. We will take the conceit out of this man; we will see how long his philosophy and lofty ideas, his notions of history, conceptions of the future, will last." You would have nothing to do but keep me on this platform and take care I did not get anything to eat or drink. You would find that as the hours passed away in spite of all my efforts to keep on a high level, the whole question of religion would gradually fade into the background of my mind, and the question of getting a drink and getting something to eat would steadily grow, and at last you might bring me to a point at which I would be prepared simply to spring on the chubbiest and nicest-looking persons in this audience and practically eat them in order to save my life. You must remember humanity is like that. The first thing you have got to do if people are to have any religious, intellectual, or artistic life, is to feed them. Until you have done that they cannot begin to have any sort of spiritual or intellectual life. You must attend to that first.

Therefore, I take it the religion of the future, the religion, what ever it is, that is to unite all the races of the Empire and to reconcile them all to one common law, will be, I may put it shortly, a thoroughly Marxist religion, in the sense that it will see that the economic question comes first.

Having said that, I want just to say a word as to how far that religion will be a tolerant religion. There is a great deal of nonsense talked in this country about toleration, and the reason of it is this, that since our national church, the Church of England, began as a heresy—it broke off [in 1534] as you know from the Roman Catholic Church, therefore it began as a heresy—it was persecuted as a heresy, it had to fight under the imputation of being heretical, and the result was it had to fight for toleration, and consequently, it has become a tradition in this country that toleration is an indispensable thing, that you must always tolerate—not that you ever do it as far as you can help it, but nevertheless we have all rather persuaded ourselves that we are tolerant. I do not think any person who has ever candidly examined his own mind would really for one moment suppose he was going to be tolerant. Take, for instance, the question how far do we tolerate the Indian religions? We do tolerate them up to a certain extent; I am not sure we are justified in doing so; but is any person here prepared to tolerate the institution of suttee [or sati, banned throughout India by Queen Victoria in 1861]? The

institution by which a woman is encouraged, when her husband dies, to burn herself on his funeral pyre? We have put
that down by simple persecution. Indians tell you that if India
became entirely self-governing and independent tomorrow,
probably there would be a return to suttee by a large class of
Indians. The moment you are brought face to face with anything of that kind you perceive you are not tolerant.

In the same way, there are institutions in this country that
I am not prepared to tolerate. I am not at all tolerant with
regard to children, for instance. In the matter of toleration
you have to draw a very distinct line between the religions,
the beliefs and creeds which you will allow to be preached
to persons who have grown up, who are able to choose and
judge, and the religions which you allow to be fed into those
children when they are very young and impressionable, when
they may have something stamped on them for life which
they may never be able to get rid of, and quite unable to resist.
If you asked me whether, if I had the power, I would tolerate teaching such a thing to a child as Calvinism [a branch
of Protestantism adhering to the tenets of French theologian
Jean (known as John) Calvin (1509–64), which include the
doctrine of predestination], which is the religion of the north
of my own country, the good old Ulster of the Calvinists, I
would reply that nothing would induce me to tolerate it for a
moment. I would not hear of it for one instant. Let the child,
if you like, when it grows up to years of discretion even before
it ceases to be going to an educational institution—there
does come a time when I would say, it is now necessary for
the child to learn, as a matter of history and understanding
its neighbors, that there is such a horrible belief in the world
as Calvinism, such an unspeakable wicked thing, at least as
I think, and he must learn also that some people think it
an exceedingly nice thing, that the Ulster and a great many
Scotch people apparently enjoy it. But as to letting a religion
of that kind—or indeed I am not sure that I am in favor of

any institutional religion—get access to children when they are very young, I am rather inclined to think children would have to be finally protected against everything but what I have called the modern religion, particulars of which I will come to presently, that is to say the general ideas of right and truth which will govern the politics of the whole Empire; undoubtedly the young children must be governed according to them, but when it comes to tolerating the teaching of religion, I think it is our first duty to protect children against that particular thing, and I should protect them if I had one of these particular creeds myself, and I daresay I have a lot of them sticking to me, I should be quite willing to have children protected against that just as much as anybody else's. I want you to think the thing out and remember that although there is a case for toleration it does not exist in the case of young children, only in the case of people who are competent to judge, and of course you must practice the widest toleration, because the probability is that the most advanced, the most hopeful direction in which your religion and intellect, your artistic doctrine or philosophy, is pushing forward and improving itself, is precisely the direction which will hold you and make you think it is blasphemy, and for that reason it is very desirable that you should not persecute movements in that way; you should only persecute in the case of things which are entirely abhorrent to your nature, and when you come to do that I am not at all sure you should not do it thoroughly.

For instance, to go back for a moment to the case of India, although there is such a tremendous lot to be said for out method of tolerating religion in India we have had no excuse for staying in India at all. As long as we are persecuting it, passionately and vigorously saying, "Your Eastern institutions are abominable, we are going to root them out with fire and sword," the probability is we are making India think, we are teaching India something. It seems to me if the Indians could only come over here and have a good persecuting go-in at a lot of our stupidities and idolatries they might improve us a good deal and in that way there may be something to be said for the domination of one civilization by another, that is to say the more bigoted and persecuting it is the more cause there is to suppose it is doing something, but the moment you get a broad, tolerant, liberal relation between the two every excuse for your intervention has gone. As long as you pretend you are in India on a great mission from God, that you are missionaries, you may have been right or wrong, at any rate it is a creditable motive. Now that you tolerate, now that you have said, "Yes, we all have the same God; it is all perfectly right; we will allow them to practice their religions in that way," where does it lead you? The Indian says, "All right, what are you here for?" We have to admit we are here looking after money, because we get money out of you, and we get berths for our sons in the Indian Service, and so on. All your excuse is gone and finally under the influence of that you will have to clear out. That is the advantage of liberal toleration, that it leads to your clearing out, which is exactly what you ought to do, and some of these days will have to do. But remember when the clearing comes about, when you have practically in India what we call a self-determining territory, when you have Egypt and Ireland with practically all their national individual aspirations satisfied, by that time the days of separate nations will have gone, by that time there will have to be bonds; the Empire will probably be a more real thing than it has ever been before. There will still be a Commonwealth, a common interest, bonds of all sorts, therefore there will still remain the necessity for a common religion, a common thing that binds them together in a common ideal of what is right and true.

Now, all this of course is a mere preliminary to my lecture. Some of you thought probably it was just going to be over; you little knew your man. Can we see any convergence towards a common faith, a common belief, on the part of modern men, especially those modern men who have practically discarded the creeds? People who go to church and who are institutionalists by instinct, like to go to a service, who are nevertheless churchmen yet do not believe the literal inspiration of the Scriptures, do not believe the Thirty-nine Articles, find it impossible for instance unreservedly and unfeignedly to believe one article which affirms transubstantiation and the next article which flatly denies it. That is your idea of an English compromise, it is a very British compromise. Nevertheless, there are many people who are sufficiently consecutive in their ideas to find certain difficulties. I suppose none of you has ever read the Articles. I have read them. They are so extremely short that it is very difficult to forget one completely before you go on to the other, and yet you find places in them where unless you can perform that feat it is not easy to see how you can accept the whole thing. But now out of the welter that has ensued on the scrapping of the old creeds, out of this breakup which is indicated by the Dean's statement that practically if you believe what your grandfather and grandmother believed you are either a fool or a bigot or a liar, that is to say if you say you believe them you are a liar and if you do believe them you are either a bigot or a fool—is there anything coming out of this and is there anything coming out of science?

When I was a young man—I was born in the year 1856—when my mind was formed, as they say, I had very great hopes of science, and the people at that time had extraordinary hopes of science, because science came to us as a deliverer from the old evangelicalism which had become entirely intolerable. There are, of course, people of the old evangelical type about, but I do not think there are any of them here because I am not the sort of preacher they run after. But I can remember when it was quite a general belief that you had a God who was a personal God, of whom they had a perfectly distinct image. He was an elderly gentleman, he had a white beard—I am an elderly gentleman and I have got a white beard, but I am not a bit like him. Nevertheless, there is a gentleman friend of mine, and a socialist, who is exactly like him, and that is my friend [the founder in 1911 of the British Socialist Party] Mr. H[enry]. M[ayers]. Hyndman [1842–1921]. Those of you who know him will recognize what the God who was believed in in my youth was like. If you have not had the privilege of meeting Mr. Hyndman you had better seek it. If you get [William] Blake's [1757–1827] illustrations to [the biblical Book of] Job [in twenty-two engraved prints (1826)] you will find a picture of the old gentleman there. You may remember how this was focused by the tremendous sensation which was made by Ibsen; the first play with which he practically stormed Europe was the play of Brand's. The one thing one always remembers is that Brand, the hero, meets a young man and they discuss a little theology and Brand says, "Your God is an old man, I have no use for him." That really I think was the first time it suddenly flashed on Europe that after all, supposing God were to be conceived as a young man?

I remember when I was young I had it pushed into me that everything that was pious was old; even when I read the [Christian allegory by John Bunyan] Pilgrim's Progress [1678], which I did when a very small child, when I came to the second part even Mr. Valiant-for-Truth I conceived as an old man, at any rate a grownup person. I remember my surprise afterwards when arriving at years of discretion to discover by carefully reading the introduction in verse, which a child always skips, that Bunyan had conceived Valiant-for-Truth as being a young man in all the glory of youth. But in those days the ruler of the universe was an elderly gentleman, and you had to be very careful about the elderly gentleman because the one thing he was watching to do at every turn was to strike you dead. You used to be told if you were not very careful—there was always one phrase used—if you said anything that implied the slightest doubt about that old gentleman, you were told that you would come home on a shutter. I had when young a vision of the blasphemer, the atheist, the infidel, always being brought home on a shutter; they were never brought home in an ambulance, a hearse, or any other way, but always on a shutter.

I can remember, too, when I was a young man I was at a bachelor party, and they began to dispute about religion. There was a pious party there and there was a young man who evidently was a bit of a secularist, and they began disputing about Charles Bradlaugh, who was the great atheist preacher of that day. It was alleged he had on one occasion in public taken out his watch and challenged this God, the old elderly gentleman, if he really existed and if he were the truth to strike him dead within five minutes. Well, you have no idea of the bitterness of the controversy. The pious people, of course, alleged it as being the most frightful and horrible defiance of God that could be conceived, but the secularist, instead of taking the line you would expect, passionately denied that Bradlaugh had done anything of the kind. He said Bradlaugh was too good a man. I said, "Look here; after all, if people do believe this crude thing, that the world is regulated by a very touchy deity who strikes people dead, is not that a very practical way of testing it?" And with that I took my watch out of my pocket. You have no idea of the effect it produced. Both the secularist party and the pious party went into transports of terror. Our host had to appeal to me as his guest, and as a gentleman, not to think of such a thing. Of course, it being my duty as a guest, I put my watch back and said, "After all, the thought has come into my head; the challenge may not have been put into words, but it has been suggested." They were exceedingly uncomfortable for the next five minutes. You, ladies and gentlemen, laugh at this, but in those days it was impossible for people to laugh at it; they were too frightened. Even the sceptical people felt extremely uncomfortable. When that is what is called religion, then you have got such a horrible oppression, the whole thing is such a nightmare, that if anybody will come and offer any kind of argument by which you can convince yourself you can get rid of it, you will jump at it without being very critical.

The argument that people found it most difficult to get over was the argument from design. You know the old argument: If a savage took up a watch and saw the way it was arranged, even he would say it was not a casual or accidental growth, that it was a thing designed by a designer. Thus in the middle of the century, evolution had been entirely forgotten. Evolution was first introduced about the year 1780, and until 1830 it was very much in men's minds; it was very much discussed. But in 1830 discussion about it had been exhausted, and it was almost forgotten. Then Charles Darwin, a grandson of one of the old evolutionists, Erasmus Darwin, suddenly made a discovery, with [naturalist, biologist and explorer] Alfred Russel Wallace [1823–1913], not of evolution, but a particular method which simulated evolution, which was called natural selection. You are all probably familiar with Darwinian natural selection, but the point that affects our argument tonight is this, that Darwin was able to show that case after case of what appeared to be the most exquisite adaptation of means to ends, the most perfect evidences of design, apparently unquestionable cases of a thing having been made and designed for a particular purpose, was nothing of the kind, that simply the pressure of environment had produced the appearance. To put it roughly, supposing there was a hole in a wall and somebody found a cannon ball near it which exactly fitted, people used to say that was the very clearest evidence that some intelligent person made that hole in the wall to fit the cannon. Darwin showed it was entirely wrong; the cannon ball knocked the hole in the wall, and nobody meant the hole to be there at all. That is what natural selection means as opposed to the old evolution, and there came, as you know, a fierce controversy between Samuel Butler, whose life some of you have been reading, and Darwin.

People are rather puzzled at the extraordinary ferocity of the quarrel. I have very often told the story, though it is not told in the biography, of Butler saying to me in the courtyard of the British Museum, in a dogged kind of way, "My grandfather quarreled with Darwin's father, I quarreled with Darwin, and my only regret in not having a son is that he cannot quarrel with Darwin's son." Many people reading the biography cannot understand why Butler was so extraordinarily bitter, but the reason was that he was one of the first men to perceive the full significance and meaning of this natural selection of Darwin's which was taken up by the scientific world and then by the whole world and embraced with the most extraordinary enthusiasm as being a new revelation of the beginning of all science and was applied to everything, so that people declared that the whole mass of evolution had been a matter of natural selection. Butler said, "This doctrine banishes mind from the universe. It presents you with a universe which no man with any capacity for real thought dares face for a moment. It takes all design, all conscience, all thought, out of it, and the whole thing becomes a senseless accident and nothing else. My mind refuses to entertain that." And then Butler set himself to work out what genuine evolution was, and although all through his life Butler was very much slighted, and everyone thought Darwin was one of the greatest men of science that ever existed, now we are all coming round to Butler's view.

But why was it people jumped at Darwin in that way? As a rule, people are not fond of science; they are not much given to studying it. The reason simply was that Darwin destroyed the old evangelicalism, the conception of the continually interfering elderly gentleman with the white beard, who was constantly sending people home on a shutter. He took that weight off the human mind, and people were so enormously relieved to get rid of it that they emptied the baby out with the bath. They practically threw aside everything, and they had a curious notion that since the old evangelical view had been taught in connection with morality, they had not only got rid of the mistakes and crudities and superstitions of the old evangelicalism, but they believed they had got rid of religion and right and wrong altogether, and we entered on a period of pragmatism and materialism which has lasted for fifty years, and which has ended in one of the most appalling wars the world has ever seen. You can trace that war exactly to these purely materialistic ideas. We are very fond of blaming the Germans for this; let us not forget it was an Englishman, Darwin, who had banished mind from the universe. We have occasionally said the Germans are only imitators of us, that they steal our inventions and ideas. I am afraid in this case it is right; they did steal scientific materialist ideas and work on them, but in that particular it is not for us to throw stones. England is undoubtedly the place those ideas came from in the first instance.

Such a thing cannot last; it is too entirely against all our poetic instincts. One knows practically as Butler knew that we cannot empty the universe out like that and make the whole thing to be a series of accidents. We know there is intention and purpose in the universe, because there is intention and purpose in us. People have said, "Where is this purpose, this intention?" I say, "It is here; it is in me; I feel it. I directly experience it, and so do you, and you need not try and look as if you didn't." It is like a man saying, "Where is the soul?" I always say to a materialist of that kind, "Can you tell me the difference between a live body and a dead one? Can you find out the life? What has happened? Here is a man struck by a shell; what has happened? He is made exactly of the same chemicals as before, the same silica, the same carbon; you can find no difference whatever. But somehow he ceases to live, and he is going to tumble to bits. What kept him that strange fantastic shape for so many years? What keeps him in this definite shape? Why do I not crumble into my constituent chemicals?" None of these material people can tell me that. It was that continual question. When people began to get frightfully bored by being told everything was sodium and carbon and all that, they said, "We are not interested in sodium and carbon except when we want it on the dinner table; can't you talk of something more interesting?" And the more interesting thing was life, the most intensely interesting thing on earth, and one began to see that right along the whole line of evolution.

You begin with the amoeba; why did it split itself in two? It is not an intelligent thing for anybody to do. You cannot pretend there is any particular accident in that. You cannot see any case that natural selection makes. But somehow the amoeba does it. It finds that perhaps two are better than one, but at any rate it does split itself in two, and from that you have a continual pushing forward to a higher and higher organization. The differentiation of sex, the introduction of backbone, the invention of eyes, the invention of systems of digestion. You have a continual steady growth, evolution of life, going on. There is some force you cannot explain, and this particular force is always organizing, organizing, organizing, and among other things it organizes the physical eye, in order that the mechanism can see the dangers and avoid them, see its food and go for it, can see the edge of the cliff and avoid falling over it. And it not only evolves that particular eye, but it evolves what Shakespeare called the mind's eye as well. You are not only striving in some particular way to get more and more power, to get organs and limbs with which you can mold the universe to your liking, you are also continually striving to know, to become more conscious, to see what it is all driving at.

And there you have the genuine thing, you have some particular force. The Chairman quoted my expression and called it the "life-force." [Henri] Bergson [1859–1941], the French philosopher, has called it [in *L'Évolution créatrice* (1907)] the vital impulse, the *élan vital*. You have many names for it, but at any rate here is a particular thing that is working this miracle of life, that has produced this evolution and is going on producing it, and it is by looking back over the long evolution and seeing that in spite of all vagaries and errant wanderings one way or another that still the line as it goes up and down seems to be always driving at more power and more knowledge, you begin to get a sort of idea; this force is trying to get more power for itself. In making limbs and organs for us, it is making these limbs and organs for itself, and it must be always more or less trying to get more perfect limbs and organs. If it goes on and on one can perceive that if it is practically given a free hand as it were, if the obstacles are not too many for it, it will eventually produce something which to our apprehension would be almost infinitely powerful and would be infinitely conscious, that is to say, it would be omnipotent and omniscient. And you get a sort of idea that God, as it were, is in the making, that here is this force driving us. You always have the humbling thought when you are told by your teachers, "God made you," you look in the looking glass, and say, "Well, why did he make me? Was that the best he could do?" And when you do not look at yourself but look at somebody else, the impression is tremendous. You really do see that somehow or other, assuming that all the organisms that have been made are visible, are sensible to us, we cannot be satisfied that we are the last word. It really would be too awful to think there is nothing more to come but us. Nevertheless, we may hope if only we give everybody the best possible chance in life, this evolution of life may go on, and after some time, if we begin to worship life, if instead of merely worshipping mammon, in the old scriptural phrase, and wanting to make money, if we begin to try to get a community in which life is given every possible chance, and in which the development of life is the one thing that is everybody's religion, that life is the thing, then cooperation with this power becomes your religion, you begin to feel your hands are the hands of God, as it were, that he has no other hands to work with, your mind is the mind of God, that he made your mind in order to work with. Then you not only get an enormous addition in courage, self-respect, dignity, and purpose, get turned aside from all sorts of vile and base things, but you get a religion which may be accepted practically by almost all the churches, as they purge themselves more or less of their superstition. Because, as I pointed out, instead of purging themselves of their superstition, their method is usually to defend themselves against attack by thickening the crust of superstition. In that they kill themselves. But new churches are formed, and in spite of all their efforts even the existing churches become more liberal.

But supposing I talk in terms of this religion which I have haltingly tried to explain to you, what is the great advantage it gives to me personally? It is this. I never have the slightest difficulty in talking to a religious man of any creed whatever; in fact, I get on perfectly well with Roman Catholics and dignitaries of the Church of England if they are really religious. I do not pretend to get on with people who have no religious sense whatever. I should bore them. But if I come across religious people, Indian, or Irish, or Mahometan, or anybody else, we can meet on this common ground. You find that this thing is in everybody, the hope of this thing. The moment you clear up people's minds and make them conscious of this, that moment you discover that the roots of this religion are in every person, and you may get a common bond all over the Empire.

This religion you will see growing up all through your literature, not only in Butler and Bergson, and even in my own works, but you find it coming in all directions, distinctly in the novels and poetry of Thomas Hardy [1840–1928], everywhere in Mr. [Herbert George] Wells [1866–1946]. Mr. Wells goes on at a tremendous rate. You never know what will come. He suddenly rushes out and says, "Hurrah! I have suddenly discovered something no one has discovered before. I have discovered God." He discovers the things that were discovered the first two centuries after Christ. There has also been a tremendous discovery of Christ himself. In the days of the old gentleman with the white beard who sent people home on shutters, Christ himself was almost as great a caricature of what we have on record of the real Christ as the elderly gentleman was of the real spirit of the universe, the life-force. There has been a sort of rediscovery of Christ. People suddenly begin to discover that his religion is a universal religion, and they also begin to discover that there have been other Christs, and that there are Christs even at the present time, that the spirit which was in Christ you will find among Buddhists, among all sorts of persons, persons whom the evangelicals used to call heathen and idolatrous, and used to give large subscriptions to convert them. Then they used to give large subscriptions to convert the Jews. The whole missionary idea of the old evangelicals was entirely wrong, and furthermore, if they had only read their gospels they would have seen it was wrong on the authority of Christ himself. Christ never attempted to establish a church; he was there in the middle of Jews and Pharisees; he never asked any Jew to become a Christian. He did not mean to establish a church. He meant practically [that] he was one of the prophets. What he was dealing with was mysticism. He wanted the Jews to accept something in addition to whatever creed or institution they believed in, to accept his universal religion. He wanted the Gentile also to accept it, the circumcised and the uncircumcised alike, and when he found people wanted to go and act as missionaries, to go somewhere else and try to tear up by the roots some man's religion and substitute their own, Christ told them quite plainly, "Do not do that; if you go and try to pull up what you think are the tares you will pull up the wheat as well." [Matthew 13:24–30] Of course, we never used to listen to that. We sent missionaries. We plucked up as we thought the tares in their religion, and the result was that the missionary's convert has become a byword throughout the world as a person with no religion at all. It turned out that the wheat had come up with the tares.

9. "Religion and Science," a toast to Albert Einstein at the Savoy Hotel, London, 28 October 1930. [SHAW: The Annual of Bernard Shaw Studies 15 (1995), pp. 232–41]

[A dinner in honor of theoretical physicist Albert Einstein (1879–1955) was sponsored by the Joint British Committee of the Societies of Ort-Oze for promoting the economic and physical welfare of Eastern European Jewry. The version in SHAW, writes editor Fred D. Crawford (p. 232), "is the most complete publication of Shaw's toast to Einstein as Shaw actually delivered it." Here Shaw wittily explains how "the whole Newtonian universe crumbled up and vanished and was succeeded by the Einsteinian universe."]

[...] Since the death of [physicist and mathematician Sir Isaac] Newton [1643–1727], three hundred years have passed, nine generations of men. And those nine generations of men have not enjoyed the privilege which we are enjoying here tonight of standing face to face with one of those eight great men, and looking forward to the privilege of hearing his voice. And another three hundred years may very well pass before another generation will enjoy that privilege. And I must—even amongst those eight men I must make a distinction. I have called them makers of universes, but some of them were only repairers of universes. Only three of them made universes. [Greco-Egyptian mathematician and astronomer Claudius] Ptolemy [c. 100–c. 170 CE] made a [geocentric] universe which lasted fourteen hundred years. Newton also made a universe, which lasted for three hundred years. Einstein has made a universe, and I can't tell you how long that will last.

These great men, they have been the leaders of one side of a great movement of humanity which has two sides. We call the one side, Religion; and we call the other, Science. Now, religion is always right. Religion solves every problem, and thereby abolishes problem from the universe because, when you have solved a problem, the problem no longer exists. Religion gives us certainty, stability, peace. It gives us absolutes, which we so long for. It protects us against that progress which we all dread, almost more than anything else. Science is the very opposite of that. Science is always wrong. And science never solves a problem without raising ten more problems to confront us.

All these great men—what have they been doing? Ptolemy, as I say, created a universe. [Polish mathematician and astronomer Nicolaus] Copernicus [1473–1543] proved that Ptolemy was wrong. [German mathematician and astronomer Johannes] Kepler [1571–1630] proved that Copernicus was wrong. [Italian mathematician, astronomer and physicist] Galileo [Galilei] proved that [Greek philosopher and scientist] Aristotle [384–322 BCE] was wrong. And now you are expecting me to say that Newton proved that they were all wrong. But, you forget, when science reached Newton, science came up against that incalculable, that illogical, that hopelessly inconsequent and extraordinary natural phenomenon, an Englishman. That had never happened to it before.

As an Englishman, Newton was able to combine mental power so extraordinary that if I were speaking fifty years ago, as I am old enough to have done, I should have said that his was the greatest mind that any man had ever been endowed with. And he contrived to combine the exercise of that wonderful mind with credulity, with superstition, with delusion, which it would not have imposed on a moderately intelligent rabbit.

As an Englishman, also, he knew his people, he knew his language, he knew his own soul. And knowing that language, he knew that an honest thing was a square thing; an honest bargain was a square deal; an honest man was a square man, who acted on the square. That is to say, the universe that he created had above everything to be a rectilinear universe.

Now, see the dilemma in which this placed Newton. He knew his universe; he knew that it consisted of heavenly bodies all in motion; and he also knew that the one thing that you cannot do to any body in motion whatsoever is to make it move in a straight line. You may fire it out of a cannon with the strongest charge that you can put into it. You may have the cannon contrived to have, as they say, the flattest trajectory that a cannon can have. It is no use. The projectile will not go in a straight line. If you take a poor man—the poorer the better—and you blindfold that man, and if you say, "I will give you a thousand pounds if you, blindfolded, will walk a thousand yards in a straight line," he will do his best for the sake of the thousand pounds to walk in a straight line, but he will walk in an elliptical orbit and come back to exactly the same place.

Now, what was Newton to do? How was he to make the universe English? Well, mere facts will never daunt an Englishman. They never have stopped one yet, and they did not stop Newton. Newton invented—invented, mind you; some people would say discovered, I advisedly say he invented—a force, which would make the straight line, take the straight lines of his universe and bend them. And that was the force of gravitation. And when he had invented this force, he had created a universe which was wonderful and consistent in it-self, and which was thoroughly British.

And when applying his wonderful genius, when he had completed the book of that universe, what sort of book was it? It was a book which told you the stations of all the heav-enly bodies. It showed their distances apart, it showed the rate at which they were traveling, it showed—gave you the exact hour at which they would arrive at such and such a point to make an eclipse or at which they would strike this earth and knock it into bits, as Sirius is going to do some day. In other words, it was not a magical marvelous thing like a Bible. It was a matter-of-fact British thing like a Bradshaw [railway timetable and travel guide, a popular series initiated in 1839].

For three hundred years, we believed in that Bradshaw and in that Newtonian universe, as I suppose no system has ever been believed in before. The more civilized, the more ed-ucated we were, the more firmly would we believe in it. I believed in it. I was brought up to believe in it.

Then an amazing thing happened. A young professor got up in the middle of Europe. And, without betraying any con-sciousness of saying anything extraordinary, he addressed himself to our astronomers. And he said, "Excuse me, gen-tlemen, but if you will attentively observe the next eclipse of the sun, you will find out what is wrong with the perihelion of Mercury." And all Europe staggered. It said, "Something wrong? Something wrong in the Newtonian universe? How can that be?" And, "Listen," we said, "this man is a blasphe-mer! Burn him alive! Confute him! Madman!"

But the astronomers only looked rather foolish. And, they said, "Oh, let us wait for the eclipse." But we said, "No, this is not a question of the eclipse. This man has said there is something wrong with the perihelion of Mercury. Do you mean to say there *is* something wrong with the perihelion of Mercury?" And then they said, "Oh yes, we knew it all along." They said, "Newton knew it." "Well," we said then, "why didn't you tell us so before?" Our faith began to shake, and we said, "If this young man, when the eclipse comes, gets away with it, then the next thing that he will be doing, he will be questioning the existence of gravitation." And the young professor smiled. And he said, "No, I—uh—mean no harm to gravitation. Gravitation is a very useful hypothesis. And, after all, it gives you fairly close results, *fairly* close results. But, personally and for my part, I can do without it."

And we said, "What do you mean, do without it? What about that apple?" The young professor said, he said, "What happened to that apple is really a very curious and interesting question. You see, Newton did not know what happened to the apple. The only *real* authority upon the subject of what happened to the apple was the apple itself! Now apples are very intelligent. If you watch apples carefully you will learn that they behave much more sensibly than men often do, but unfortunately we do not know their language, and," the professor said, "what Newton ought to have done would be to see something fall that could tell the story afterwards, could explain itself. He should have reflected that not only apples fall, but *men* fall. And," he said, "I, instead of sitting about in orchards and watching apples fall, what did I do? I frequented cities in quarters where building operations were going on. I knew as a man of science that it was statistically certain that, sooner or later, I should see a man fall off a scaffolding. And I did.

"And I went to that man—in hospital—and, after condoling with him in the usual fashion, saying how sorry I was for his accident, and how he was, I came to business. I said, 'When you came off that scaffolding, did the earth attract you?' The man said, 'Certainly not! *Gar nicht!* On the contrary, the earth repelled me with such violence that here I am in hospital with most of my bones broken!'" And the Professor could only say, "Well, my friend, you have been lucky enough to escape without breaking your own back, but you have broken Newton's back."

That was very clear. And, we turned round and we said, "Well! This is all very well, but what about the straight line? If there is no gravitation, why do not the heavenly bodies travel in a straight line right out of the universe?" The Professor said, "Why should they? That is not the way the world is made. The world is not a British rectilinear world. It is a curvilinear world. And the heavenly bodies go in curves because that is the natural way for them to go." And, at that word, the whole Newtonian universe crumbled up and vanished and was succeeded by the Einsteinian universe. [...]

Now I come to my peroration. I have spoken enough. Within the last month or so, there has come to me, and come to many of you, our visitor's profession of faith, his creed [in his essay, "What I Believe" in *Forum and Century* 84.4 (October 1930), 193–94]. And that has interested me very much because I must confess to you that there is not a single creed of an established church on earth at present that I can subscribe to. But to our visitor's creed I can subscribe to every single item.

I rejoice at the new universe to which he has introduced us. I rejoice in the fact that he has destroyed all the old sermons, all the old absolutes, all the old cut-and-dried conceptions even of time and space, which were so discouraging because they seemed all so solid that you never could get any further. I want to get further always, I want more and more problems. And our visitor has raised endless and wonderful problems, and has begun solving them. [...]

Now, my lords and ladies and gentlemen, are you ready for the toast? I now give you: Health and length of days to the greatest of our contemporaries: Einstein.

10. "Bradlaugh and Today," address at Friends House, Euston Road, London, 23 September 1933. [*Religious Speeches*, pp. 89–93]

[*Smith notes (p. 89): "It is quoted from a memorial pamphlet issued for the Centenary Committee by C. A. Watts & Co., Ltd., and The Pioneer Press." Shaw fondly remembers Charles Bradlaugh, a man who "saw that the religious question was the question."*]

One of the things that one has to do at this distance of time in speaking of Charles Bradlaugh is to find out what he really stands for in the memories of those who, like myself, personally remember him and in the memories of those who know nothing about his personality and to whom he is only a name. [...]

Now we are not here tonight to discuss the merits of this or that belief or disbelief. We are here to celebrate the memory of a political genius. Political genius consists in a sense of values, of knowing the relative importance of things. Bradlaugh saw the fundamental importance of the religious question in this country: that was what made him before all things an Anti-Fundamentalist.

Since his death [in 1891], things have marched his way. A week or so ago a couple of very eloquent sermons were broadcast from London. One of them was by that great man in his way, the Dean of St. Paul's, and the other by that eminent churchman, [George Bell (1883–1958)] the Bishop of Chichester [1929–58]. They were both preaching, and preaching with their utmost seriousness, because they were addressing many millions of people. The subject with which they were dealing was the life of Christ, the example of Christ, the possibility of living the Christian life. The sermons were very good sermons, but neither of them contained one single word from which a stranger to our religions and institutions could have gathered that Jesus Christ was anything more than a man. There was not the slightest hint of his being a supernatural event. The Dean of St. Paul's even went a little out of his way to emphasize that the promises made by Jesus Christ at the end of his career, that he would return and establish his kingdom on earth, had not been fulfilled, and that in future we must face the question of Christ's life and example in the light of that fact.

Clearly we have traveled some distance since the death of Charles Bradlaugh; yet few of those who remember him notice that they have changed their opinions. They remember only that it was not considered respectable to agree with him when he was alive, and as they quite forget why—if they ever knew—they still remember Bradlaugh as being a man with whose opinions it was not respectable to agree. They are not conscious of the fact that there has been such a shift of opinion that many church dignitaries have reached a point which I really think would rather have shocked Charles Bradlaugh. [...] What really made Charles Bradlaugh the great man that he was was not so much those extraordinary heroic personal qualities which made him an almost superhuman figure for his contemporaries as well as a great platform artist, but that he saw that the religious question was *the* question. It was certainly the question he had the most at heart. (*Hear, Hear*) He spoke as a matter of duty about other questions, but on this one he spoke with passion and conviction, facing every peril to himself for the sake of making his opinions known and denouncing and trying to destroy the Bible worshipping superstition they called religion at that time.

It is a curious point that his devotion to this great social service proves that he must have been a deeply religious man, and this is why we could not have chosen a more appropriate place of meeting to celebrate the centenary of Charles Bradlaugh than Friends House. (*Applause*) Our friends the [Religious Society of Friends, the] Quakers [founded by George

Fox (1624–91)] have got nearer to real religion than any other professedly religious body. (*Hear, Hear*)

His work is not finished. The spadework he did on its foundations was mostly negative work, that is to say that he had to deny. A great deal of it was necessarily denial of falsehoods and exposure of all sorts of irrationalities and superstitions. I wish he were with us today, because he brought us to the point at which we see that negatives are not enough. (*Hear, Hear*) One of the worst of the crimes we are still committing is that we deliberately go on teaching our children lies. (*Applause*) Those of us who are carrying on Bradlaugh's work are like the unfortunate man in the classical inferno, whose punishment it was throughout all eternity to roll an enormous stone up a hill, only to have it crash back on him again every time. That is what is happening to us, and what happened continually to Charles Bradlaugh. He could get at his own audiences and could convert them, but all round him the new generations of children were going into church schools and into all sorts of schools where the Bible was being put into their hands, not as a collection of old literature and fairy tales, as it is, but as a divine revelation. (*Hear, Hear*) If you want to know what it means to get the campaigns of [military general] Joshua [the leader of the Israelite tribes following the death of Moses], rubbed into you in your youth as the work of God, you have nothing to do but read the history of the [World War I] years 1914 to 1918. (*Applause*)

[...] We shall have to see that in future children shall not only not be told lies but told truths. (*Applause*) Bradlaugh would approve of that because what made him great was that he could not tolerate falsehood. (*Hear, Hear*) [...] There are many men who, in their earliest days, are intellectually honest and, like Bradlaugh, have told the truth and fought for the truth, but they end by going into Parliament. They are classed as eminent statesmen when they learn how to give the public what it wants, and that is bunk. (*Applause*) Whatever you got from Charles Bradlaugh you never got bunk. You never got anything that he did not believe. The only thing I regret in his career is that he went into Parliament. It was just the one place that was not fit for him, nor he fit for it. [...]

I do not, like [socialist politician] Lord [Henry] Snell [1865–1944], owe my conversion to Charles Bradlaugh, because I was ten times as much an atheist as he was before I ever met him, but I do say that he was a great figure, and there he remains, when a great many of his parliamentary contemporaries have completely faded out of our memory and out of history. We have not got any single man of his stamp now. [...]

11. "Religion and War," an untitled BBC broadcast, 2 November 1937. [*Religious Speeches*, pp. 94–99]

[*Published as "As I See It" in* The Listener 18 (10 November 1937) *and as "So Long, So Long" in* Vital Speeches of the Day (15 November 1937). *Reprinted as "Shaw Speaks on War" in* The Shavian 1 (December 1953), *as "This Danger of War" in Dan H. Laurence,* Platform and Pulpit (New York: Hill and Wang, 1961) *and in* Bernard Shaw on War, *edited by J. P. Wearing (London: Hesperus Press, 2009), and as "As I See It" in L. W. Conolly,* Bernard Shaw and the BBC (Toronto: University of Toronto Press, 2009). *Shaw comments here that one cannot "depend on any sort of divine providence to put a stop to war."*]

What about this danger of war which is making us all shake in our shoes at present? I am like yourself. I have an intense objection to having my house demolished by a bomb from an aeroplane and myself killed in a horribly painful way by mustard gas [the chemical compound used by the Germans in World War I]. I have visions of streets heaped with mangled corpses in which children wander crying for their parents and babies gasp and strangle in the clutches of dead mothers. That is what war means nowadays. It is what is happening in Spain [the Spanish Civil War (1936–39)] and in China [the Second Sino-Japanese War (1937–45)] whilst I speak to you, and it may happen to us tomorrow.

And the worst of it is that it does not matter two straws to nature, the mother of us all, how dreadfully we misbehave ourselves in this way or in what hideous agonies we die. Nature can produce children enough to make good any extremity of slaughter of which we are capable. London may be destroyed, Paris, Rome, Berlin, Vienna, Constantinople may be laid in smoking ruins, and the last shrieks of their women and children may give way to the silence of death. No matter: nature will replace the dead. She is doing so every day. The new men will replace the old cities and perhaps come to the same miserable end. To nature, the life of an empire is no more than the life of a swarm of bees, and a thousand years are of less account than half an hour to you and me.

Now the moral of that is that we must not depend on any sort of divine providence to put a stop to war. Providence says, "Kill one another, my children, kill one another to your heart's content. There are plenty more where you came from." Consequently, if we want the war to stop, we must all become conscientious objectors.

I dislike war, not only for its dangers and inconveniences, but because of the loss of so many young men, any of whom may be a Newton or an Einstein, a [Ludwig van] Beethoven [1770–1827], a Michelangelo [Buonarroti (1475–1564)], a Shakespeare, or even a Shaw. Or he may be, what is of much more immediate importance, a good baker or a good weaver or builder. If you think of a pair of combatants as a heroic British St. Michael [the archangel] bringing the wrath of God upon the German Lucifer, then you may exult in the victory of St. Michael if he kills Lucifer, or burn to avenge him if his dastardly adversary mows him down with a machine gun before he can get to grips with him. In that way, you can get intense emotional experience from the war.

But suppose you think of the two as they probably are, say two good carpenters taken away from their proper work to kill one another. That is how I see it, and the result is that whichever of them is killed, the loss is as great to Europe and to me.

In nineteen hundred and fourteen I was sorry for the young Germans who lay slain and mutilated in no man's land as for the British lads who lay beside them, so I got no emotional satisfaction out of the war. It was to me a sheer waste of life. I'm not forgetting the gratification that war gives to the instinct of pugnacity and that admiration of courage that are so strong in women. [...]

The pacifist movement against war takes as its charter the ancient document called "The Sermon on the Mount," which is almost as often quoted as the speech which Abraham Lincoln [1809–65] is supposed to have delivered on the battlefield of Gettysburg [in Pennsylvania on 19 November 1863]. The sermon is a very moving exhortation, and it gives you one first rate tip, which is to do good to those who despitefully use you and persecute you. I, who am a much hated man, have been doing that all my life, and I can assure you that there is no better fun; whereas revenge and resentment make life miserable and the avenger hateful.

But such a commandment as "Love one another," as I see it, is a stupid refusal to accept the facts of human nature. Are we lovable animals? Do you love the rate collector? Do you love [Liberal PM (1916–22)] Mr. Lloyd George [1863–1945], and if you do, do you love [eminent statesman] Mr. Winston Churchill [1874–1965]? Have you an all-embracing affection for [military statesmen] Messrs. [Benito] Mussolini [1883–1945], [Adolf] Hitler [1889–1945], [Francisco] Franco [1892–1975], [Mustafa Kemal] Atatürk [1881–1938], and the Mikado [or Emperor of Japan, Hirohito (1901–89)]? I do not love all these gentlemen, and even if I did, how could I offer myself to them as a delightfully lovable person? I find I cannot like myself without so many reservations that I look forward to my death, which cannot now be far off, as a good riddance. If you tell me to be perfect, as my Father in Heaven is perfect, I can only say that I wish I could. That will be more polite than telling you to go to the zoo and advise the monkeys to become men and the cockatoos to become birds of paradise.

The lesson we have to learn is that our dislike for a certain person, or even for the whole human race, does not give us any right to injure our fellow creatures, however odious they may be. As I see it, the social rule must be: Live and let live. And as people who break this rule persistently must be liquidated, the pacifists and non-resisters must draw a line accordingly.

When I was a young man in the latter part of the nineteenth century, war did not greatly concern me personally, because I lived on an island far away from the battlefield and because the fighting was done by soldiers who had taken up that trade in preference to any other open to them. Now that aeroplanes bring battle to my housetop, and governments take me from my proper work and force me to be a soldier, whether I like it or not, I can no longer regard war as something that does not concern me personally, though they say that I am too old to be a soldier. And if nations had any sense, they would begin a war by sending their oldest men to the trenches. They would not risk the lives of their young men except in the last extremity.

In nineteen hundred and fourteen it was a dreadful thing to see regiments of lads singing [the popular World War I music hall song] "Tipperary" [full title "It's a Long Way to Tipperary"] on their way to the slaughter house. But the spectacle of regiments of octogenarians, hobbling to the front, waving their walking sticks and piping up to the tune of [singing] [the lyrics in Rudyard Kipling's novel *The Light That*

Failed (1890)] "We'll never come back no more, boys, we'll never come back no more." —wouldn't you cheer that enthusiastically? I should. And let me not forget that I should be one of them.

It has become a commonplace to say that another great war will destroy civilization. Well, that will depend on what sort of war it will be. If it is to be like the nineteen hundred and fourteen war, a war of nations, it will certainly not make an end of civilization. It may conceivably knock the British Empire to bits and leave England as primitive as she was when [Roman Emperor] Julius Caesar [100–44 BCE] landed in Kent [in 55 and 54 BCE during the Gallic Wars]. Perhaps we should be happier then, for we are still savages at heart and wear our thin uniform of civilization very awkwardly.

But anyhow, there will be two refuges left for civilization. No national attack can seriously hurt the two great federated republics of North America and Soviet Russia. They are too big, the distances are too great. But what could destroy them is civil war—wars like the wars of religion in the seventeenth century. And this is exactly the sort of war that is threatening us today. It has already begun in Spain, where all the big capitalist powers are taking a hand to support General Franco through an Intervention Committee, which they think it more decent to call a Nonintervention Committee. This is only a skirmish in the class war. The war between the two religions of capitalism and communism, which is at bottom a war between labor and landowning.

We could escape that war by putting our house in order as Russia has done, without any of the fighting and killing and waste and damage that the Russians went through. But we don't seem to want to. I have shown exactly how it can be done and, in fact, how it must be done. But nobody takes any notice. Foolish people in easy circumstances flatter themselves that there is no such thing as the class war in the British Empire, where we are all far too respectable and too well protected by our parliamentary system to have any vulgar unpleasantness of that sort. They deceive themselves. We are up to the neck in the class war.

What is it that is wrong with our present way of doing things? It is not that we cannot produce enough goods. Our machines turn out as much work in an hour as ten thousand hand workers used to. But it is not enough for a country to produce goods. It must distribute them as well. And this is where our system breaks down hopelessly. Everybody ought to be living quite comfortably by working four or five hours a day, with two Sundays in the week. Yet, millions of laborers die in the workhouse or on the dole after sixty years of hard toil so that a few babies may have hundreds of thousands a year before they are born.

As I see it, this is not a thing to be argued about or to take sides about. It is stupid and wicked on the face of it, and it will smash us and our civilization if we do not resolutely reform it. Yet we do nothing but keep up a perpetual ballyhoo about bolshevism, fascism, communism, liberty, dictators, democracy, and all the rest of it.

The very first lesson of the new history dug up for us by [Egyptologist] Professor Flinders Petrie [1853–1942] during my lifetime is that no civilization, however splendid, illustrious, and like our own, can stand up against the social resentment and class conflict which follow a silly misdistribution of wealth, labor, and leisure. And it is the one history lesson that is never taught in our schools, thus confirming the saying of the German philosopher, [Georg Wilhelm Friedrich] Hegel [1770–1831]: "We learn from history that men never learn anything from history." Think it over.

So long. So long.

Part II. Essays and Journalism

1. From "On Going to Church," *The Savoy* 1 (January 1896), pp. 13–28. [*Shaw on Religion*, pp. 19–25]

[*Published as* On Going to Church *(Boston: John W. Luce & Co., 1905). Recalling the intolerable services of his youth that "prejudiced me so violently against church-going," Shaw yet maintains that only in church can our need for "refreshment and recreation... be truly met, ...going in without thought or belief or prayer or any other vanity."]*

There is still one serious obstacle to the use of churches on the very day when most people are best able and most disposed to visit them. I mean, of course, the services. When I was a little boy, I was compelled to go to church on Sunday; and though I escaped from that intolerable bondage before I was ten, it prejudiced me so violently against church-going that twenty years elapsed before, in foreign lands and in pursuit of works of art, I became once more a churchgoer. To this day, my flesh creeps when I recall that genteel suburban Irish Protestant church, built by Roman Catholic workmen who would have considered themselves damned had they crossed its threshold afterwards. Every separate stone, every pane of glass, every fillet of ornamental ironwork—half-dog-collar, half-coronet—in that building must have sowed a separate evil passion in my young heart. Yes; all the vulgarity, savagery, and bad blood which has marred my literary work, was certainly laid upon me in that house of Satan! The mere nullity of the building could make no positive impression on me; but what could, and did, were the unnaturally motionless figures of the congregation in their Sunday clothes and bonnets, and their set faces, pale with the malignant rigidity produced by the suppression of all expression. And yet these people were always moving and watching one another by stealth, as convicts communicate with one another. So was I. I had been told to keep my restless little limbs still all through those interminable hours; not to talk; and, above all, to be happy and holy there and glad that I was not a wicked little boy playing in the fields instead of worshipping God. I hypocritically acquiesced; but the state of my conscience may be imagined, especially as I implicitly believed that all the rest of the congregation were perfectly sincere and good. I remember at that time dreaming one night that I was dead and had gone to heaven. The picture of heaven which the efforts of the then Established Church of Ireland had conveyed to my childish imagination was a waiting room with walls of pale sky-coloured tabbinet, and a pew-like bench running all around, except at one corner, where there was a door. I was, somehow, aware that God was in the next room, accessible through that door. I was seated on the bench with my ankles tightly interlaced to prevent my legs dangling, behaving myself with all my might before the grown-up people, who all belonged to the Sunday congregation, and were either sitting on the bench as if at church or else moving solemnly in and out as if there were a dead person in the house. A grimly-handsome lady who usually sat in a corner seat near me in church, and whom I believed to be thoroughly conversant with the arrangements of the Almighty, was to introduce me presently into the next room—a moment which I was supposed to await with joy and enthusiasm. Really, of course, my heart sank like lead within me at the thought; for I felt that my feeble affectation of piety could not impose on Omniscience, and that one glance at that all-searching eye would discover that I had been allowed to come to heaven by mistake. Unfortunately for the interest of this narrative, I awoke, or wandered off into another dream, before the critical moment arrived. But it goes far enough to show that I was by no means an insusceptible subject: indeed, I am sure, from other early experiences of mine, that if I had been turned loose in a real church, and allowed to wander and stare about, or hear noble music there instead of that most accursed Te Deum [Laudamus] of [William] Jackson's [1730–1803] and a senseless droning of [the hymn, associated with the 100th Psalm, that begins "All People That on Earth Do Dwell"] the Old Hundredth, I should never have seized the opportunity of a great evangelical revival, which occurred when I was still in my teens, to begin my literary career with a letter to the Press (which was duly printed), announcing with inflexible materialistic logic, and to the extreme horror of my respectable connections, that I was an atheist. When, later on, I was led to the study of the economic basis of the respectability of that and similar congregations, I was inexpressibly relieved to find that it represented a mere passing phase of industrial confusion, and could never have substantiated its claims to my respect if, as a child, I had been able to bring it to book. To this very day, whenever there is the slightest danger of my being mistaken for a votary of the blue tabbinet waiting-room or a supporter of that morality in which wrong and right, base and noble, evil and good, really mean nothing more than the kitchen and the drawing-room, I hasten to claim honourable exemption, as atheist and socialist, from any such complicity.

When I at last took to church-going again, a kindred difficulty beset me, especially in Roman Catholic countries. In Italy, for instance, the churches are used in such a way that priceless pictures become smeared with filthy tallow-soot, and have sometimes to be rescued by the temporal power and placed in national galleries. But worse than this are the innumerable daily services which disturb the truly religious visitor. If these were decently and intelligently conducted by genuine mystics to whom the Mass [or sacrament of the Eucharist, the divine service of worship] was no mere rite or miracle, but a real communion, the celebrants might reasonably claim a place in the church as their share of the common human right to its use. But the average Italian priest, personally uncleanly, and with chronic catarrh of the nose and throat, produced and maintained by sleeping and living in frowsy, ill-ventilated rooms, punctuating his gabbled Latin only by expectorative hawking, and making the decent guest sicken and shiver every time the horrible splash of spitten mucus echoes along the vaulting from the marble steps of the altar: this unseemly wretch should be seized and put out, bell, book, candle and all, until he learns to behave himself. The English tourist is often lectured for his inconsiderate behavior in Italian churches, for walking about during service, talking loudly, thrusting himself rudely between a worshipper and an altar to examine a painting, even for stealing chips of stone and scrawling his name on statues. But as far as the mere disturbance of the services is concerned, and the often very evident disposition of the tourist—especially the experienced tourist—to regard the priest and his congregation as troublesome intruders, a week spent in Italy will convince any unprejudiced person that this is a perfectly reasonable attitude. I have seen inconsiderate British behavior often enough both in church and out of it. The slow-witted Englishman who refuses to get out of the way of the Host, and looks at the bellringer going before it with 'Where the devil are you shoving to?' written in every pucker of his freeborn British brow, is a familiar figure to me; but I have never seen any stranger behave so insufferably as the officials of the church habitually do. It is the sacristan who teaches you, when once you are committed to tipping him, not to waste your good manners on the kneeling worshippers who are snatching a moment from their daily round of drudgery and starvation to be comforted by the Blessed Virgin or one of the saints: it is the officiating priest who makes you understand that the congregation are past shocking by any indecency that you would dream of committing, and that the black looks of the congregation are directed at the foreigner and the heretic only, and imply a denial of your right as a human being to your share of the use of the church. That right should be unflinchingly asserted on all proper occasions. I know no contrary right by which the great Catholic churches made for the world by the great church-builders should be monopolized by any sect as against any man who desires to use them. My own faith is clear: I am a resolute Protestant; I believe in the Holy Catholic Church; in the Holy Trinity of Father, Son (or Mother, Daughter) and Spirit; in the Communion of Saints, the Life to Come, the Immaculate Conception, and the everyday reality of Godhead and the Kingdom of Heaven. Also, I believe that salvation depends on redemption from belief in miracles; and I regard St Athanasius [of Alexandria (c. 296–373)] as an irreligious fool—that is, in the only serious sense of the word, a damned fool. I pity the poor neurotic who can say, 'Man that is born of a woman hath but a short time to live, and is full of misery' [from the Anglican *Book of Common Prayer* (1549), the first to give the complete forms of services of worship], as I pity the maudlin drunkard; and I know that the real religion of today was made possible only by the materialistic-physicists and atheist-critics who performed for us the indispensable preliminary operation of purging us thoroughly of the ignorant and vicious superstitions which were thrust down our throats as religion in our helpless childhood. How those who assume that our churches are the private property of their sect would think of this profession of faith of mine need not describe. But am I, therefore, to be denied access to the place of spiritual recreation which is my inheritance as much as theirs? If, for example, I desire to follow a good old custom by pledging my love to my wife in the church of our parish, why should I be denied due record in the registers unless she submits to have a moment of deep feeling made ridiculous by the reading aloud of the *naïve* impertinences of St Peter, who, on the subject of Woman, was neither Catholic nor Christian, but a boorish Syrian fisherman. If I want to name a child in the church, the prescribed service may be more touched with the religious spirit—once or twice beautifully touched—but, on the whole, it is time to dismiss our prayer-book as quite rotten with the pessimism of the age which prescribed it. In spite of the stolen jewels with which it is studded, an age of strength and faith and noble activity can have nothing to do with it: Caliban [in Shakespeare's *The Tempest*] might have constructed such a ritual out of his own terror of the supernatural, and such fragments of the words of the saints as he could dimly feel some sort of glory in.

My demand will now be understood without any ceremonious formulation of it. No nation, working at the strain we face, can live cleanly without public-houses in which to seek refreshment and recreation. To supply that vital want we have the drinking-shop with its narcotic, stimulant poisons, the conventicle with its brimstone-flavoured hot gospel, and the church. In the church alone can our need be truly met, not even there save when we leave outside the door the materialisms that help us to think the unthinkable, completing the refuse-heap of 'isms' and creeds with our vain lust for truth and happiness, and going in without thought or belief or prayer or any other vanity, so that the soul, freed from all that crushing lumber, may open all its avenues of life to the holy air of the true Catholic Church.

2. "On Miracles: A Retort," *The New Age* (10 December 1908), pp. 129–30. [*Shaw on Religion*, pp. 42–48]

[The original title was "A Retort on Mr Chesterton." After discussing certain "classes" of miracles, and though some miracles "so please our imaginations or promise us relief or profit of some sort that we believe them in spite of experience," Shaw concludes that

"there is nothing to be got out of miracles, either one way or the other, by special pleaders for or against any particular religion."]

In the course of his encounter with [socialist and historian] Mr [Ernest] Belfort Bax [1854–1926], Mr Chesterton takes the opportunity to tread on the tail of my coat. Lest the humorous ingenuity of the attack should be lost on the careless reader, let me quote it. "Ask Bernard Shaw," says Mr Chesterton, "to speak on any other subject, and he explodes with epigrammatic sagacity: ask him why he denies miracle, and his answer is a curious and dreary compound of a Hyde Park Secularist and a Broad Church [or liberal] Bishop." The humour of this lies in the fact that nobody ever asks me why I deny miracles, because I never do deny them, but, on the contrary, spend my life largely affirming them. And I do not see why a compound of a Hyde Park Secularist and a Broad Church Bishop need be dreary or even curious: the Victorian Broad Church Bishops who had a dash of the Hyde Park Secularist in them were particularly lively Bishops; and the combination has not become conventional, though I quite agree that the type is obsolescing. But I have never in my life heard either a Broad Church Bishop or a Hyde Park Secularist put forward my view of miracles. I will now proceed to lay down the law on the subject of miracles; and I defy Mr Chesterton to braze his cheerful countenance to the extremity of telling me that it is a relic of that Victorian past which he imagines, but which I remember.

The world is full of miracles. Consciousness, for instance, is a complete miracle. Birth is a miracle; life is a miracle; and death was a miracle until quite recently, when [German evolutionary biologist August] Weismann [1834–1914] made out a very plausible case for regarding it as a rather late product of natural selection. Anyhow, there are lots of miracles about; and the man who denies their existence is always a man who is simply wrong in his definition of a miracle. By a miracle he means only something that he is not accustomed to and did not expect.

Miracles can be divided into two main classes: (1) Miraculous events as to the actual occurrence of which there is no question and no doubt. (2) Miraculous events of which the occurrence is not generally admitted. For instance, it is alleged that Lazarus rose from the dead at the command of Jesus. Though this was a very much simpler feat than to get born and up, yet nobody believes that he actually did it except people who would believe anything.

The reason of this is obvious enough. None of us has ever seen a man raised from the dead except on the banks of the Serpentine [lake in London] by a policeman skilled in the art of inducing artificial respiration; and even this exception we try to get out of by the manifestly futile contention that the resurrected one was not dead—that he was only drowned. Still, the distinction between a familiar miracle and an unprecedented one accounts roughly for a good deal of the fact that we are credulous as to some miracles and incredulous as to others. But it does not account for all of it. There are certain kinds of miracles that so please our imaginations or promise us relief or profit of some sort that we believe them in spite of experience. Doctors, like witches, profess to perform all the miracles attributed to founders of religions; and though they fail daily, people are actually sent to prison for doubting such professions.

Finally, one observes that the moment you get beyond the range of those miracles which everybody has seen performed often enough to have lost all sense of their being miracles, credulity and incredulity are entirely temperamental and dogmatic. It was my grasp of this fact that enabled me to deflate Mr Chesterton recently at [an Inn of Chancery in London] Clifford's Inn. Like the old-fashioned Secularist, he started arguing about miracles. He argued, in effect, that it is ridiculous for us, gorged as we are daily by unquestionable miracles, to make a difficulty about believing in this or that event merely because it is a miracle. And he was quite right. If you believe that the sun will rise tomorrow morning, you give up all right to deny that I can turn a dog into a cat merely on the ground that such a metamorphosis is a miracle. But that does not alter the fact that everybody believes that the sun will rise tomorrow, and that nobody believes that I can turn a dog into a cat. I quite grant that the Victorian Secularist who tries to make out that the one event is a miracle and the other is not, can be controversially spifflicated by Mr Chesterton, who is nevertheless not a bit more credulous than [physicist John] Tyndall [1820–93] or [historian and critic] Leslie Stephen [1832–1904]. But Mr Chesterton, overshooting his conclusion with his usual impetuosity, not only devastated the gasping Rationalists and Materialists in the audience by demonstrating this, but went on to imply that since he might as well be hanged for a sheep as for a lamb, he was prepared to swallow all the miracles of religious legend, holding himself up as one who had risen into a mystic sphere in which vulgar incredulity as to miracles had fallen off him as a garment.

I ruined this transfiguration in a very simple manner. I am by this time a sufficiently good judge of men to be able to guess the place at which they will draw the line between their dogmatic credulity and their dogmatic incredulity. I took a particular miracle, one just as well vouched for as any other particular miracle, and not a bit more miraculous than dozens of miracles in which Mr Chesterton and I believe, but one in which, nevertheless, I dogmatically do not believe and in which I knew that Mr Chesterton did not believe. I asked him did he believe in that miracle. He could easily have floored me by telling a direct lie and saying he did. But it was miraculously impossible for him to do so, as I knew it would be. He made a gallant attempt to shake my teeth out of his calf, so to speak, by saying that there were just as good reasons for his believing in this particular miracle as for his believing in many other things which I and everybody else in the room believe in as well. But I knew too much about miracles to be shaken off. I kept repeating, both when I was in order and out of order, the flat question as to whether he believed or did not believe in that particular miracle. He could not say that he believed in it. Nobody believed in it. Nobody believed that he could believe in it. And the impression produced was—most unfairly and erroneously—that Mr Chesterton's argument had fallen to pieces.

A point to be observed about miracles is that mankind may be divided into people who, like [empiricist philosopher David] Hume [1711–76], consider that any "natural" explanation of an event is to be preferred to the no-explanation that it is miraculous, and the other sort of people who have the opposite preference, and think it much more likely that the spirit of their late grandmother is rapping on the table than that I am tapping my boot against the leg of my chair, as I generally am on such occasions. These marvellors will not believe in a religion unless its apostles entertain them with conjuring tricks: the other sort will not believe in religion at all because concessions have been made by all religions to the other party. And of course these two sorts of people are mostly the same sort. Professor Tyndall would not believe in spontaneous generation on any terms; but he made no bones about attributing to every atom a positive and negative magnetic pole, and a consequent self-arrangement of atoms into crystals, and mountains, and sunsets, and vertebrate animals, stopping short quite unaccountably of cherubim and seraphim, who, if they exist, may surely be as atomic and magnetic as anybody else. Other learned doctors are quite ready to believe that when St Paul's head was chopped off it bounded away, leaving a new spring of fresh water to mark the place of each ricochet; but they will not believe the simplest fact of natural history discovered by Darwin.

Let us confess, then, that the man who argues that miracles must be either credible or incredible, and that if some miracles are credible (as they undoubtedly are), then all miracles must be credible, is the most hopelessly unreal kind of logician. The plain facts are that some miracles are credible and some are incredible, and that every different sort of man draws the line in a different place. Therefore there is nothing to be got out of miracles, either one way or the other, by special pleaders for or against any particular religion.

Further, it is inevitable that a man's quality shall be judged by the situation of the boundary between his credulity and his incredulity. We cannot help saying, concerning any given miracle, either "the man who believes this would believe anything," meaning, "the man who believes this must be a silly fool," or "the man who will not believe this will not believe anything," meaning, "the man who cannot feel the truth of this must be a damned fool." (Need I say that I am using the word damned literally and not abusively?) But these sayings are inevitable only because it is inevitable that men should express their opinions. Each miracle remains a separate matter of opinion after all; and every brace of miracles is like the two women grinding in the field [in Luke 17:35]: one shall be taken and the other left by that capricious human appetite which we call faith. When I was taken to the pantomime at a very early age, I believed piously in the fairy queen and ecstatically in the clown; but I did not believe in the clown *because* I believed in the fairy queen, nor would I have forsaken her if I had found the clown out. I no longer believe in either of them in that particular way. And these are not the only options I changed. I have gained beliefs and lost beliefs; but I never took on a new belief merely because I already entertained beliefs just as incredible; and I never threw off a belief merely because I had already thrown off others just as credible. That is not the way the human imagination works.

Such is my position about miracles. I offer it as completely up-to-date, although it was probably held by Adam, or would have been if Adam had had my opportunities of observation. And I challenge Mr Chesterton to name any Victorian Secularist or Broad Church Bishop who anticipated me in it. Not that it would be any the worse for having been so anticipated; but, as a matter of fact, both Secularists and Broad Church Bishops always struck me as resolutely binding themselves to it because they had jumped to the conclusion that you could not discredit any miracle without discrediting all miracles, and that if you admitted all the rest, not noticing, apparently, that whether you were bound to or not, you just didn't.

3. "God Must be Non-Sectarian and International," *The Christian Commonwealth* (17 July 1912), p. 683. [*Shaw on Religion*, pp. 54–59]

[Shaw's original letter was headed, "The Idea of God / Mr G Bernard Shaw's Surrejoinder to Mr Campbell." Shaw offers a number of viewpoints on the crucifixion and on Jesus, including that of the Jew ("a seditious carpenter whom my people executed") and Moslem ("a very worthy prophet," but "so timid and helpless personally that he was defeated by a second-rate high priest") and Shaw's own ("the cruelty and bigotry of the high priest and his supporters").]

"The difference between Mr R. J. Campbell's position and mine is really part of the fact that we have a different job, and that the theology that suffices for his job will not suffice for mine. Mr Campbell, as pastor of the Christian congregation of the City Temple, knows that Christianity is a first necessity of spiritual life for its members, because to them no spiritual life is intelligible except in terms of Christianity. But my congregation is as wide as the English language, and, indeed, wider. It includes Jews, Mohammedans, Agnostics, and all sorts of non-Christians with whom the first condition of an acceptable theology, or biology, or psychology, or whatever they call it (for I am not free even to use the word theology) is that it shall be entirely independent of Christianity. If I were to write about Jesus as Mr Campbell does, and pray to him, I should presently be up against a Jewish reader who would say to me: "My good sir, all this is no use to me. I see nothing in this man Jesus but a seditious carpenter whom my people executed, very properly in my opinion, exactly as your Christians executed [Italian Dominican friar Girolamo] Savonarola [1452–98] and [Dutch Anabaptist leader] John of Leyden [1509–36], because he was upsetting all law and order without having any clear or practicable idea of what to put in their place. Your Mr Campbell is simply an idolator; and, though he may find that his idolatry is a convenient instrument for saving the souls of congregations of Christians who have been taught from their earliest childhood to associate all their highest idealism with the personality of Jesus, I and my co-religionists have not been trained in that way; we crucified Jesus, and have never recanted that very practical criticism of him; so if you wish to draw us into your communion you must not ask us to rate Jesus higher generically that any other historical character. You must even be content to find that many of us consider that we are making too great a concession in admitting that Jesus was a historical person, and not a mere excuse for robbing, outlawing, and murdering the chosen people." On which some good Moslem will cry: "I do not at all agree with our Israelite friend about Jesus. He was a very worthy prophet, and to some extent the forerunner of The Prophet, who spoke very handsomely of him. But you will surely not contest the enormous superiority of Mahomet. Jesus, as your most enthusiastic Christian, Mr Campbell, admits, preached to a highly civilized people a gospel which had been propagated among them for several hundred years. But he was incapable of organization, and so timid and helpless personally that he was defeated by a second-rate high priest, and beaten and executed. Mahomet preached God to hordes of fierce idolators who worshipped stones. He began with two followers: his wife and a boy of sixteen; and he ended on one of the greatest temporal and spiritual thrones the world has ever seen, having not only taught the people, but fought for them and conquered for them, and put the Caiaphases and Pilates of Arabia under his feet." [Caiaphas was the powerful Jewish high priest said to have organized the plot to kill Jesus.] And yet a third critic will come and say: "Really, Mr Shaw, I am surprised to find you pretending to listen respectfully to these two imbeciles, one of them worshipping an Arab camel driver who divided the year into lunar months and thought the mountains were weights to keep the earth from being blown away, and the other prating about his wretched tribe being the chosen people of a long since demolished idol. Pray, have you ever heard of modern science? Have you ever heard of Evolution? Do you really believe? does anybody worth counting really believe? in the Resurrection, in a sky rocket Ascension [forty days later of the resurrected Jesus up to Heaven], in the commercial theory of the Atonement, in the Garden of Eden, and the miracles, and all the rest of it? Do you expect me to associate myself with a propaganda that gives the slightest countenance to these absurdities for the sake of conciliating ignorant labourers and petty tradesmen and the priestly exploiters of their credulity?" And so on, and so forth.

What am I to say to these people? They are all as right as Mr Campbell: that is, they feel exactly as they say. Some of the ablest of our young musicians and writers tell me that they find Beethoven's harmony intolerably uninteresting, and that they cannot read [novelist Charles] Dickens [1812–70]. Well, they are none the less entitled to their sensations because I am saturated with Dickens and Beethoven. Evidently, if I am to work with them at all, I must take care not to make my views on music and literature hinge on an adoration of

Beethoven and Dickens. But for the purpose of a Beethoven society or a Dickens Fellowship I might safely disregard them, and do very good work by appealing to the love of Beethoven and Dickens. Just so can Mr Campbell do good work by appealing to the love of Jesus felt by the congregation of the City Temple. But this very thing that helps him so powerfully would be fatal to me.

For the same reason I must not talk about "The Father." If I do, my friend [the prominent socialist and atheist Robert] Blatchford [1851–1943] will promptly say: "Let us understand one another, Shaw. A father is evidently a mature person of the male sex. That is the beginning of definiteness. Let us follow up that beginning. If we are looking for a person, and a male person, let us inform the police. They will want to know his age, his height, the colour of his hair and eyes, the place where he was last seen and who saw him, his customary habits and resorts, his race, colour, and language, and any other information that may lead to his identification, and, if necessary, arrest." At the City Temple it is easy to dispose of all this by crying "Throw the blasphemer out" and throwing him out. But the great majority of the subjects of the British Empire (do not forget the East) would laugh quite good-humouredly and consider that Mr Blatchford had reduced "The Father" to absurdity very successfully, wittily, and properly. I cannot unite even the sexes on a male Life Force; and as to uniting the nations on a black or white or yellow one (I should like to see the City Temple congregation confronted with a picture of the Trinity represented as a German, a negro, and a Chinaman), such an idolization is hopeless. I repeat, a combination of a white Father and a white Madonna may serve very well for the purpose of European Christian congregations. But for my purpose, which is to find a common faith for Mr Campbell and Mr Blatchford—both obviously good men, who should be helping instead of hindering one another—"The Father" is out of the question.

I really cannot accept Mr Campbell's apology for the crucifixion. If I were a deity, and anyone made such a plainly desperate attempt to whitewash me I should throw thunderbolts. The crucifixion manifested nothing but the cruelty and bigotry of the high priest and his supporters, and the impotence of imperial power and culture face to face with cruelty and bigotry. Mr Campbell's view seems to imply that if there had been a little more cruelty the effect would have been still more complete. As a matter of fact many more horrible executions are on record. John of Leyden was so hideously tortured to death at Munster that the wretched Christian bishop who had to preside over the execution went home and died of horror. The torture [for six weeks by red-hot irons, burning coals and other means] and execution [by public impalement in 1718] of [Major Stepan] Gliebof by [Russian Tsar (1682–1721) and Emperor (1721–25)] Peter the Great [(1672–1725), who had learned of Gliebof's nine-year love affair with Peter's ex-wife, Eudoxia] was much more horrible than the crucifixion; and even Gliebof's fate was less horrible than that of several of the women [including Eudoxia] on whom Peter wreaked his vengeance. We are ourselves responsible for the executions [by hanging, on 27 June 1906, of four Egyptians] at Denshawai [in Egypt], which were less defensible politically than the execution of Jesus, and were, relatively to our customs and the morality we profess, much more deliberately wicked and cruel. Mr Campbell's apology applies to all those horrors just as much as to the crucifixion. He will admit this, and repeat that Omnipotence could manifest its benevolence in no other way. But if he really means Omnipotence, he must write would instead of could; and that change turns his Omnipotent into "the almighty fiend" of Shelley.

I do not deny that the intentions of the Life Force have been good all through; and therefore Mr Campbell may say that all the good it has done was intended from the beginning. But he says also that all the bad it has done (and I have just cited some sensational examples) was intended from the beginning. That is not so cheering. I know only one method of finding out how to do anything. It is the method of Trial and Error. If the City Temple maintains that the Life Force intended its errors, it will not be long before not one stone of it shall be left on another; for this is the doctrine that killed religion in the nineteenth century, and may bury it in the twentieth if we do not root it out.

Finally, may I say that my mind is so constituted that if I could conceive a god as deliberately creating something less than himself, I should class him as a cad. If he were simply satisfied with himself, I should class him as a lazy coxcomb. My god must continually strive to surpass himself.

4. From *Common Sense About the War*, *The New Statesman* (14 November 1914). [*Shaw on Religion*, pp. 60–62]

[Shaw reprinted his thirty-five-thousand-word New Statesman *supplement in* What I Really Wrote About the War *(1932). Here he suggests that all churches close their doors in time of war.]*

In no previous war have we struck that top note of keen irony, the closing of the Stock Exchange [from 31 July 1914 to 4 January 1915] and not of the Church. The pagans were more logical: they closed the Temple of Peace when they drew the sword. We turn our Temples of Peace promptly into temples of war, and exhibit our parsons as the most pugnacious characters in the community. I venture to affirm that the sense of scandal given by this is far deeper and more general than the Church thinks, especially among the working classes, who are apt either to take religion seriously or else to repudiate it and criticize it closely. When a bishop at the first shot abandons the worship of Christ and rallies his flock round the altar of Mars [the Roman god of war], he may be acting patriotically, necessarily, manfully, rightly; but that does not justify him in pretending that there has been no change, and that Christ is, in effect, Mars. The straightforward course, and the one that would serve the Church best in the long run, would be to close our professedly Christian Churches the moment war is declared by us, and reopen them only on the signing of the treaty of peace. No doubt to many of us the privation thus imposed would be far worse than the privation of small change, of horses and motor cars, of express trains, and all the other prosaic inconveniences of war. But would it be worse than the privation of faith, and the horror of the soul, wrought by the spectacle of nations praying to their common Father to assist them in sabring and bayoneting and blowing one another to pieces with explosives that are also corrosives, and of the Church organizing this monstrous paradox instead of protesting against it? Would it make less atheists or more? Atheism is not a simple homogeneous phenomenon. There is the youthful atheism with which every able modern mind begins; an atheism that clears the soul of superstitions and terrors and servilities and base compliances and hypocrisies, and lets in the light of heaven. And there is the atheism of despair and pessimism: the sullen cry with which so many of us at this moment, looking on blinded deafened maimed wrecks that were once able-bodied admirable lovable men, and on priests blessing war, and newspapers and statesmen and exempt old men hounding young men on to it, and saying, "I know now there is no God." What has the Church in its present attitude to set against this crushed acceptance of darkness except the quaint but awful fact that there are cruder people on whom horrifying calamities have just the opposite effect, because they seem the work of some power so overwhelming in its malignity that it must be worshipped because it is mighty? Let the Church beware how it plays to that gallery. If all the Churches of Europe closed their doors until the drums ceased rolling they would act as a most powerful reminder that though the glory of war is a famous and ancient glory, it is not the final glory of God.

5. "A Catechism on My Creed," St. Martin-in-the-Fields Review (May 1922). [Shaw on Religion, pp. 128–31]

[Published in the St. Martin-in-the-Fields Review (May 1922). According to Laurence (Bibliography I: 310), the text was pre-published, as "Bernard Shaw on Religion," in The Observer (30 April 1922). A catechism is a series of fixed questions and answers summarizing the principles and beliefs of the Christian religion and used for instruction. Shaw again invokes "the God who is still struggling with the work of Creative Evolution."]

Do you believe (a) That there must be "somebody behind the something"? (b) In a First Cause? (c) That the universe made itself and that our world is a pure accident?

(a) No: I believe that there is something behind the somebody. All bodies are products of the Life Force (whatever that may be); and to put the body behind the thing that made it is to reverse the order of Nature, and also to violate the first article of the Church of England ["Of Faith in the Holy Trinity"], which expressly declares that God has neither body, parts, nor passions.

(b) A First Cause is a contradiction in terms, because in Causation every cause must have a cause; and therefore there can no more be a First Cause than a first inch in a circle. If you once admit a cause that is uncaused, you give up Causation altogether. And if you do that, you may as well say that everything makes itself. But you can only do that if it is alive; so you are back again at your mystery, and may as well confess that to your ignorance and limited faculty the universe is unaccountable. I daresay every blackbeetle thinks it must have a complete explanation of the world as one of the indispensable qualifications of a respectable cockroach; but it will have to do without it for a while yet.

(c) All life is a series of accidents; but when you find most of them pointing all one way, you may guess that there is something behind them that is not accidental.

Do you believe that given enough data to go on we could account for everything?

No. As a matter of fact we have data enough, from the Alps to the electrons, to account for everything fifty times over; but we have not the brains to interpret them.

You think the Church has "failed grossly in the courage of its profession," and therefore you disbelieve in it. But the Labour Party has equally missed its opportunity, yet you believe in it. Why?

The Church has failed infamously: I can hardly imagine how it has the face to exist after its recreancy during the war. But what has that to do with belief or disbelief? The Church of England is only a Society of gentlemen amateurs, half of them pretending to be properly trained and disciplined priests, and the other half pretending that they are breezy public schoolboys with no parsonic nonsense about them. They profess to sustain and propagate religious faith; but their failure or success, their honesty or dishonesty, their sense or their folly, cannot affect the faith: it can only affect the attendance in the buildings in which they pontificate. If a man sells me a bad motor car, I can take my custom away from him, and denounce him as an impostor, without ceasing to believe in the science of mechanics. There are churches where the parson snarls the service and bullies God like a barrister at the Old Bailey [the Central Criminal Court in London]. There are churches where he is a duffer, and churches where he is a snob. But that does not prevent people going to St Martin's. The Church is what the parsons make it; and when a man says he does not hold with the Church, and that parsons are frauds, we generally find either that he never goes to church, or else that his particular parson *is* a fraud.

The same thing is true of the Labour Party. It, also, is what the Labour men make it. But the truths it stands for remain none the less true.

Do you agree with [French philosopher and satirist] *Voltaire* [(1694–1778), who wrote bitterly against established religion], *who said, "To believe in God is impossible, not to believe in him is absurd"?*

No. Voltaire's remark was witty—that is, true—when he made it; and it is still true of the Omnipotent Personality, with body, parts, and passions, which the word God meant in Voltaire's time. But our God, the God who is still struggling with the work of Creative Evolution, and using us as his labourers, having created us for the purpose, and proceeding by the method of trial and error, presents no such difficulty. Unfortunately, many of our people have not yet caught up with Voltaire, much less with the twentieth century; and for them it would be a considerable advance if they were to become Voltaireans.

What effect do you think it would have on the country if every Church were shut and every parson unfrocked? Do you think a Religion is a necessity for the development of a nation? and if so, must it not have some organization for its development? Or do you believe that nothing can be organized in the realm of the Spirit in this present existence?

A very salutary effect indeed. It would soon provoke an irresistible demand for the Re-establishment of the Church, which could then start again without the superstitions that make it so impossible today. At present the Church has to make itself cheap in all sorts of ways to induce people to attend its services; and the cheaper it makes itself the less the people attend. Its articles are out of date; its services are out of date; and its ministers are men to whom such things do not matter because they are out of date themselves. The marriage service and the burial service are unbearable to people who take them seriously—and please do not conclude that I am thinking now of the current foolish and prudish objections to the sensible and true parts of the marriage service. Your main point is what would happen if the people suddenly found themselves without churches and rituals. So many of them would find that they had been deprived of a necessity of life that the want would have to be supplied; and there would presently be more churches than ever, and fuller ones. The only people who can do without churches are the simple materialists on the one hand, and on the other those who have no use for institutional worship because their churches are their own souls. That is the Quaker position; but you find such people in all circles. They are sometimes artists, sometimes philosophers; and the irony of circumstance has landed one of them in the extraordinary predicament of being a Dean.

Do you think Christ is still a living influence in the present day?

Yes; but there are, as he expected there would be, a good many very unchristlike people trading under his name: for instance, St. Paul. The wholesale rebellion against Christ's teaching which culminated in the war has turned out so very badly that just at present there are probably more people who feel that in him is the only hope for the world than there ever were before in the lifetime of men now living.

6. "On Ritual, Religion, and the Intolerableness of Tolerance," 1922. [*Shaw on Religion*, pp. 148–71]

[Smith notes (p. 238) that the essay is "from an edited typescript, but an extra copy bears the alternative title, 'The Church Versus Religion', and both are dated 'Ayot St. Lawrence. 16/10/22'." Shaw contrasts Quaker and Ritualist extremes to explain "the position of the persons who are somewhere on the scale between them" and offers examples to show that "no man will tolerate what he believes to be a false and mischievous religion whilst he has the means of perse-

cuting and suppressing it." Although "a common religion" would do away with the "persecution problem," the problem is that for many "it is not enough to believe in God: you must call him God and nothing else: if you call him Allah or Vishnu or... Gott, you are a heathen." Shaw concludes that we must be careful how we "put ourselves in the place of God by dictating how our neighbour should serve Him."]

Such a caption as The Church Versus Religion begs the question whether the Churches are really opposed to religion. Proverbs like "The nearer the Church, the further from God," or, "Heaven for holiness: hell for company" are happy witticisms; but no statesman could legislate on them, unless both had given up religion altogether as a bad job. [Russian novelist and Christian anarcho-pacifist Count Leo] Tolstoy [1828–1910], whose letters to certain churchmen have provoked the present discussion, did not shake the dust of the Greek Church off his feet because it was religious, nor even because, on its political side, it was violently and shockingly irreligious. On that ground he would have had to leave, not only the Greek Church, but the world. Churches can repent and can reform; can purify their hearts and ennoble their rituals; can defy ambitious and tyrannical princes and either make them come to Canossa [in Italy, where in 1077 the Holy Emperor Henry IV famously did penance (standing three days in the snow) to reverse his excommunication by Pope Gregory VII] or suffer the worst they can inflict; can, in short, raise themselves from "harmful sects," as Tolstoy rightly called the [Russian Orthodox] Church he left [in 1901, when he was excommunicated], to mighty spiritual powers, without committing suicide and abandoning their flocks to the world, the flesh, and the devil.

Tolstoy's real reason for leaving the Church was that he had no personal use for it. Its ritual, which helped others to a religious mood, only exasperated him, much as Jackson's

Te Deum might have exasperated Beethoven. The preacher who seemed to the moujik [or muzhik, a Russian peasant] and the little shopkeeper a wise and holy man must have often seemed to Tolstoy a noodle making an absurd mess of his job.

But even if the music had been by a Beethoven, and the preacher another Peter or even another Christ, Tolstoy would have appreciated them only as a connoisseur appreciates a masterpiece of art. He would not have needed them for the making of his soul. That was his own business, which he could do so well for himself that a ritual and a priest could only distract him. For this reason he was an anti-Ritualist [opposed to excessive focus on ritual objects and symbolic acts in religious worship], and in England or America would have been a Quaker if he could have endured even a Quaker's meeting [where attendees are encouraged to speak if "the Spirit finds you"].

He need not have gone far to find men no less religious than himself to whom the forms in which he apprehended his religion seemed as idolatrous as the [venerated religious] ikons [depicting Christ, Mary, saints, angels, etc.] of the Greek Church seemed to him. "I believe," said Tolstoy, "in God the Father, who sent me in to this world so that I should fulfil His law." A Bergsonian evolutionist would have replied, "This conception of a Father is the superstition of a cottager. The *élan vital* in which I believe cannot be represented by anything so corporeal, though as I, too, believe that it sent me into the world to do its will, I am as religious a man as you."

Beside the Bergsonians he might have found many people at the opposite extreme of intellectual development, to whom even so familiar a concept as a Father is no use unless he is seen and felt as well as conceived. They can pray to some material object only, were it only a stone that overhangs them threateningly or has something uncanny about its shape.

All the religious conflicts and bigotries and persecutions and wars of religion and [the Inquisition's] *autos da fé* ["acts of faith" (Portuguese), public penance of condemned heretics and apostates followed by torture or burning at the stake] and so forth are misunderstandings between the men who apprehend God directly and intimately in the abstract (say Platonically), and those who can reach him only through symbols and ceremonies.

Let me state the case in due order from the beginning, using for convenience sake, the term Quaker (it is more homelike than Platonist) to denote the man at one end of the scale, and the term Ritualist to denote the man at the other.

There has always been, and always will be, a division between the Ritualist and the Quaker. There is no reason for quarrelling over it. There is room in the world for George Fox and the Pope. The trouble begins only when an attempt is made to force ritual on Fox, or to smash the statues and extinguish the candles in the Pope's chapel. Religion takes different men in different ways; and if they would accept that fact instead of trying to force their ways on one another, a process which involves the utter extinction of the religious spirit the moment it is even contemplated, both the Ritualist and the Quaker would be free to develop their states of grace to the utmost.

The first thing to grasp is that ritual is not religion, nor the absence of ritual irreligion. One man will not enter a church on any persuasion: he will not even call it a church: he calls it a steeplehouse. Another man haunts churches because he finds that in them he can meditate or pray better than anywhere else; but he flies from them the moment he is interrupted by the entry of the priest and the choristers in procession. Yet another man goes to church for the service alone: he never dreams of entering a church at any other time; and until the ritual begins he will busy himself disposing of his hat and umbrella, and noting that old Jones must be still down with lumbago as he has not come to church, and that the young Smith has bought a new coat at last. But at the first word of the service he will buckle-to and be as pious as he can. Far from feeling that the priest and the service are coming between him and his God, and resenting them as a distracting illusion, he clings to them because they are doing for him something that he cannot do for himself. The fact that the priest is there, and is not dressed as men of the world are dressed, and does not speak as they do, makes him feel that God must be there in the background, just as the sight of a liveried butler on the doorstep of a great man, and of the sentries at the palace gates, convinces him that the great man exists, and that the king is a reality. For what more convincing proof of a nearness of God can there be than the bodily vision of His house and of His servants?

Now it is very hard for these three different men to believe in one another's religiousness. To Number Three Number One must be an atheist, because he not only does not go to church, but denies its sacredness. Number Two, who prowls about churches when there is no service going on, and leaves them when the congregation arrives, is clearly either a lunatic or a thief watching for an opportunity to break open the money-boxes or steal the Communion plate. Number One and Number Two regard Number Three as a Pharisee and a hypocrite. Number One suspects Number Two, who prays in the steeplehouse, of being half ritualist, half dilettant. When they go to extremes, Number One becomes an iconoclast, smashing everything in the cathedrals that he can reach, and insulting and murdering priests; and Number Three makes laws that Number One shall come to church whether he likes it or not, on pain of pillory, mutilation, outlawry, or the stake. Number Two is never powerful enough to go to extremes. If he were, he would keep Number Three and his priests out of the church, and keep Number One in the county jail.

When this sort of thing begins, there is an end of religion. Number Three, who, being usually in the majority, has most power of social and political coercion, attacks not only the man who does not go to church, but the man who goes to church at which the service differs in the slightest detail from that at his own church. In Ulster, men who go to the Protestant church throw bombs into groups of little children because the parents of those children go to the Roman Catholic church. They do so as champions of God, to the great amusement of the devil. They are provoked to this by the records of the Holy Office, or Inquisition, the proceedings of which moved the humane and genuinely religious Voltaire, who himself erected a church of God, to exclaim, as he contemplated the established Church of his country, *Écrasez l'infâme!* [crush the infamous or vile (individual)] Whereupon Number Three concluded that Voltaire must be an atheist, and believed that he died in horrible terror and remorse, not because this was true, but because Number Three liked to believe that an atheist died that way, even when he also believed that God had warned him that there were no bands in death for the wicked; that their strength is firm; that they are not troubled as other men.

Number One cannot mistake Number Three for an atheist. He mistakes him for something much more revolting than an atheist: an idolator. An Ulster Protestant, when he sees a Papist (as he calls him) lighting a candle before a statue of the Blessed Virgin, feels exactly as Robinson Crusoe [hero of Daniel Defoe's 1719 novel of the same name] did when he burnt the tribal idol, or as Moses did when he found his people worshipping the golden calf. Mahomet in his reaction against idolatry stamped on Islam a law that makes it impossible today to place any image of man or beast in a mosque. [Italian diplomat, historian and politician Niccolò] Machiavelli [1469–1527], an ultra-Ulsterman, though he was never in Ulster, hated priests with a mortal hatred, and might logically have adopted the creed of Mahomet, who excluded priests from his system as religiously as images. In vain does the Laodicean [lukewarm or indifferent to religion] man of the world, the Gallio [see Acts 18:12–17], or the impatiently Protestant [Anglo-Irish satirist] Jonathan Swift [1667–1745], ask what these people are quarrelling about? what it matters whether a man prays and preaches in a black gown or a white vestment? whether he raises a winecup above his head before drinking or not? whether the [sacramental] wafer [in the rite of the Eucharist, or Holy Communion] is regarded as bread eaten in memory of the bread that Christ broke at his last supper or as the body of God? Men who understand the issues behind the symbolism are not indifferent: their intense abhorrence of idolatry on the one hand, and of atheism on the other, is at stake on every one of these details; and they will slaughter and lay waste, burn women alive, beat children savagely, sink and demolish, act so as to make the tiger and the serpent, the lightning and the earthquake, seem beneficent in comparison; and all this with the name of God not only on their lips, but in their hearts.

When we have the two extremes of a case clearly in mind, we have no difficulty in understanding the position of the persons who are somewhere on the scale between them. These are the great majority; for there are relatively few out-and-outers in religion. Anyone who has been in a mosque can testify that though there is nominally no priest there, the Imaums who lead the prayers and conduct the ceremonies fill, in the imagination of the worshippers of Allah, the place of the clergy and priests in the Christian churches, and that a Moorish Marabout [a Muslim leader of the Maghreb region of Africa] has all the powers and all the sanctity of a medieval Christian bishop. True, there are no graven images or likenesses of anything that is in heaven above or in the earth beneath or in the water under the earth; but the elaborate decoration, the symbols and texts, the majestic architecture that is made homelike for Allah by the carpeted floor, are capable of influencing the mind of the spectators quite as powerfully as the imagery in Christian cathedrals.

The mass of mankind must have something to worship that the senses can apprehend. The Church of England began with a resolute effort to repudiate the anthropomorphic conception of God: its first article of belief is that God is a spirit without body, parts, or passions. Yet if it were to exclude from its communion today the people to whom God is the figure we see in [Italian painter] Raphael's [1483–1520] Vision of Ezekiel [c. 1518, depicting the prophet's vision of God], and in Blake's illustrations to the Book of Job, it would be a negligible sect instead of a national Church. The four articles numbered 28 to 31 were a desperate attempt to make room in the same Church for Puritans who, though they lived too soon to read [social anthropologist] Sir James Frazer's [1854–1941] Golden Bough [subtitled "a Study in Magic and Religion" (1890)], yet identified the Mass with the heathen Mexican [Aztec] ceremony of eating the god, and for Catholics who believed literally in transubstantiation. There are High churches to please the Anglican Catholics and Low churches to please the Protestants. Those who cannot stomach prelacy will not join an Episcopalian Church [(led by bishops), whose members adhere to the Scriptures as the revealed word of God]; but they can become Presbyterians [(led by elders), whose members adhere to the Book of Common Prayer]. The last straw that breaks the churchgoer's back is often a very light one. A single candle on the Communion table, or a right or left turn of the celebrant reading the service, may drive one worshipper away to a church where there is neither candle on the table nor pivot in the parson, and attract another to it.

The persecuting spirit acts in opposite directions. At first it meant an attempt to force heretics into churches. [Holy Roman Emperor] Charlemagne [c. 742–814] offered his heathen prisoners of war the choice between baptism and death. [Anglican] Queen Elizabeth [I (1533–1603)] told the Catholics and Puritans that she had done her best to make a Church that would satisfy both of them, and that they must come to it every Sunday or go to prison. As she overlooked the fact that there was a third alternative, America, Puritan Massachusetts and Catholic Maryland were among the consequences; but the point is that she wanted to compel people to come to her Church, not to repel them from its doors. Yet the inevitable result of treating as enemies the people who will not come to your Church is that you end by refusing to let them come even when they want to. Mahomet summoned the whole world to [the Holy City of] Mecca [in Saudi Arabia]; but when [explorer and orientalist] Captain [Sir Richard Francis] Burton [1821–90] went there in 1853 he did so at the risk of his life, carefully disguised as a Mussulman. I have seen an Englishman in Tangiers dragged violently away from the door of a mosque into which he was peeping. Thus the heretic is so hated that he is denied his right to conversion and salvation: he is killed because he will not worship in the temple, and killed equally if he attempts to enter it.

The evils of intolerance are so monstrous and so well advertised that the Laodicean Centre, as we may call the easygoing majority, have set up Toleration as a virtue, and established it in law to some extent. But their success is only apparent. What is called Toleration is only submission to the fact that after many bloody trials Catholics and Protestants, Churchmen and Dissenters, Hindus and Mahometans, Buddhists and Shintos, have found that they cannot exterminate one another, and must agree to live and let live until luck gives one of them a decisive upper hand. The Laodiceans have never been able to prevent the religious people from dragging them sooner or later into wars of religion; and civilization does nothing to diminish the ferocity of these wars. The British Empire is specially hampered by the number and variety of its fanaticisms. White Christians are only about 11 per cent of the population. In India alone 33 native languages are more spoken than English. In addition to the 17-or-so varieties of Christians which the United States have to handle, the British Empire has to drive in single harness hundreds of millions of Hindus, Sikhs, Jains, Buddhists, Parsees, and Mahometans, to say nothing of divisions that the compilers of western books of reference have been unable to classify. The Jew is everywhere; and the attempt to shepherd him into a definitely localized Zion [mentioned in 2 Samuel 5:7] in Palestine has only brought his faith into a definitely localized conflict with the Islam of its native Arabs. It is natural for the American to preach Toleration to all these fanatics, because his very existence is due to a flight of persecuted but utterly intolerant men from intolerance; but his sermons are wasted breath. We must face the fact that no man will tolerate what he believes to be a false and mischievous religion whilst he has the means of persecuting and suppressing it.

Let the American who, fancying himself tolerant, is surprised by this statement, consider a little. If he were ruling India, would he tolerate Suttee and the car of Juggernaut [a gigantic chariot carrying statues of the god Jagannath]? Would he tolerate Thuggee [the act of a Thug, or professional assassin], the worship of Kali, goddess of blood, who demands from her devotees not prayers and good works, but murders? Does he tolerate Voodoo? These questions answer themselves in the negative: nobody but a lunatic dreams of toleration for such beliefs in practice.

Bring it nearer home. If he is a materialist atheist, would he tolerate the Plymouth Brethren if he could help it? If he is a Plymouth Brother, would he tolerate atheism if he could help it? Is he quite sound on the Jewish question? Even if he is a Laodicean, and is prepared to tolerate all religions and irreligions for the sake of a quiet life, is that a reason for tolerating Ulster Calvinism and [the papal supremacy advocated by] Ultramontanism? I cannot exhaust all the particular cases which raise the question of toleration; but I do not believe there is a man or woman on earth who cannot be fitted with a case in the which he or she is an uncompromising advocate of ruthless persecution. To be convinced of this it is only necessary to turn from the adults to the children. Granted that your neighbour must be left undisturbed in his belief that he may be predestined to spend eternity in boiling brimstone, driving himself half mad by continually thinking about it, is he to be allowed to lay his children's souls waste by urging that doctrine on them before they are old enough to dare go upstairs by themselves in the dark? If Shelley's children were taken away from him because he held that the god of Calvinistic Predestination [God having ordained one's destiny as salvation or damnation] is a fable, and if he were not, would be a fiend, are the people who agree with Shelley now that he is accepted as a prophet and a saint, likely to allow Calvinism to be taught to infants as divine truth in the public elementary schools for which they have to pay?

No. Toleration as an expediency may be very advisable; but as a principle it is out of the question. Persecution may be so inexpedient in many cases that no sane person would insist on it; but when expediency is on the side of persecution, as, for example, on the Prohibition [1920 to 1933 in the United States] issue, everyone can see that there is not the smallest difference in principle between persecuting a toper [or drunkard] and persecuting a Thug. In prejudice, of course, there is all the difference in the world. Speaking as a man of prejudice I should say that when you prevent me from doing anything I want to do, that is persecution; but when I prevent you from doing anything you want to do, that is law, order, and morals. After [the Russian Revolution of] 1917 in America there was a savage persecution of Bolshevism [or Soviet Communism, advocating the violent overthrow of capitalism]. Several of its victims are still in prison. Do you, respectable Yankee, call that persecution? Are you going to have those victims released? Of course not. You believe in Toleration; but you draw the line at Bolshevism. I blame you for this; but I am not blaming your intolerance: I am blaming your ignorance. If you believe that Bolshevism means theft, murder, communism in women, and everything horrid (your English great-grandfather believed the same things about [the radical republicanism of] Jacobinism, and talked about [George] Washington [1732–99] as you do about Lenin) why then you are right to persecute Bolshevism. But you are not right to believe such manifest guff and bugaboo.

Is there then no remedy for the evils brought on us by our bigotry? None, in my opinion, except a hair of the dog that bit us. What we need is more religion to get us to the root of the matter. There is a science of religion in which we should all be instructed. When [Christian Science founder] Mrs [Mary Baker] Eddy [1821–1910] set up the Church of Christ Scientist [in 1879], she was very well inspired indeed. Christ was not tolerant: he was not prepared to tolerate money-changers and traders in sacrificial beasts in the Temple [in Mark 11:15–19]. He warned the Pharisees that there were blasphemies that are unpardonable, and denounced them as vipers: that is, creatures whom the most tolerant cannot tolerate. But he refused altogether to make any distinction on the point of eligibility for salvation between Jew and Gentile, baptized and circumcized. He not only refrained from proselytizing, but expressly warned the proselytizers that a man's religious consciousness is like a fertile field, so that if they tried to root up the tares in it they would root up the wheat as well and leave him without any religion at all. It never occurred to him to ask a Jew to cease being a Jew: he simply exhorted him to become a Christian as well as a Jew. Christianity as Christ preached it is applicable to all the Churches and religions that are consistent with human society. A Thug cannot be a Christian; but a Mahometan can: a Buddhist can: a Parsee can: a Jain can; and though there are greater difficulties in the case of varieties of pseudo-Christians now overrunning the world outside Asia, there is hope even for them.

When men are united in a common religion, there will be no persecution problem. What we have to deal with now is the fact that they cannot be so united until the common religion presents itself to them in many different forms. If you ask me why not, I reply that all men's minds have not the same scope. The form of worship that brings one man into communion with God may move another to impatient derision as a childish mummery or even as a blasphemy. God without body, parts or passions, though legally the God of the Church of England, is no god at all to the man who can apprehend no moral force that is not anthropomorphic. [French philosopher Jean-Jacques] Rousseau [1712–78] told us that if we would only get rid of our miracle stories the whole world would fall at the feet of Christ; but he was wrong: there are multitudes of simple people—Italian peasants for example—who cannot be induced to worship any saint or Saviour who does not prove his title to their veneration by performing miracles; so that their Church has actually to provide sham miracles to save their souls. The popular fiction of hell is a very horrible one: so much so that if it were not tacitly dropped in cultured urban congregations, the Churches would die of it; but Mahomet, though personally humane to a degree that makes his personal career somewhat scandalous to Western tastes, was forced to elaborate the story of the brimstone lake by the most ingeniously disgusting inventions, knowing that men who are morbidly attracted by tragically terrible punishments, will recoil from the ridicule that attends squalor, dirt, stench, and infirmity. And what drove him to this was that he had to govern men of whom many were quite incapable of conceiving divine displeasure unless it had what modern diplomatists call sanctions: that is, unless it was visited on those who incurred it in extremely unpleasant ways.

These are only the more obvious cases of the rule that no two men can have exactly the same faith unless they have exactly the same mental capacity. [Theologian, philosopher and Dominican friar] St Thomas Aquinas [1225–74] was an Italian Catholic; and the peasants of the Abruzzi were Italian Catholics; but as St Thomas was a very subtle schoolman, and the peasants were very superstitious fieldmen, they understood Catholicism quite differently, and had not in fact the same religion at all; whilst the avowed differences between the Italian peasant and the Tibetan peasant, between St Thomas and Plato or Aristotle, were no deeper than differences of dialect.

To take a less extreme contrast, there are men of wide culture and reading, and of considerable achievement in physical science, who are so matter-of-fact in their mental constitution that they can see nothing in the Athanasian Creed [professing the belief in the Holy Trinity] but an arithmetical impossibility. They say that if there is one god there is one god, and if there are three gods there are three gods, but there cannot be one and three at the same time. But the three in one and the one in three presented no difficulty to Athanasius: it seemed so simple to him that he went the length of declaring that anyone with so little intellect as to boggle at it would be damned. To many of us the notion of a man being damned for purely intellectual inadequacy is revolting: we feel that everything will be forgiven to him whose heart is in the right place, and that Athanasius himself deserved to be damned for his uncharitableness, in spite of his having written the most intellectually subtle page in the Prayer Book of the Church of England; but there is a great deal to be said for a sharp reminder to us that good intentions are no excuse for stupidity, and that if people are to be damned at all, it had better be the fools than the rascals.

If we try to group all these differences, and scores of others which it would be wearisome to state, so as to arrive at some generalization by which our mind can deal compendiously with them, we will find that, as to worship, they arrange themselves along the scale at one end of which is the Quaker and at the other the Ritualist, and, as to belief, along the scale from the abstract to the concrete. At one end of this scale of belief is a Creative Spirit, a Force of Nature, as immaterial until incarnated in its living works as a part without an actor; and at the other the visible corporal humanly-emotional figure depicted by Blake and Raphael, or fashioned with a hundred hands and an elephant's trunk by Hindoo artificers, or as a man with a hawk's head by the Egyptians, until you come to the mere block of stone on which the human imagination fastens as sacred in the stage in which it must have something concrete to cling to to save it from madness.

In the understanding and recognition of this inequality of apprehension between men lies the secret of tolerance. Take my own case. When affairs do not oblige me to be in London, I live in [Ayot St Lawrence, in Hertfordshire] a little village of 130 scattered inhabitants. It has a church and a Rector. My own house was for a long time the Rectory; and my tenancy of it endowed the church. When the churchwardens apply to me at the usual seasons I contribute; and when the hat goes round for special expenses for repairs to the building, I pay my share of what may be necessary to keep it standing. I am on intimate terms with the Rector. I am, in short, a local pillar of the Church; and I visit it occasionally. But I have never attended a service there. Whether from defect or excess of intellect, I cannot use the Church of England ritual either as spiritual food or to express and demonstrate my religion. The last time I tried was when my mother died. She was not a Church of England ritualist; but she had no prejudices nor bigotries; and she would have agreed with me that when there was a chaplain attached to the crematorium, it would have been a little shabby to save his fee and consign her body to the fire without any ceremony at all. And so the Church of England burial service was read. But I found it morbid and heathenish. It was all wrong for my mother and all wrong for me. Later on, my sister followed my mother; and she left a will in which she expressly barred any ritual. But here I found myself up against a religious need. When I found myself in the chapel of the crematorium surrounded by her friends, many of them suffering from a distress that needed some recognition and expression, I found that it was not possible to order the officials to dispose of the remains that still had my sister's shape as if they were a scuttleful of coals. I had to improvise a ceremony which was none the less a funeral ceremony because it consisted of an address by myself in my own words. This was possible for me: I am a practised public speaker, and by profession an author. But of the relatives of those who die not one in a thousand could compose a suitable address, or dare utter it in public if he or she could. For the vast majority there must be a form of words provided and a professional speaker to utter them impressively. To bury without a word or gesture would be to them to bury "like a dog." How then could I possibly live in a village and refuse my share in the provision of a ceremony to my neighbours merely because the ceremony did not fit my own case, and I was able to supply one for myself? It would be the act not merely of a bigot, but of a curmudgeon.

Later still a friend of mine induced me to go to the nuptially famous London church of St George's, Hanover Square [Benjamin Disraeli, Theodore Roosevelt and other notables were married there], to see him married. Here my feelings were quite decisive. I felt that I would live and die celibate rather than take part in such a ceremony and thereby seem to assent to its unwholesome and nonsensical comparison of my mating to the mystical union of Christ with the Church, and to that very disingenuous reference to St Paul by which the author of the Prayer Book tried to make the best of what they evidently considered (as he did) a rather questionable business. I congratulated myself on having had the alternative of civil marriage open to me. But in the view of strict

Catholics, Anglican and Roman, I am not married at all. Only, they need not go on to say that I am living in sin; for on my part the sin would lie in giving a false expression to my religious feeling. But what is false for me may be true for another; and I have not the smallest objection to its being provided for him out of the common funds to which I contribute. He has to contribute to the common fund out of which the civil registrar who marries me is paid; and if this reciprocal fiscal toleration works smoothly I do not see why reciprocal spiritual toleration should be impossible.

If I were asked to fill up an ordinary official form containing a column for my religion I should probably save the officials trouble by writing The Episcopal Church of Ireland, of which I am a member by baptism. But if I were asked to describe myself for the purposes of a serious investigation of the religious condition of the country, I should call myself a Creative Evolutionist for reasons which I have already sufficiently explained in my [1921] Preface to Back to Methuselah; but I might quite fairly write myself down a Platonist or amateur Quaker, using the word amateur to imply that I am not an enlisted member of the Society of Friends, in which, by the way, genuine Quakers are hardly commoner than they are elsewhere, because, as membership of the Society is largely hereditary, and genuine Quakerism is a gift of God, I suspect that in most Quaker meetings, if the Spirit moved a young man to get up and say anything unexpected, or indeed to say anything at all, there would be as much scandalized indignation as if he had "brawled" in a cathedral. In essentials I am Protestant and Quaker, because the intervention of any priest between me and my God would be to me the most unbearable of impertinences, and because I need no visible image, no temple made with hands, no acted fable, to enable me to apprehend as much of my relation to the universe as is humanly apprehensible. Nor do I use or need forms of prayer. When I was a child, and said my prayers at night as I had been taught to do, I composed my own prayers, ending up with [the venerated prayer beginning "Our Father" (see Matthew 6:9–13 and Luke 11:2–4) and known as] the Lord's Prayer: rather, I think, as a gesture of politeness to its author, than as a prayer. Thus, even in my nonage, I was independent of the set forms of heavenly communion; and my religion, for what it is worth, needs no ceremonial aid from writer, builder, musical composer, priest, or Church, though nobody has been more nourished by their works than I. Nothing must come between me and the spirit that moves within me; and though I do not walk by the inner light alone, but by all the light I can get, from without or within, yet I must interpret what I see for myself. And if that is not the quintessence of Quakerism, and indeed of genuine Quakerism, I do not know what Quakerism means.

But what could be more unreasonable and cruel than for me to try to deprive my ritualist neighbours of their set prayers, their praises, their legends, their temples and masses, their anthems, their coloured windows, their pictures and statues, and their hierarchies of vestured priests, especially as all these give extraordinary delight to my sense of art when their poets and painters and sculptors and orators have been religiously inspired, and often awaken my religious sense as sun and rain awaken seed? It would be no less unreasonable and cruel on their part to force their ritual on me and persecute me because another fashion of religion is natural to me.

The mischief of persecution lies, not in our different ways, but in the unfounded inferences we draw from them. A friend of mine, since dead, an army officer with the education and knowledge and experience of the world implied by that position, once said to me, "Well, Shaw, I don't know what you think about religion; but I know for a fact that the son of the Vicar up at —— is the father of the housemaid's illegitimate child; and you may tell me that the Bible is true after that if you like; but I shan't believe you." To this man the whole validity of his religion, and indeed of all religion, depended on the success of one of its ministers in imposing conventional chastity on his son. We cannot laugh at him because we all know that such grotesque tests of religion are too common to be a laughing matter. Immense numbers of people would conclude unhesitatingly that because I do not attend Church services I can have no religion and therefore no conscience. Of these numbers many believe that if a man prays to the Blessed Virgin to intercede for him with God, he is an idolator who, if he had the power, would consign thousands of his fellow citizens to the rack and stake. To such sophisticated souls it is not enough to believe in God: you must call him God and nothing else: if you call him Allah or [the supreme Hindu deity] Vishnu or (of late years) even Gott, you are a heathen.

The difficulty is an old one. Everybody is sincerely in favour of religion, of duty, of goodness and justice, of all things that are lovely and of good report; but it is not enough to be in favour of these things: you must be able to recognize them when you meet them. Annas [the Roman high priest from 6 to 15 CE] and Caiaphas [his son-in-law] had a remarkable opportunity in that way; but they missed it because they mistook a man [Jesus] more religious than themselves, though in a different fashion, for a blasphemer and a scoundrel.

Nowadays intolerance is rife between sects so anti-clerical that the mere suggestion of their possibility would have made Caiaphas tear himself beardless and naked. Take for example the formulas of the Church of Christ Scientist as prescribed by Mrs Eddy. Mrs Eddy, as it is now appearing, was much sounder in her science than the medical profession in her day, with its materialistic view of the living body as a purely mechanical and chemical phenomenon; yet she is denounced and reviled not only by the materialistic doctors and surgeons, but by the disciples of [French psychologist and pharmacist] M. [Émile] Coué [(1857–1926), whose psychotherapy involved optimistic auto-suggestion], who makes invalids cure themselves by the formula "I am getting better and better every minute." The cures of Christian Science are obviously fundamentally identical with the cures of M. Coué; but Mrs Eddy's formula will not start the self-healing process in Smith, who is subsequently cured triumphantly by M. Coué; and Jones, who has told himself in vain for weeks that he is getting better from hour to hour, is no sooner taken in hand by one of Mrs Eddy's ministers than he makes a perfect recovery. The plan of St James, as practised by the Peculiar People, succeeds where both Mrs Eddy and M. Coué's plan fail. Even a doctor's prescription has been known to succeed with people who have faith in it, and would succeed much oftener if doctors did not persist in poisoning the chalice by putting drugs into it. None of these plays cure me, because they have not found the exact sort of hocus-pocus that starts the miracle of healing and recreation in me; but I owe a great deal to the fact that having in my happily irreverent youth dismissed all the religions, and subsequently the scientific formulas as hocus-pocus, there was nothing to hinder me from going on to discover that all the hocus-pocuses are equally good for the people whose capacities and idiosyncrasies they hit off. Thus they are at once all wrong and all right; and he who calls his brother a fool for clinging to one of them is a fool himself. The texts to hang out like banners to confound bigots are (from [Poet Laureate Alfred, Lord] Tennyson [1809–92]), "God fulfils himself in many ways," [from "Idylls of the King"] and (my favourite Scripture) "What doth the Lord require of thee but to do justly, and to love mercy, and to walk humbly before thy God?" [Micah 6:8]

Though the moral of all this is that you must suffer your neighbour to serve God in his own way, however different it may be from yours, let no Church lazily conclude that its ritual needs no revision merely because it is sure to supply somebody's want. If the Church of England, for example, consoles itself for the loss of another hundred of the British intelligentsia by the accession of another million Polynesian and African converts from crude anthropophagy, her state will not be the more gracious. I take, after my manner, the extreme instance to make the position clear; but the danger lies in more insidious changes. If the Church is losing its hold on relatively clever and cultured people and filling their pews with relatively stupid and ignorant people, then, however slight the difference may be from year to year, it will tell perceptively from lustrum to lustrum. The Dean of St Paul's, himself the greatest Platonist of us all, has said that if ordination be refused to all candidates who do not believe literally and unequivocally what they now have to profess to believe before they can be ordained, the ministry will presently consist exclusively of fools, bigots, and liars. This, which is so obviously true that the Church dares not rebuke the Dean for affirming it, however much it may wish he had said nothing, is not a wholesome state of things. And the Prayer Book has gone bad in the course of three centuries in other places than in the creeds and articles. The people they are good enough for are not good enough for a Church aiming at representing what is best in Christendom.

Then there is the quaint anarchy of the parsons by whose conduct most of their neighbours judge the Church. The Rector is the freeholder of his Rectory; and he may also be a rampant freethinker in politics and sociology. He claims and exercises all the liberties of a country gentleman, and wallows openly in class prejudices. Often he snubs the poor, and sides with the squire against them; he sees to it that servility and imperialist militarism are inculcated in the Church schools; he pitches the emblems of Christian peace into the cellar and waves the Union Jack the moment there is any question of war; he supports the way of the police as God's appointed way of dealing with crime; and he is equally free to preach the most extreme Bolshevist views in opposition to all this if his congregation will stand it. In the late war British clergymen who had to bury certain German soldiers who were killed in aeroplane raids actually altered the words of the burial service to express their personal refusal to admit that Englishmen and Germans, as the children of the Father of us all, are brothers; and though this was clearly either treachery to Christ or cowardice in the face of the mob: that is to say, a betrayal of duty for which a soldier would be shot, it was taken as a matter of course that a clergyman should behave like any irresponsible tramp if he had in mind to. It was this sort of thing that made Tolstoy so bitter against the Greek Church, and which makes all the revolutionary movements anti-clerical, in spite of the fact that Socialism, the main revolutionary movement of today, bases its policy on the conception of a truly Catholic Church for the workers of all nations.

There is, in fact, no effective modern discipline in any of the Churches. A Roman Catholic priest can be silenced; but he is much more likely to be silenced for advocating the wholesome practice of cremation, or declaring that animals have quite soul enough to have rights against cruel and thoughtless men, than for making his Church ridiculous or odious by insisting on such crudely literal acceptance of all the Church's dogmas as must put them in the light of silly superstitions before reasonably humane and well informed people. As to a Church of England rector, he cannot be silenced at all: his rectory is his castle; and he can be driven from it only by general social pressure.

Up to a certain point this freedom of the individual priest or minister, unless he is a hopeless crank, does more good than harm. And beyond a certain point Churches will be what their members, clerical and lay, make them, no matter what their creeds, articles, and disciplines may be. But the same may be said of any human organization; and yet an organization that does not draw certain lines in faith and conduct is not an organization at all, but a mob. The British navy allows its admirals a latitude in writing to The Times which can be explained only by its recognition of the fact that no man can go through the ordeal of the quarter-deck without becoming more or less crazy; but an admiral who altered the Articles of War to suit his own political prejudices, or who allowed rich officers to shirk their share of the risks run by those who were the sons of parsons and suchlike hard-ups (like [Vice Admiral Horatio] Nelson [1758–1805]), would be dismissed from the service or certified as insane and sent to Copenhagen Hospital. You may be a very eccentric naval officer: you may swear like a fighting mate on an ocean tramp, and shake your fist in the king's face, and even flatly disobey orders if you can win a battle thereby; but you may not fight for the enemy when the battle is joined (however much you may sympathize with him), nor, in time of peace, may you, by example and precept, devote yourself to the subversion of the principles of national defence and the encouragement of the slackers and shirkers as the most respectable persons in the ship. Consequently the navy has never fallen into contempt in England as the Church has, and as the courts have; and the explanation is that clergymen are not effectively restrained from bringing religion, nor judges from bringing the law, into contempt. To the naval and military officer we do effectively and convincingly say, "Be faithful to your profession, or get out." To the officers of the Church and the Law, we say, "Do what you please, and be damned." With the result that it is we who are damned, unless we keep carefully out of the churches and out of the courts. And it is not possible for all of us to keep out of either.

The end of the discussion then is, for the present, that as some of the most religious men in the world have been mistaken for atheists, like Voltaire, for mere gluttonous winebibbers, like Christ [see his miracle at Cana (John 2:1–11)], for impostors, like Mahomet, and for superstitious humbugs, like many very honest nameless parsons and priests, we had better be careful how we judge one another, or put ourselves in the place of God by dictating how our neighbour should serve Him. And also that any Church which makes a great fuss when a cathedral pillar sinks or a wall cracks, and collects a great sum to have the building under-pinned and made safe, but sees its creeds and services going crazy with age, and sinking and rifting and tumbling in all directions without saying a word about them except to swear that they are as safe as the Pyramids, and that those who are complaining that they will presently fall and bury the nation in their ruins are disreputable liars, that Church will end, as many churches have ended in England, in having buildings without congregations. Also, since people want up-to-date creeds and rituals, but care for nothing later than the fifteenth century in architecture (or, if they are connoisseurs, the twelfth), the carefully "restored" churches will not attract even the better sort of sight-seeing tourists to fill the places of worshippers their obsolete rituals have driven away.

7. "The Infancy of God," an essay written around 1922. [*Shaw on Religion*, pp. 132–42]

[From a typescript edited in Shaw's hand and marked by him "Hitherto Unpublished." According to Smith (pp. 132 and 238), the essay "was apparently written especially for inclusion in the abandoned religious volume of the Collected Works." It appears to have been written "about the same time" as "On Ritual, Religion, and the Intolerableness of Tolerance" (see "page 147). Here Shaw makes the distinction between religion and reverence. "To obtain the utmost satisfaction for your passion of veneration, you conceive a God who is omnipotent, omniscient, and infinitely good." This Shaw cannot

do, and he provides examples from history of the consequences of "the idolatry which conceives God as perfect and omnipotent."]

I wish at the outset to clear myself of all suspicion of that confusion of religion with Veneration which enables most men to imagine themselves religious when they are only reverent. I am myself, and always have been, as religious a man as Voltaire; but as I have also been, like him, an extremely irreverent one, most Englishmen are unable to conceive me as religious. I have no power to alter this state of things. Many years ago I found myself in a vegetarian restaurant in Barbican [in London], sitting opposite a man who began to discuss religion with me. Before I had at all shewn my hand on the subject, he said: "I can see you are a sceptic." "How do you know?" said I. "I am a bit of a phrenologist," said he. "Oh," I said, "have I no bump of veneration?" [in phrenology, a cranial protuberance supposedly indicating respect for what is great and good, giving rise to religious emotion] "Bump of veneration!" he exclaimed: "Why, it's a hole." And as a matter of fact that part of the scalp which in very devout worshippers and very obedient moralists rises into a dome or a ridge like a church roof, is on my scalp a majestic plain with a slight depression in the centre.

To ask me to be reverent, with whatever moving appeals to good taste, is like asking me to hang from a tree by my tail. In me nature has discarded the tail, having higher uses for me than hanging on trees upside down. She has also discarded the bump of veneration, having nobler attitudes for me than kneeling and groveling. I have achieved at least one of the characteristics of the Superman: the upright posture of the soul; and I am as proud of it as the first monkey who achieved the upright posture of the body, and so felt himself a stage nearer to the Supermonkey, man.

Yet I am not so far evolved that I cannot understand veneration. It is important that every statesman (and I write always for statesmen) should know that veneration is a passion; and that its satisfaction brings a comfort so ineffable that its voluptuaries never stop to think out what it implies, and are consequently not degraded by it as they would be if they had thought it out—as I should be by it, for example. Let me think it out for the purpose of this book, on paper. To venerate, you must have something higher than yourself before you do. To obtain the utmost satisfaction for your passion of veneration, you conceive a God who is omnipotent, omniscient, and infinitely good. And you think no more about it, but worship and are happy. But I, having no such use for this ideal, and having, instead, an instinct for criticism, immediately begin to reflect. I see that the veneration scheme implies that an all-powerful God, to whom nothing is impossible, has deliberately created something lower than himself for the sake of enjoying his own superiority to them, just as a snob surrounds himself with footmen or an unkingly king with flatterers. Immediately my chin goes up; and my back stiffens. I, with all my faults and follies, am at least better than this; for, being man, I strive to surpass myself and produce Superman; whilst this God of the people with ridged and domed heads, does not try to produce a Supergod, but produces subgods, giving them all sorts of ridiculous and disastrous weaknesses so that he may despise them. This God will not do for me at all: to be quite frank, I consider him a cad. Unless I can bring you to the knowledge of some higher divinity than that, I may as well shut up my treatise on religion, and write farces.

Yet such a God is at present indispensable to the statesman, and, as I have said, to the venerators also. To the statesman, because the ridged and domed men, of whom there are many, will not obey laws or officials through a comprehension of the need for subordinators, but only through veneration for the lawgiver and the official. To induce them to do anything subordinate, you have to set up a golden calf for them to adore, and persuade them that your officials are its ministers, to which end you must deck the officials in the best trappings your stage managers can devise, and set them apart by every device of caste and money that can make them appear awful and venerable. And you will find the task a very easy one; for the passion of veneration is so strong that the ridged heads and what Shakespear called the pregnant knees [*Hamlet* 3.ii] will bend and crook before the most pitiful and grotesque makeshifts. Humanity has not yet produced a creature so cruel, so disgusting, so silly, or even so common, but it will find adorers as loyal as the noblest kings and bishops known to history. Just as the amorous voluptuary soon comes to care nothing for the lover and everything for the passion, so the ridged and domes care everything for loyalty and piety and nothing for the king or bishop. [Roman Emperor] Nero [37–68] will serve their turn as well as [King of Wessex] Alfred [the Great (849–99)]. The blacking on the shoes of "Great Catherine, whom the world still adores" [title and subtitle of Shaw's 1913 one-act play about Catherine the Great of Russia (1729–96)] is as sweet to their lips as that on the shoes of the virgin Elizabeth. Neither their loyalty nor their devotion affords the smallest guarantee of good government or lofty religion. It guarantees nothing but its idol; and if the idol deepens the emotional effect from time to time by some appalling crime, his hold is all the surer; the cult of pleasure is near akin to the cult of pain. What finally wrecks all republics, and is now struggling fiercely with Democracy, is this Idolatry, abhorred of all the prophets. The English Commonwealth of the XVII century failed because it starved the idolator; it took away his king and his bishop; and [military commander and Lord Protector of the Commonwealth, the intensely religious Oliver] Cromwell [1599–1658], had he lived, would have had to crown himself or perish; for he could not have gone on much longer with his armed heel on the throat of an idolatrous nation without pretending that he was something more than a man of the like passions to themselves.

Democracy is fundamentally a proposal that we should live without idols, obeying laws and doing justly because we understand the need for doing so, and making an end of purely lascivious veneration and idolatry. In every democratic revolution the democrats instinctively begin by rushing to the cathedral and knocking off the heads of the statues. It then proceeds to the residences of the human idols—the official persons—and knocks off their heads also. When, as often happens, these unlucky living idols are excellent functionaries and estimable, kindly, or at worst quite commonplace individuals, such acts of mob violence seem as senseless as they are cruel. Even those who care little about the slaughter of men are infuriated by the destruction of priceless works of art. All the same, there must be some logic in the action of a thousand men who all do the same thing without stopping to paralyse thousands with inept arguing. In Paris, in 1789, there was not in [the medieval fortress called] the Bastille [when it was stormed on 14 July] a single prisoner about whom the mob cared a rap; and the governor [Bernard-René de Launay (1740–89)] was no worse a man than any other military gentleman with a good place. But when the mob demolished the Bastille and hacked off Delaunay's head, they were demonstrating that the Bastille was only a heap of stones and its governor only a man who would die when you cut his throat: a demonstration which had been made necessary by the success with which the Bastille had been imposed on France as the inviolate temple of a terrible and irresistible idol called the King, and the Governor as a High Priest wielding the idol's power vicariously. In the same way, if no one had ever thought [King] Charles I [(1600–49), condemned on charges of high treason and beheaded] more than a man, Cromwell would never have taken the trouble to prove that his neck, at all events, was mortal, and that one could shear through it without being struck by lightning. And when Cromwell, having in due course become something of an idol, was dug out of his grave [two years after his death] and hung up in chains [and beheaded], that, too, was thought necessary to shew people that what he had done was no more than any common criminal could have done. It is but a few years since [in 1898], in the Sudan, we desecrated the tomb of [Muhammad Ahmad Abd Allah (1844–85), who in 1881 had proclaimed himself] the Mahdi [the messianic redeemer of Islam], and mutilated his corpse to prove that Mahomet would not avenge him; and no doubt we shall yet see the statue of [Major-General Charles George] Gordon [(1833–85), famously defeated by the Mahdi's army at Khartoum, where he was killed (and decapitated)] we set up in his place duly defiled and decapitated by the next Mahometan conqueror to prove that it, too, is under no special supernatural protection.

All these tides of idolatry and iconoclasm are to me, and therefore presumably to many other people, stupid and disgusting. To us idolatry, though easy, and, for the mere mechanical purposes of law and order, effective, is a rotten and degrading basis for society, and reduces religion to "a rhapsody of words," as Shakespear put it. We want intelligent obedience instead of idolatrous obedience, as that is our only guarantee against the abuse of power for the private ends of those whom we must trust with it.

So far, this is mere political commonplace. The need for political intelligence in order to secure rebellion the moment our governors betray their trust has been demonstrated quite often enough, in spite of the fact that the Ridged and Domed remain constitutionally impervious to it. What has been less noticed is the danger that arises from the fact that idolators always expect too much from their idols, and in the fury of their disappointment often outdo the iconoclasts when an insurrection is provoked by famine or defeat. [Popular French novelist] Anatole France [1844–1924] tells the story of a peasant who, praying before a statue of the Virgin and Child, addressed the latter in these terms: "It is not to thee, son of a wanton, that I offer my prayer, but to thy sainted mother." On a previous occasion he had made his petition to the Infant Christ without success; and when it was not granted he abused the obdurate deity just as Russian peasants, when they have prayed in vain for good weather to their Ikons, take them into the fields and beat them.

We have the same phenomenon in politics, where it takes the form of "the swing of the pendulum" at general elections. Our Party leaders are idolized. The inevitable consequence is that impossibilities are expected from them. They are held accountable for the harvests, for the fluctuations of trade, for the fortune of war, for every private mishap and every public calamity, whilst at the same time they get no credit for beneficial measures that are beyond the comprehension of their idolators. Consequently they are thrown down and smashed, and the Opposition set up on their pedestals and worshipped until the pendulum swings again, when they are set up again and given another turn. At last the governing classes become entirely cynical as to democracy and set themselves deliberately to perfect themselves in the art of exploiting idolatry.

This also is something of a commonplace as far as politics are concerned. But its application to religion is less familiar. How about the man who expects too much from his God?

How are atheists produced? In probably nine cases out of ten, what happens is something like this. A beloved wife or husband or child or sweetheart is gnawed to death by cancer, stultified by epilepsy, struck dumb and helpless by apoplexy, or strangled by croup or diphtheria; and the looker-on after praying vainly to God to refrain from such horrible and wanton cruelty, indignantly repudiates faith in the divine monster, and becomes not merely indifferent and skeptical, but fiercely and actively hostile to religion. This result is inevitable when once the level is passed beneath which idolatry is intensified by cruelty. For all people are not driven from religion by calamity; many are driven just the other way by it. Whilst their circumstances are happy they never think of religion; but "plague, pestilence and famine, battle, murder, and sudden death" impress them with such a dread of the majesty and power of God, that they spend the rest of their lives in worship and propitiation. It is the stronger spirits, the thinkers, those with a high ideal of God and the power and courage to criticize and judge God by the standard of that high ideal, who revolt against his cruelty, denouncing him as "the Almighty Fiend" of Shelley; and finally rejecting the tale of his existence as a hideous dream. Although atheism may be mere stupidity, yet the intelligent atheist is generally superior to the average worshipper in intellect, and in character as well. When the [quarterly] Westminster [1824–1914] and Fortnightly [1865–1954] Reviews were distinctly atheistic reviews, they were as superior to their orthodox competitors in intelligence and culture as the extinct [secularist weekly] National Reformer [1860–c. 1890] and the Freethinker [founded 1881] of today to the Parish Magazine. The association of scepticism with high mental gift soon became so firmly established that orthodoxy was a positive disadvantage in a scientific career, a useless qualification in medicine and law, and a thing not to be too strongly insisted on even by clergymen and schoolmasters. The Bishop who reminded people, however unintentionally, of the sceptical abbés of the French salons of the XVIII century, was much more fashionable than any of his evangelical colleagues could hope to be. It became necessary to invent a polite euphemism for the terms atheist and atheism; and we now speak of Agnostics and Agnosticism [the view that the existence a divine being is unknown and unknowable], representing sometimes, no doubt, an entirely honest confession of ignorance as to the ultimate problems of existence, but mostly the state of mind of those who have neither faith to believe nor courage to deny. But whether the attitude was frankly and boldly negative or timidly non-committal, what was at the back of it in nine cases out of ten was the horror of a God who was not only the God of honour, of love, and of light, but also the God of epilepsy, of cancer, of smallpox, of madness, of war, of poverty, of tyranny; in short, of the huge burden of pain and evil under which the world has always groaned and is still groaning more pitifully than ever. In vain did the orthodox attempt to propitiate the agnostics by throwing over the imaginary hell of everlasting brimstone: they could not throw over the real hell which was flaming all around them. And so, as [German philosopher Friedrich] Nietzsche [1844–1900] put it, the news went round that God was dead.

Now this whole difficulty was created by the idolatry which conceives God as perfect and omnipotent. If he is omnipotent, then he is a hopeless puzzle. He is not the Almighty Fiend of Shelley's *Queen Mab*, because he is also the God of veracity, honour, and kindness. And he is not the God of love and mercy because he is also the god of the tubercle bacillus, and the guilty butt of the sarcasms of Mephistopheles [a demon in German folklore made famous by Johann Wolfgang von Goethe (1749–1832) in his drama *Faust* (1808, 1832)]. Now a god who is a puzzle is no use. It is easy to say "If I could understand him, he would not be a god: how can a creature understand the creator?"; but if you do not understand God, you may as well be an atheist for all practical purposes, because you must leave the thing you do not understand out of account. The moment you make any law or give any counsel on the ground that the thing you enjoin or forbid will please him or offend him, you are pretending to understand him to that extent; that is, you are treating him, not as a puzzle, but as a consistent, understood, ascertained character. And with what assurance can you undertake to say that any given conduct will please or displease a deity who is responsible for all the cruelty and evil of life as well as for all the good? It ends inevitably, as it always has ended, either in ignoring him altogether or making him the excuse for whatever you feel inclined to do, whether it happens to be a crime or a benefaction. The latter course, which prevailed as long as God was exempt from criticism, is now so revolting to the Opposition that God is never mentioned in Parliament, and very seldom out of it, except to give emphasis to an expletive.

In the old times, God was not really conceived as omnipotent, but as the divine antagonist of a malign power which wrestled with him for the souls of men. The Father of Lies and the Author of Evil was not God but Satan, who was so vividly imagined that [German theologian Martin] Luther [1483–1546] threw his inkpot at him [while sequestered at Wartburg Castle in 1521–22 translating the Bible]. Fortunately a malignant god—a devil—is too grotesquely horrible a thing to be believed in. A god with horns and a tail is ridiculous; and a fallen archangel is not really a devil: people began to defend him and make him into the hero of the piece instead of the villain.

The moment this point is reached it is all over with the old childish way of accounting for evil as the work of Old Nick the mischief maker. And yet that nurse's tale has made us familiar with a conception of immeasurable value. When he wanted to do anything he had to tempt man or woman to do it. Failing that instrument, he could do nothing. Now one glance at the world as it exists, or at the pages of history, will shew that this is also the method of God. You may call it inspiration in the one case and temptation in the other, out of politeness to God; but the two things are as identical as steadfastness and obstinacy. When a hungry and penniless man stands between his good and his bad angel in front of a baker's shop, the good angel cannot seize and drag him away, nor can the bad angel thrust the loaf into his hands. The victory of honesty or the consummation of a theft must be effected by the man; and his choice will depend a good deal on the sort of man he is. Not only is he an indispensable agent; not only is he the vehicle of the force that moves him; but he is also the vehicle of the force that chooses. He is, in the old phrase, the temple of the Holy Ghost. He has, in another old phrase, the divine spark within him.

Now, to the extent that a man is the temple of the Holy Ghost and the agent of the Holy Ghost, he is necessarily also the limitation of the Holy Ghost. Not even the Holy Ghost can lift ten pounds with a baby's arm or ten tons with a man's. Not even the divine spark can solve a problem in fluxions with the brain of an actor, or play Hamlet with the brain of a mathematician. When "the word became flesh" [John 1:14] it had to take on all the weaknesses of flesh. In all ages the saints and prophets have had to protest against the demand made on them for miracles. John Bunyan's inspiration could make him write better than Shakespear; but it could not make him write always grammatically. It could nerve Mahomet to convert the fierce tribes of Arabia from worshipping stones to an exalted monotheism; but it could not make him say No to a pretty woman. The sword will snap in the hand of God at just the point at which it will snap in a testing machine; and all the swords of God bend and snap at one point and another, or cut the wrong throats at the bidding of the ape or tiger from whom they are evolved.

Now if God (so to speak) were omnipotent, it is clear that he would provide himself with a perfectly fashioned and trustworthy instrument. And it is also clear that such an instrument would be nothing less than God himself incarnate. The fact that man is his best instrument so far on this planet, and that 999 out of every 1000 men are so stupid and cruel, so clumsy and imbecile, that they drive the thousandth to despair even when they do not murder him in sheer dread and hatred of his superiority, proves that God is as yet only in his infancy.

8. "A Note on the Prayer Book," an essay written around 1922. [*Shaw on Religion*, pp. 143–47]

[From a typescript edited in Shaw's hand and marked by him "Hitherto Unpublished." Smith notes (pp. 143, 238) that the essay "was apparently prepared as a commentary on the proposals of [Anglican priest] H[ugh]. R[ichard]. L[awrie]. Sheppard [1880–1937], Vicar of the Church of St. Martin-in-the-Fields from 1914 to 1927," and appears to have been written "about the same time" as "On Ritual, Religion, and the Intolerableness of Tolerance" (see page 147). Shaw here criticizes the Anglican Book of Common Prayer (1549) and concludes that as "Creative evolution has no place in it," the book "has no place in modern religious thought."]

Certain comments from the church of St Martin-in-the-Fields on the Book of Common Prayer have startled the people who have never given the subject five minutes serious consideration, and who are indeed so little interested in the Church that they have been too much occupied with the city news or the sporting news or the fashionable news or the parliamentary news to notice that the demand for the revision of the Prayer Book has been clamorous for many years, and that the work has been actually taken in hand by the Church bodies and has given rise to many heated debates and exciting divisions in the fullest publicity. Now that a beneficed clergyman has reached their consciousness they rise up wailing that the Church is about to be destroyed. But they will soon forget their panic; and when revision is carried out they will never notice it, as the Legend of the Jabberwock [a creature made famous by Lewis Carroll (1832–98) in *Through the Looking-Glass* (1871)] and The Dying Christian to His Soul [a poem by Alexander Pope (1688–1744)] are all the same to them, provided they are read by a surpliced person [wearing the liturgical vestment called a surplice (a white tunic)] with occasional diversions on the organ, and relieved by standings up and sittings down with a bout or two of kneeling.

Those to whom the Church ritual and services mean something know that the Prayer Book as it stands is indefensible, and that civil marriage, civil registration, and funerals at which there is either no service at all or one improvised by the friends of the deceased are preferred by many people to Church marriage, baptism, and burial, not because these people are irreligious, but on the contrary because they are too religious to be able, at the most solemn moments of their lives, to bear listening to a clergyman saying things which they do not believe, and which he does not believe unless he is an imbecile in such matters. An example is given by the clerical Revisionist from the marriage service, in which, after receiving from the bridegroom a pledge of life-long monogamy, he has to exhort him to take for his model in domestic conduct a polygamous oriental patriarch; and this illustrates with comic vividness the paralysis of thought which religion produced in the authors of the Prayer Book, and still produces in our worshippers; for though many vulgarly prudish people have objected to the marriage service because it necessarily mentions matters which are taboo at the nursery teatable, I cannot remember anyone before Mr Sheppard pointing out that the household of Abraham, Sarah, and Hagar [the Egyptian handmaid of Sarah, with whose husband, Abraham, she bore Ishmael], if taken seriously and literally as a model of our suburbs, would lead to a multiplication of *ménages à trois*. The polygamy [among members of the Church of Jesus Christ of Latter-day Saints (or Mormons)] of Salt Lake City [Utah, made public in 1852] was in fact defended by citing the examples of the patriarchs.

But whilst admitting all these points, and some more that my Revisionist friend might have made, the fact remains that it seems almost impossible to bring the Prayer Book into harmony with modern thought without spoiling it. It is saturated from beginning to end with a magical belief in transubstantiation; and it is from this that it derives all its beauty and impressiveness. Take that magic away, and the residue will be as dull as an average ethical tract, which is perhaps the dullest thing on earth. Leave it in, and the service glows, repeatedly with a thrilling and consoling faith, and changes the unbearable void of infinite space into a vision of paradise.

The difficulty is that there is in the human soul an imperative demand for reality which no sweetness of consolation or beauty of vision can satisfy or silence. No matter how beautifully a story is worded or said or sung, if it is only a fairy story its charm will not last; and those who, like Mr Sheppard, have to repeat it again and again, or, like his congregation, listen to it again and again, will finally lose patience with it and demand something real and credible told in terms of their own daily life.

Let me make quite clear what scope I am giving to the word transubstantiation [the Catholic belief that the sacramental bread and wine of the Eucharist actually become the body and blood of Christ]. If I do not, all my readers will assume that I am thinking only of the elements in the Mass, of the bread and wine on the Lord's table. But this is only the very crudest part of the ritual: a curious survival of the practice of the warrior who ate his enemy to acquire his fighting qualities and of the refinement upon it of the Central American who ate his God symbolically to acquire some of his divinity, kept alive by the more subtle doctrine of the Epistle to the Corinthians [1 Corinthians 11:17–34]. Transubstantiation does not mean merely that bread turns into flesh and wine into blood, as that do every day by simple metabolism, but that our corruptible body and mortal flesh and blood, which is such a trouble to us, can be changed by faith into an incorruptible and immortal spiritual body. If this transfiguration and transubstantiation is once accepted as a possibility every consideration beside its achievement sinks unto utter insignificance. Our corruptible body with its needs and plea-sures becomes an abomination to be cast off at the earliest possible moment, and meanwhile to be despised, mortified, shamed, and held in subjection and contempt, and all the services of the Church have only one object, the prepara-tion for the great change, the hastening of it, and the ritual symbolizing of it. The baptism of the child, though it may incidentally enlist it as Christ's soldier and servant, is essen-tially to change it symbolically by water and the spirit from an abhorred little bundle of original sin to an immortal and incorruptible child of God. A clergyman who is a natural born Pelagian [a follower of ascetic theologian Pelagius (c. 390–418), who denied original sin and believed that our free will can choose good or evil] objects strongly to be compelled to call on a mother to loathe her child's body in this fashion, and would rather read [nature poet William] Wordsworth's [1770–1850] Intimations of Immortality [or *Ode: Intimations of Immortality from Recollections of Early Childhood* (1807)] to her, in which her child is trailing clouds of glory as it comes from God in innocence and loveliness. But if the mother believes in transubstantiation, she will rejoice in the hope that this very troublesome little physical body of her baby, which is by no means to her the exquisite amorino it is to the male painter or poet, can be transfigured into an angel. All the apparent morbidities of the service become reasonable and natural on the basis of this belief; and those who grasp it fully can understand not only why a clergyman has to treat the natural body of the infant he baptizes as a tainted survival of "the old man," or "the old Adam," to be exchanged as soon as possible for a more glorious spiritual body; they can also un-derstand how in the first days of the gospel, men were seen by [influential theologian and philosopher] St Augustine [of Hippo (354–430)] blackening their wives' eyes for tempting them, or when they escaped the snare of matrimony, volun-tarily lived in bodily filth and misery in caves or on the tops of pillars, chastising and shaming the old Adam so that it might give way the more easily to the new Christ.

But if the Prayer Book stands with transubstantiation, it also falls with it. As long as we believe in transubstantiation the Prayer Book will be sacred to us; and we shall overlook such slips as the one about Abraham sooner than suffer anyone to lay a finger on it. But if on a candid self-examination we find that we do not believe it, then the whole Prayer Book crumples; and there is no longer any question of mere revision: what we need is virtually a new Wordsworthian prayer book.

It is, however, very difficult to take seriously a document which is nearly 300 years old in its latest passages and 400 in the main. The physical universe it contemplates is not merely pre-Einsteinian but pre-Newtonian, not merely pre-Newtonian, but pre-Copernican. Creative evolution has no place in it; and this means that the Book of Common Prayer has no place in modern religious thought. Frankly, the book is worn out. It is past repair. And if and when a new one is established by Act of Parliament a clause should be added making revision compulsory every six years at most. I have said elsewhere that the law of change is the law of God; and Churches which deny this and try to keep their hold on the people by rituals stereotyped for eternity will presently find their already quarter-filled temples quite empty.

9. "Where Darwin Is Taboo: The Bible in America," *New Leader* (10 July 1925). [*The Shavian* 2.2 (1960), pp. 3–9]

[*The State of Tennessee v. John Thomas Scopes (decided 21 July 1925), often referred to as the Scopes Trial or Scopes Monkey Trial, took place in Dayton, Tennessee. John Scopes (1900–70) stood accused of violating the state's Butler Act (of 21 March 1925), intro-*

*duced in the House of Representatives by John Washington Butler
(1875–1952), which prohibited public-school teachers from teaching
evolution in place of the biblical account of creation. Devout Pres-
byterian William Jennings Bryan (1860–1925) argued for the pros-
ecution, while famous defense attorney (and agnostic) Clarence
Darrow (1857–1938) spoke for Scopes, who was found guilty and
fined $100 (about $1,350 today). Shaw inveighs here—with biblical
examples aplenty—against Bryan and "this monstrous nonsense of
Fundamentalism."]*

It is not often that a single State can make a whole Continent
ridiculous, or a single man can set Europe asking whether
America has ever really been civilised. But Tennessee and
Mr. Bryan have brought off the double event. We have always
had our suspicions of American civilization on this side of
the Atlantic. The statute books of the federated States are
museums of freak legislation, defended by travelling Ameri-
cans on the ground that nobody ever dreams of putting the
freak laws into operation. The public assemblies of America
abound in monumental men who have every quality of an
imposing statue (including the solidity of its head) except its
silence. We have asked ourselves sometimes, are all Amer-
icans like that? If so, who keeps the place going? Is it run
by Irish policemen, Chinese laundrymen, Scottish engineers,
Jewish bankers, and dagoes of every degree? For clearly, if it
were run by Tennessean legislators like Mr. John Washington
Butler, and remarkable men like Mr. Bryan, it would be in ruins in a week.

Tennessee and Mr. Butler have had a nasty jolt. They have
come up against a modern idea. Not a new idea, of course;
only the idea of Evolution, which has attained the respectable age of one hundred and thirty-five years. It came
into modern thought in 1790, and is therefore a little older
than the State of Tennessee. It got a set-back from Charles
Darwin in the middle of the nineteenth century. Charles, or

rather his followers, tried to make out that the changes attributed to Evolution were a mere chapter of accidents with no sort of sense in them. But that was only a soulless episode in the investigation of the facts. Charles Darwin did indeed, as Samuel Butler said, for a time "banish mind from the universe" (which perhaps accounts for Mr. Bryan, who was born thenabouts); but nobody under seventy now believes that life as we know it could have been produced by what Charles Darwin called Natural Selection. Evolution to-day means Creative Evolution, the operation of an aspiring and creative purpose which is sure to have the last word, for all that it proceeds by the method of Trial and Error.

Mr. Bryan, Mr. Butler, and the legislators of Tennessee do not believe in any sort of evolution. They believe that God invented and constructed them once for all in the Garden of Eden, and that He looked on His work and saw that it was good [Genesis 1:31]; and they have ordered that the school children of Tennessee be taught to look forward to an eternity of incorrigible and unimprovable (because perfect) Bryans and Butlers leading and governing that happy state until the Day of Judgment. And they have decreed dreadful penalties against any teacher who shall suggest to the young that Mr. Bryan is any better than his fathers, or that he is any advance on a rattlesnake. God made a fancy assortment of creatures in the garden, including a pair of rattlesnakes and a pair of Bryans, and endowed them with a strong reciprocal antipathy, giving the snake a poison bag to kill the Bryans and a rattle to warn them of its approach, and giving the male Bryan a stick-wielding hand to kill the snake, and a powerful voice and a copious supply of words to warn the snake when he is around.

For these wildly absurd proceedings Mr. Bryan and the law-givers of Tennessee claim the authority of the Bible. Europe stares half-incredulously, yet with a pleasant sense of superiority, and wonders how soon these American barbarians will begin to sacrifice their daughters, like Jephtha[h] [whose rash vow to God led to his murdering his daughter (Judges 11)], or their sons, like Abraham [whose obedience was rewarded by God, who stopped him from murdering his son, Isaac (Genesis 22)], on the same authority. After all, that would be more poetic than witch burning, which had a considerable vogue at one time even in Europe, because the Bible says that we must not suffer a witch to live. Then there is Communism, which the Apostles enjoined so strongly on the authority of Christ that they struck Ananias and [his wife] Sapphira dead [in Acts 5:1–11] for holding back their little private capital from the common stock. The Bible does not forbid the teaching of Evolution; but it prescribes fruit and seed bearing herbs as the proper food of Man, and flatly forbids the eating of pork. As this interdict is not raised anywhere in the New Testament, visions of a Holy War between Tennessee and Illinois arise. Which side would South Carolina take? South Carolina is Scriptural in the matter of divorce, on which both Tennessee and Illinois fly in the face of the Gospel. Is the Volstead Amendment [establishing Prohibition in the United States on 16 January 1920] consistent with the miracle of Cana in Galilee?

I need not go through the elaborate codes [or *mitzvoth* (commandments)] of [the third and fifth books of the Torah (or Pentateuch)] Leviticus and Deuteronomy, nor the polygamous institutions adopted by the American Latter Day Saints on the authority of [the biblical prophet and a king of Israel] Solomon [reigned c. 970–931 BCE] (and most unscripturally suppressed by the Federal authorities), nor the injunctions to mutilate ourselves rather than let our members sin, to make it as obvious in America as it is in Europe that no modern civilized State could exist if it substituted the Bible for its statute roll.

The real difficulty about the Bible in America is that, though nobody reads it, everybody imagines he knows what is in it. In Europe those who do not read it carefully attach no importance to it and claim no authority for it. Those who do attach importance to it know what it really says. But in America the Bible has become a figment of the American imagination. To Mr. Bryan and Mr. Butler it is a book by a single omniscient and infallible author who has written for us a straightforward narrative in which there are no inconsistencies, no contradictions, no repetitions, no ambiguities, and in which there is only one God, who is the author in question.

To those who have read the Bible it is not a book but a literature written by a succession of authors differing in their religious beliefs, worshipping different gods, representing different phases of civilization, writing hopelessly irreconcilable biographies of the same persons and histories of the same events, furiously denouncing one another's rituals as abominable in the sight of God and contradicting one another's views of His nature, and occasionally passing suddenly from Christian sentiments to outbursts of vindictiveness so atrocious that popular clergymen in London refuse to read them or allow them to be read in their churches, and Bishops are appealed to by the most earnest of their flocks to have them struck out of the Prayer Book. The authors wrote, not in Elizabethan English but in an ancient Hebrew, of which, in many places, the Elizabethans could make no sense, and in a later Syrian dialect (that spoken by Christ), of which we have only Greek translations copied four centuries after the event.

Of all this Mr. Bryan is frankly innocent. He sticks to an imaginary Book of Books, learnt at his mother's knee, with an imaginary simple and single narrative of an imaginary simple and single Christ, which he calls "The Bible Christ: the only Christ mentioned in the Bible," adding emphatically, "People may accept Him or reject Him; but they cannot change His character."

Sancta simplicitas! [Holy simplicity (Latin)]

If I could induce Mr. Bryan to turn from his party newspaper to the real Bible he would discover to his astonishment that it contains four separate biographies of Christ by different authors, and that they differ from one another, both as to the facts of Christ's career and as to His character and manners, more than any four existing biographies of George Washington. For example, Mr. Bryan specifies belief in the Virgin Birth as a test of that acceptance of his imaginary Bible which he calls Fundamentalism. By this he means that Christ is to be classed with [founding Roman Emperor] Augustus Caesar [63 BCE–14 CE] and [Macedonian king] Alexander the Great [355–23 BCE] as the son, not of His mother's husband, but of a divine personage. I turn to the Bible to verify the reference. What do I find? Out of the four biographers only two claim that Christ was begotten of the Holy Ghost. The other two make no mention of this extraordinary circumstance; and none of the four represents Christ as being aware of anything abnormal about his incarnation, or of having any special affection or respect for his mother. His "Woman: what have I to do with thee?" [John 2:4] is typical of his general teaching as to family relationships other than the common relationship of all men as the children of God.

But the two biographies which allege the parentage of the Holy Ghost also allege the descent of Jesus from King David [of Israel (c. 1040–970 BCE)]. Each gives a complete genealogy tracing that descent through David from Abraham. Yet instead of tracing it to Mary they trace it to Joseph! Mr. Bryan is therefore committed as a Fundamentalist to believing that Jesus was the son of the Holy Ghost and also the son of Joseph. That is, he is committed to the ultra-Modernist view that Joseph was the vehicle of the Holy Ghost. To the modern Creative Evolutionist who believes that all fathers are vehicles of the Holy Ghost, and that all conceptions are immaculate, such a conclusion presents no difficulty; but the term Virgin Birth is not applicable to it.

I shall not press the further difficulty that the two genealogies are not the same, either as to names or numbers of generations, because Mr. Bryan may plead that though the names differ the men may be the same and that mere omissions from the list of generations are not discrepancies. But the Tennessean school-teachers know that children are matter-of-fact little animals, without the afflatus that carries Mr. Bryan over all prosaic contradictions. They will want to know exactly where they are on this and other points on which Matthew and Luke differ from Mark and John and from one another.

"What story are we to tell the children," they will ask, "about the birth of Jesus?" "You will teach the simple Bible story, or out you go," replies honest John Washington Butler. "But excuse us, Mr. Butler," say the teachers: "there are two Bible stories. Are we to teach that Jesus was born at home in His father's house, where He was visited by wise men, bringing Him princely gifts, and led by a star, or that Jesus was born in the stable of an inn on a journey from His distant home in Nazareth, and was visited by shepherds directed by an angel?" "You will teach the children," Mr. Butler answers, "that if the Bible says that Jesus was born at home He *was* born at home, because the Bible cannot err; and if the Bible says He was born in a stable when travelling He *was* born in a stable when travelling, for the same unanswerable reason; so get on with your work and let me hear no more of your atheistic blasphemies."

Experience shows that this way of handling the teachers will work perfectly. The children will accept as many birthplaces for Jesus as for Homer without noticing any discrepancy; they will grow up under the impression that such acceptance constitutes them religious persons; and in that capacity they will vote for Bryan and the Bible, or go out with the [white supremacist vigilante organization] Ku-Klux Klan [founded 1865 in Pulaski, Tennessee, and 1915 in Atlanta,

Georgia] and tar-and-feather Roman Catholics *ad majorem Dei gloriam* ["for the greater glory of God," the Latin motto of the Society of Jesus (Jesuits)]. We in Europe know what "wars of religion" this tarring and feathering business may develop into, and how much reason the Roman Catholic Church had and has for insisting that to put the Bible into the hand of every fool is as dangerous as to put a gas bomb in the hand of every mischievous child.

America having decided, as against the Roman Catholic Church, to put the Bible into the hands of the people, finds itself committed to popular distaste for serious reading, not to the real Bible, but to the Bible of Mr. Bryan's imagination. And now that Mr. Bryan has been rash enough to demand legislation on the subject, in which the terms must be defined in plain black and white for use in the courts, it becomes necessary to require Mr. Bryan to write his Bible out, in order that it may be inserted in the schedules to the proposed legislative Acts in Tennessee and elsewhere.

He will have to start with an account of the Creation: that is, of the development of life on our globe. Now the real Bible begins with two chapters on this subject, giving the two different accounts by two different writers. The first, which gives the creation of Man as the climax, is for its date the work of a scientific mind, clear, orderly, carefully thought out, and wide in its grasp and scope. The second, which says that God began His creation of living things by Man, and afterwards created the animals and brought them to Man to be named, is the work of a story-teller with no turn for science. What sort of muddle of the two is in Mr. Bryan's mind nobody can guess. Rumors of both must have reached him; but then rumors of the modern account given in Mr. H. G. Wells's *Outline of History* [1920] must have reached him also; and it is highly probable that when Mr. Bryan and Mr. John Washington Butler are finally compelled to set down their notion of the Bible account for inclusion in the Act, large chunks of Wells will be found swimming in their infusion of the two authors whom they generalize (without scriptural authority) under the impossible heading of Moses.

I am more anxious about Mr. Butler than about Mr. Bryan, because Mr. Butler seems just the simple sort of honest man who might take up the Bible to refresh his memory and make sure, whereas that is the very last thing Mr. Bryan will dream of doing, seeing that in his moments of ecstatic American uplift he loses all sense of distinction between the Bible and his own platform inspirations. Now if Mr. Butler once open the Bible he will not only be bothered by the conflicting accounts of the facts in it, but may even become unsettled as to his belief in God. As he will begin with a corporeal god who has to be propitiated with blood sacrifices, including human sacrifices, his first cry will be "Back to the Aztecs!" He will then come upon a poem of doubt and disillusion in which God gets so completely worsted in an argument with Job on the problem of evil, that another writer has had to save the situation by a sort of happy ending in which Job apologises. A still greater surprise awaits him in [one of the books of the Tanakh (the canon of the Hebrew Bible)] the Book of Ecclesiastes [the anonymous treatise on how to lead one's life], which gives the authority of the Bible to the most uncompromising pessimistic atheism. [The Old Testament prophet] Micah [c. 737–695 BCE] will rescue him from this by leading him to a God who abhors sacrifices, and requires no more from us than to do justice and love mercy and walk humbly with our God (not a word about prosecuting schoolmasters for picking fruit from the tree of knowledge and handing it to incipient citizens of the United States). When he has reached this highest moral point in the Bible he will be led from the corporeal conception of God to the Father who is a spirit ("without body, parts, or passions" as the Church of England insists in its first Article) [of the Westminster Confession of Faith (1646)], yet who is still so haunted with the idea of sacrifice that He compounds with it once and for all by the blood sacrifice of Christ.

Now I have not the privilege of knowing Mr. Butler personally, and therefore cannot guess what effect all these complications of what now seems to him to be a simple and straight-forward matter may have on him. But I can describe what happens in England when a boy who has been taught to believe what Mr. Butler believes about the Bible, discovers, as he must discover when he grows up if he ever troubles himself about the matter at all, that he has been mistaught and deceived, and that no Churchman or scholar of any distinction now regards that view of the Bible as other than grossly ignorant and superstitious. In ninety-nine cases out of a hundred, instead of rising to the occasion and entering into his heritage of our superb English translation of a famous, and, in many passages, nobly inspired ancient oriental literature as such, he empties the baby out with the bath by declaring that the parsons are a pack of frauds, the Bible a parcel of lies, and God and Religion inventions, like hell and the flood, and the whale that swallowed [the prophet] Jonah [in Jonah 2], and all the rest of it.

Please remark that he does not become an Evolutionist nor a Rationalist nor a Scientist nor a cultivated Bostonian Pragmatic Agnostic. He just throws all metaphysical ideas overboard because he has been cheated once and is determined not to be cheated twice.

That is the danger of Fundamentalism. I do not believe that it is a danger peculiar to England. I have met American workmen as well as English ones. I have seen the same cynical stamp on their faces, and heard the same blasphemies and obscenities from their lips when the name of religion was mentioned. And this is because their teachers lied to them and taught them the false religion of Fundamentalism instead of the truths revealed by the inspiration of their own day. They were taught that God retired from business when the Bible was finished, and left our succeeding generations to walk in darkness. For this dead Syrian God they have no use: they need a live American one. Meanwhile, left godless, they say "Let us eat and drink; for tomorrow we die."

Let America look to it; and let the newspapers and pulpits of Tennessee rally to their duty lest their State become a mere Reservation of Morons and Moral Cowards. They can put a stop to this monstrous nonsense of Fundamentalism in a single Sunday if they have the courage of their professions; and no Sunday in America can ever be better spent.

10. "Personal Immortality," *Daily News* (6 June 1928). [*Shaw on Religion*, pp. 181–83]

[A contribution to a newspaper discussion entitled "Where Are the Dead."]

I am butting into this controversy not with any intention of settling it, but merely to suggest a variation on its method. I have noticed that the point under discussion is stated as whether "we" are immortal, whether "the dead" survive, or whether "the soul" perishes with the body.

The style is the leading article style, the royal style, or the style of Italian and Highland politeness, in which the individual is not you but she, the she denoting an abstraction of honour and excellency, as to which anything is credible and arguable.

This gives immense scope to the discussion and elasticity to its terms; but it takes our feet off the earth so completely as to enable the controversialists to prove that there may be such a thing as immortality without producing the faintest conviction that any particular Tom, Dick or Harry, Susan, Sophronia or Jane ever was or will be immortal.

What I propose is that your next few contributors shall discuss, not whether "we" are immortal, or whether the soul is immortal, or whether the dead are still seeking lodgings in infinite space, but whether I, Bernard Shaw, am going to persist to all eternity in a universe utterly unable to get rid of me, no matter how desperately tired it may become of Shavianismus, or how intolerably bored I may be by myself. Can there never be enough of me? Never too much of me?

Also, am I myself to have any say in the matter? Am I or am I not to be allowed to hand myself back to my creator, and say "Will you be so kind as to pulp this worn out article, and re-manufacture it, if possible, without any of the glaring defects which have made it so troublesome to myself and others?"

For the guidance of those who will undertake this discussion, I had better say that as far as I know no person has ever doubted that I did not exist before [conception in] October 1855. Now the arguments that prove that I cannot have an end seem to me to prove equally that I cannot have had a beginning. Many persons think that it would have been better if I could not have had a beginning. But I most certainly had a beginning. The event can be precisely dated.

Nobody but a lunatic would maintain that a brick existed before it was baked, or will still be a brick when it has crumbled into dust. Consequently, all the arguments that prove that my non-existence is impossible must be ruled out.

As a matter of fact, I have non-existed; and the discussion must address itself to proving or disproving that the non-existence that was possible before 1855 can never be possible again.

With this hint I leave your contributors to their stupendous theme: an eternity of G. B. S. Imagine it, if you can! Millions upon millions of Shaw plays! Billions upon billions of letters to the Press, intensely irritating to many worthy citizens! To be "a fellow of infinite jest," [Hamlet 5.i] not, like poor Yorick, figuratively, but literally!

Chesterton, too. He also will be bombinating for ever and ever, world without end. And Wells and Belloc in sempiternal controversy! How if we became really convinced of it—not on paper, where anybody can be convinced of anything, but genuinely in the centre of our life—and immediately went off our chumps, as I for one most certainly should?

[King of Prussia] Frederick the Great [1712–86] was very far from being in all respects a trustworthy spiritual guide; but when he said to the soldier who was running away, "Confound you, do you want to live for ever?" he said a mouthful.

One word more. Let no controversialist try to evade the point by assuring that I shall survive, not as myself, but as the just man made perfect. He might as well tell me that the chariot of Pharaoh survives in the Rolls Royce.

When I use the word "I" (as I frequently do) I mean myself, with all my imperfections (if any) on my head, and my eyebrows turning up, and not down like those of my friend [comedian, singer, and renowned music hall performer] Mr George Robey [1869–1954]. I mean the celebrated G. B. S., almost unbearably individualized, with his consciousness and his memories, his tricks and his manners, complete and exact in his G. B. Essence.

Otherwise the controversy is about nothing.

11. Afterword to *The Adventures of the Black Girl in Her Search for God* (London: Constable, 1932), pp. 59–75.

[Shaw was decried as a blasphemer for his satirical Adventures, which recounts the experiences of a young African girl, newly converted to Christianity, and her many encounters, among them God, Job, Micah, Jesus, Muhammad, an old gentleman (Voltaire), and a red-haired Irishman (Shaw). In his afterword (dated "Ayot St Lawrence, 9th October 1932"), Shaw expounds at length on the Bible—instead of keeping it "in the clouds in the name of religion" or "trying to get rid of it altogether in the name of Science," he sug-

gests it should be read in "the spirit of intellectual integrity that obliges honest thinkers to read every line which pretends to divine authority with all their wits about them"—including the Ten Commandments, "vicarious and hideously cruel blood sacrifice," the Bible and science, and the crucifixion (and "Crosstianity").]

I was inspired to write this tale when I was held up in Knysna [South Africa] for five weeks in the African summer and English winter of 1932. My intention was to write a play in the ordinary course of my business as a playwright; but I found myself writing the story of the black girl instead. And now, the story being written, I proceed to speculate on what it means, though I cannot too often repeat that I am as liable as anyone else to err in my interpretation, and that pioneer writers, like other pioneers, often mistake their destination as [Italian explorer Christopher] Columbus [c. 1450–1506] did. That is how they sometimes run away in pious horror from the conclusions to which their revelations manifestly lead. I hold, as firmly as St Thomas Aquinas, that all truths, ancient or modern, are divinely inspired; but I know by observation and introspection that the instrument on which the inspiring force plays may be a very faulty one, and may even end, like Bunyan in The Holy War, by making the most ridiculous nonsense of his message.

However, here is my own account of the matter for what it is worth.

It is often said, by the heedless, that we are a conservative species, impervious to new ideas. I have not found it so. I am often appalled at the avidity and credulity with which new ideas are snatched at and adopted without a scrap of sound evidence. People will believe anything that amuses them, gratifies them, or promises them some sort of profit. I console myself, as Stuart Mill did, with the notion that in time the silly ideas will lose their charm and drop out of fashion and out of existence; that the false promises, when broken, will pass through cynical derision into oblivion; and that after this sifting process the sound ideas, being indestructible (for even if suppressed or forgotten they are rediscovered again and again) will survive and be added to the body of ascertained knowledge we call Science. In this way we acquire a well tested stock of ideas to furnish our minds, such furnishing being education proper as distinguished from the pseudo-education of the schools and universities.

Unfortunately there is a snag in this simple scheme. It forgets the prudent old precept, "Don't throw out your dirty water until you get in your clean" which is the very devil unless completed by "This also I say unto you, that when you get your fresh water you must throw out the dirty, and be particularly careful not to let the two get mixed."

Now this is just what we never do. We persist in pouring the clean water into the dirty; and our minds are always muddled in consequence. The educated human of today has a mind which can be compared only to a store in which the very latest and most precious acquisitions are flung on top of a noisome heap of rag-and-bottle refuse and worthless antiquities from the museum lumber room. The store is always bankrupt; and the men in possession include [the first Norman King of England] William the Conqueror [c. 1028–87] and Henry the Seventh, Moses and Jesus, St Augustine and Sir Isaac Newton, Calvin and Wesley, Queen Victoria [1819–1901] and Mr H. G. Wells; whilst among the distraining creditors are Karl Marx, Einstein, and dozens of people more or less like Stuart Mill and myself. No mind can operate reasonably in such a mess. And as our current schooling and colleging and graduating consists in reproducing this mess in the minds of every fresh generation of children, we are provoking revolutionary emergencies in which persons muddled by university degrees will have to be politically disfranchised and disqualified as, in effect, certified lunatics, and the direction of affairs given over to the self-educated and the simple-tons.

The most conspicuous example of this insane practice of continually taking in new ideas without ever clearing out the ideas they supersede, is the standing of the Bible in those countries in which the extraordinary artistic value of the English translation has given it a magical power over its readers. That power is now waning because, as sixteenth century English is a dying tongue, new translations are being forced on us by the plain fact that the old one is no longer intelligible to the masses. These new versions have—the good ones by their admirable homeliness and the ordinary ones by their newspapery everydayness—suddenly placed the Bible narratives in a light of familiar realism which oblige their readers to apply common sense tests to them.

But the influence of these modern versions is not yet very wide. It seems to me that those who find the old version unintelligible and boresome do not resort to modern versions: they simply give up reading the Bible. The few who are caught and interested by the new versions, stumble on them by accidents which, being accidents, are necessarily rare. But they still hear Lessons read in church in the old version in a specially reverent tone: children at Sunday School are made to learn its verses by heart, and are rewarded by little cards inserted with its texts; and bedrooms and nurseries are still decorated with its precepts, warnings, and consolations. The British and Foreign Bible Society [formed in 1804 to encourage wider circulation of the Scriptures] has distributed more than three million copies annually for a century past; and though many of these copies may be mere churchgoers' luggage, never opened on weekdays, or gifts in discharge of the duties of godparents; yet they count. There is still on the statute book a law which no statesman dare repeal, which makes it felony to question the scientific truth and supernatural authority of any word of Holy Scripture, the penalties extending to ruinous outlawry; and the same acceptance of the Bible as an infallible encyclopedia is one of the Articles of the Church of England, though another Article, and that the very first, flatly denies the corporeal and voracious nature of God insisted on in the Pentateuch.

In all these instances the Bible means the translation [begun 1604, completed 1611] authorized by King James the First [1566–1625] of the best examples in ancient Jewish literature of natural and political history, of poetry, morality, theology, and rhapsody. The translation was extraordinarily well done because to the translators what they were translating was not merely a curious collection of ancient books written by different authors in different stages of culture, but the Word of God divinely revealed through his chosen and expressly inspired scribes. In this conviction they carried out their work with boundless reverence and care and achieved a beautifully artistic result. It did not seem possible to them that they could flatter the original texts; for who could improve on God's own style? And as they could not conceive that divine revelation could conflict with what they believed to be the truths of their religion, they did not hesitate to translate a negative by a positive where such a conflict seemed to arise, as they could hardly trust their own fallible knowledge of ancient Hebrew when it contradicted the very foundations of their faith, nor doubt that God would, as they prayed Him to do, take care that his message should not suffer corruption in their hands. In this state of exaltation they made a translation so magnificent that to this day the common human Britisher or citizen of the United States of North America accepts and worships it as a single book by a single author, the book being the Book of Books and the author being God. Its charm, its promise of salvation, its pathos, and its majesty have been raised to transcendence by Handel, who can still make atheists cry and give materialists the thrill of the sublime with his Messiah. Even the ignorant, to whom religion is crude fetishism and magic, prize it as a paper talisman that will exorcise ghosts, prevent witnesses from lying, and, if carried devoutly in a soldier's pocket, stop bullets.

Now it is clear that this supernatural view of the Bible, though at its best it may achieve sublimity by keeping its head in the skies, may also make itself both ridiculous and dangerous by having its feet off the ground. It is a matter of daily experience that a book taken as an infallible revelation, whether the author be Moses, Ezekiel, Paul, [Swedish scientist, philosopher and theologian Emanuel] Swedenborg [1688–1772], [American founder of Mormonism] Joseph Smith [1805–44], Mary Baker Eddy, or Karl Marx, may bring such hope, consolation, interest and happiness into our individual lives that we may well cherish it as the key of Paradise. But if the paradise be a fool's paradise, as it must be when its materials are imaginary, then it must not be made the foundation of a State, and must be classed with anodynes, opiates, and anaesthetics. It is not for nothing that the fanatically religious leaders of the new Russia dismissed the religion of the Greek Church as "dope." That is precisely what a religion becomes when it is divorced from reality. It is useful to ambitious rulers in corrupt political systems as a sedative to popular turbulence (that is why the tyrant always makes much of the priest); but in the long run civilization must get back to honest reality or perish.

At present we are at a crisis in which one party is keeping the Bible in the clouds in the name of religion, and another is trying to get rid of it altogether in the name of Science. Both names are so recklessly taken in vain that [mathematician, scientist and theologian Ernest Barnes (1874–1953)] the Bishop of Birmingham [1924–53] has just warned his flock that the scientific party is drawing nearer to Christ than the Church congregations. I, who am a sort of unofficial Bishop of Everywhere, have repeatedly warned the scientists that the Quakers are fundamentally far more scientific than the official biologists. In this confusion I venture to suggest that we neither leave the Bible in the clouds nor attempt the impossible task of suppressing it. Why not simply bring it down to the ground, and take it for what it really is?

To maintain good humor I am quite willing to concede to my Protestant friends that the Bible in the clouds was sometimes turned to good account in the struggles to maintain Protestant Freethought (such as it was) against the Churches and Empires. The soldier who had his Bible in one hand and his weapon in the other fought with the strength of ten under Cromwell, William of Orange [1650–1702], and [King of Sweden (1611–32)] Gustavus Adolphus [1594–1632]. The very old-fashioned may still permit themselves a little romance about the Ironsides at Dunbar singing "O God, our help in ages past," [a hymn by Isaac Watts paraphrasing Psalm 90, sung by the soldiers whom Oliver Cromwell, nicknamed "Old Ironsides," led to victory in the Battle of Dunbar of 3 September 1650], about the ships that broke the boom and relieved the siege of Londonderry [18 April to 28 July 1689], and even about [soldier of fortune Captain] Dugald Dalgetty [in the historical novel A *Legend of Montrose* (1819) by Sir Walter Scott].

But the struggle between [late medieval Italy's warring factions] Guelph [supporting the pope] and Ghibelline [supporting the Holy Roman emperor] is so completely over that in its last and bloodiest war the ministers of the Guelph king did not even know what his name meant, and made him discard it in the face of the Ghibelline Kaiser and the Holy Roman Empire. And the soldier fought with the trigger of a machine gun in one hand and a popular newspaper in the other. Thanks to the machine gun he fought with the strength of a thousand; but the idolized Bible was still at the back of the popular newspaper, full of the spirit of the campaigns of Joshua, holding up our sword as the sword of the Lord and Gideon [Judges 7:20], and hounding us on to the slaughter of those modern Amalekites and Canaanites [whom God ordered destroyed in 1 Samuel 15:3 and Deuteronomy 20:17], the Germans, as idolators, and children of the devil. Though the formula (King and Country) was different, the spirit was the same: it was the old imaginary conflict of Jehovah against [the Canaanite deity] Baal [in Kings 18:21]; only, as the Germans were also fighting for King and Country, and were quite as convinced as we that Jehovah, the Lord strong and mighty, the Lord mighty in battle, the Lord of Hosts (now called big battalions), was their God, and that ours was his enemy, the fighting, though fearfully slaughterous, was so completely neutralized that the victory had to be won by blockade. But the wounds to civilization were so serious that we do not as yet know whether they are not going to prove mortal, because they are being kept open by the Old Testament spirit and methods and superstitions. And here again it is important to notice that the only country which seems to be vigorously recovering is Russia, which has thrown the Old Testament violently and contemptuously into the waste paper basket, and even, in the intensity of its reaction against it, organized its children into a League of the Godless [an atheistic organization formed in 1925 in Soviet Russia that included members of the Komsomol youth movement], thereby unexpectedly suffering them to obey the invitation of Jesus to come unto him, whilst we are organizing our children in Officers' Training Corps: a very notable confirmation of the Bishop of Birmingham's observation that scientific atheism moves towards Christ whilst official Christianity pulls savagely in the opposite direction.

The situation is past trifling. The ancient worshippers of Jehovah, armed with sword and spear, and demoralized by a clever boy with a sling, could not murder and destroy wholesale. But with machine gun and amphibious tank, aeroplane and gas bomb, operating on cities where millions of inhabitants are depending for light and heat, water and food, on centralized mechanical organs like great steel hearts and arteries, that can be smashed in half an hour by a boy in a bomber, we really must take care that the boy is better educated than Noah and Joshua. In plain words, as we cannot get rid of the Bible, it will get rid of us unless we learn to read it "in the proper spirit," which I take to be the spirit of intellectual integrity that obliges honest thinkers to read every line which pretends to divine authority with all their wits about them, and to judge it exactly as they judge the Koran [or Quran, the central religious text of Islam revealed by God to Muhammad through the angel Gabriel from 609 to 632], the Upanishads [the collection of texts containing the central concepts of Hinduism forming the core of Indian philosophy], the Arabian Nights [or *One Thousand and One Nights*, the collection of tales compiled during the Islamic Golden Age (c. 622 to 1258)], this morning's leading article in *The Times*, or last week's cartoon in [the popular satirical weekly (1841–2002)] *Punch*; knowing that all written words are equally open to inspiration from the eternal fount and equally subject to error from the mortal imperfection of their authors.

Then say, of what use is the Bible nowadays to anyone but the antiquary and the literary connoisseur? Why not boot it into the dustbin as the Soviet has done? Well, there is a *prima facie* [at first sight (Latin)] case to be made out for that. Let us first do justice to it.

What about the tables of the law? the ten commandments? They did not suffice even for the wandering desert tribe upon whom they were imposed by Moses, who, like Mahomet later on, could get them respected only by pretending that they were supernaturally revealed to him. They had to be supplemented by the elaborate codes of Leviticus and Deuteronomy, which the most fanatically observant Jew could not now obey without outraging our modern morality and violating our criminal law. They are mere lumber nowadays; for their simpler validities are the necessary commonplaces of human society and need no Bible to reveal them or give them authority. The second commandment ["Thou shalt not make unto thee any graven image"], taken to heart by Islam, is broken and ignored throughout Christendom, though its warning against the enchantments of fine art is worthy [of] the deepest consideration, and, had its author known the magic of word-music as he knew that of the graven image, might stand as a warning against our idolatry of the Bible. The whole ten are unsuited and inadequate to modern needs, as they say not a word against those forms of robbery, legalized by the robbers, which have uprooted the moral foundation of our society and will condemn us to slow social decay if we are not wakened up, as Russia has been, by a crashing collapse.

In addition to these negative drawbacks there is the positive one that the religion inculcated in the earlier books is a crudely atrocious ritual of human sacrifice to propitiate a murderous tribal deity who was, for example, induced to spare the human race from destruction in a second deluge by the pleasure given him by the smell of burning flesh when Noah "took of every clean beast and of every clean fowl, and offered burnt offerings on the altar." [Genesis 8:20] And though this ritual is in the later books fiercely repudiated, and its god denied in express terms, by the prophet Micah, shewing how it was outgrown as the Jews progressed in culture, yet the tradition of a blood sacrifice whereby the vengeance of a terribly angry god can be bought off by a vicarious and hideously cruel blood sacrifice persists even through the New Testament, where it attaches itself to the torture and execution of Jesus by the Roman governor of Jerusalem, idolizing that horror in Noah's fashion as a means by which we can all cheat our consciences, evade our moral responsibilities, and turn our shame into self-congratulation by loading all our infamies on to the scourged shoulders of Christ. It would be hard to imagine a more demoralizing and unchristian doctrine: indeed it would not be at all unreasonable for the Intellectual Co-operation Committee [(1922–46), to promote cultural exchange] of the League of Nations [1920–46] to follow the example of the Roman Catholic Church by objecting to the promiscuous circulation of the Bible (except under conditions amounting to careful spiritual direction) until the supernatural claims made for its authority are finally and unequivocally dropped.

As to Bible science, it has over the nineteenth-century materialistic fashion in biology the advantage of being a science of life and not an attempt to substitute physics and chemistry for it; but it is hopelessly pre-revolutionary; its description of the origin of life and morals are obviously fairy tales; its astronomy is terracentric; its notions of the starry universe are childish; its history is epical and legendary: in short, people whose education in these departments is derived from the Bible are so absurdly misinformed as to be unfit for public employment, parental responsibility, or the franchise. As an encyclopedia, therefore, the Bible must be shelved with the first edition of the Encyclopedia Britannica as a record of what men once believed, and a measure of how far they have left their obsolete beliefs behind.

Granted all this to Russia, it does not by any means dispose of the Bible. A great deal of the Bible is much more alive than this morning's paper and last night's parliamentary debate. Its chronicles are better reading than most of our fashionable histories, and less intentionally mendacious. In revolutionary invective and Utopian aspiration it cuts the ground from under the feet of [influential art critic John] Ruskin [1819–1900], Carlyle, and Karl Marx; and in epics of great leaders and great rascals it makes Homer seem superficial and Shakespear unbalanced. And its one great love poem [the Song of Solomon] is the only one that can satisfy a man who is really in love. Shelley's [long poem celebrating ideal love] Epipsychidion [1821] is, by comparison, literary gas and gaiters.

In sum, it is an epitome, illustrated with the most stirring examples, of the history of a tribe of mentally vigorous, imaginative, aggressively acquisitive humans who developed into a nation through ruthless conquest, encouraged by the delusion that they were "the chosen people of God" and, as such, the natural inheritors of all the earth, with a reversion to a blissful eternity hereafter in the kingdom of heaven. And the epitome in no way suppresses the fact that this delusion led at last to their dispersion, denationalization, and bigoted persecution by better disciplined states which, though equally confident of a monopoly of divine favor earned by their own merits, paid the Jews the compliment of adopting the Hebrew gods and prophets, as, on the whole, more useful to imperialist rulers than the available alternatives.

Now the difference between an illiterate savage and a person who has read such an epitome (with due skipping of its genealogical rubbish and the occasional nonsenses produced by attempts to translate from imperfectly understood tongues) is enormous. A community on which such a historical curriculum is imposed in family and school may be more dangerous to its neighbors, and in greater peril of collapse from intolerance and megalomania, than a community that reads either nothing or silly novels, football results, and city articles; but it is beyond all question a more highly educated one. It is therefore not in the least surprising nor unreasonable that when the only generally available alternative to Bible education is no liberal education at all, many who have no illusions about the Bible, and fully comprehend its drawbacks, vote for Bible education *faute de mieux* [for want of anything better (French)]. This is why mere criticism of Bible education cuts so little ice. Ancient Hebrew history and literature, half fabulous as it is, is better than no history and no literature; and I neither regret nor resent my own Bible education, especially as my mind soon grew strong enough to take it at its real value. At worst the Bible gives a child a better start in life than the gutter.

This testimonial will please our Bible idolaters; but it must not for a moment soothe them into believing that their fetishism can now be defended by the plea that it was better to be Noah or Abraham or Sir Isaac Newton than a London street arab [a homeless child who begs or steals for survival]. Street arabs are not very common in these days of compulsory attendance at the public elementary school. The alternative to the book of Genesis at present is not mere ignorant nescience, but Mr H. G. Wells's Outline of History, and the host of imitations and supplements which its huge success has called into existence. Within the last two hundred years a body of history, literature, poetry, science, and art has been inspired and created by precisely the same mysterious impulse that inspired and created the Bible. In all these departments it leaves the Bible just nowhere. It is the Bible-educated human who is now the ignoramus. If you doubt it, try to pass an examination for any practical employment by giving Bible answers to the examiners' questions. You will be fortunate if you are merely plucked and not certified as a lunatic. Throughout the whole range of Science which the Bible was formerly supposed to cover with an infallible authority, it is now hopelessly superseded, with one exception. That exception is the science of theology, which is still so completely off the ground—so metaphysical, as the learned say—that our materialist scientists contemptuously deny it the right to call itself science at all.

But there is no surer symptom of a sordid and fundamentally stupid mind, however powerful it may be in many practical activities, than a contempt for metaphysics. A person may be supremely able as a mathematician, engineer, parliamentary tactician or racing bookmaker; but if that person has contemplated the universe all through life without ever asking "What the devil does it all mean?" he (or she) is one of those people for whom Calvin accounted by placing them in his category of the predestinately damned.

Hence the Bible, scientifically obsolete in all other respects, remains interesting as a record of how the idea of God, which is the first effort of civilized mankind to account for the existence and origin and purpose of as much of the universe as we are conscious of, develops from a childish idolatry of a thundering, earthquaking, famine striking, pestilence launching, blinding, deafening, killing, destructively omnipotent Bogey Man, maker of night and day and sun and moon, of the four seasons and their miracles of seed and harvest, to a braver idealization of a benevolent sage, a just judge, an affectionate father, evolving finally into the incorporeal word that never becomes flesh, at which point modern science and philosophy takes up the problem with its *Vis Naturae* [more properly *vis medicatrix naturae*, the healing power of nature (Latin)], its [Bergsonian] *Élan Vital*, its Life Force, its Evolutionary Appetite, its still more abstract Categorical Imperative [the concept of an absolute, unconditional requirement, justified as an end in itself, introduced in 1785 by German philosopher Immanuel Kant (1724–1804)], and what not?

Now the study of this history of the development of a hypothesis from savage idolatry to a highly cultivated metaphysic is as interesting, instructive, and reassuring as any study can be to an open mind and an honest intellect. But we spoil it all by that lazy and sluttish practice of not throwing out the dirty water when we get in the clean. The Bible presents us with a succession of gods, each being a striking improvement on the previous one, marking an Ascent of Man [likely an allusion to Darwin's *The Descent of Man* (1871)] to a nobler and deeper conception of Nature, every step involving a purification of the water of life and calling for a thorough emptying and cleansing of the vessel before its replenishment by a fresh and cleaner supply. But we baffle the blessing by just sloshing the water from the new fountain into the contents of the dirty old bucket, and repeat this folly until our minds are in such a filthy mess that we are objects of pity to the superficial bur clearheaded atheists who are content without metaphysics and can see nothing in the whole business but its confusions and absurdities. Practical men of business refuse to be bothered with such crazy matters at all.

Take the situation in detail as it develops through the Bible. The God of Noah is not the God of Job. Contemplate first the angry deity who drowned every living thing on earth, except one family of each species, in a fit of raging disgust at their wickedness, and then allowed the head of the one human family to appease him by "the sweet savour" of a heap of burning flesh! Is he identical with the tolerant, argumentative, academic, urbane, philosophic speculator who entertained the devil familiarly and made a wager with him that he could not drive Job to despair of divine benevolence? People who cannot see the difference between these two Gods cannot pass the most elementary test of intelligence: they cannot distinguish between similar and dissimilars.

But though Job's God is a great advance on Noah's God, he is a very bad debater, unless indeed we give him credit for deliberately saving himself from defeat by the old expedient: "No case: abuse the plaintiff's attorney." Job having raised the problem of the existence of evil and its compatibility with impotent benevolence, it is no valid reply to jeer at him for being unable to create a whale or to play with it as with a bird. And there is a very suspicious touch of Noah's God in the offer to overlook the complicity of Job's friends in his doubts and consideration of a sacrifice of seven bullocks and seven rams [Job 42:8]. God's attempt at an argument is only a repetition and elaboration of the sneers of Elihu [who rebukes his friend Job (Job 32–37)], and is so abruptly tacked on to them that one concludes that it must be a pious forgery to conceal the fact that the original poem left the problem of evil unsolved and Job's criticism unanswered, as indeed it remained until Creative Evolution solved it.

When we come to Micah we find him throwing out the dirty water fearlessly. He will not have Noah's God, nor even Job's God with his seven bullocks and seven rams. He raises the conception of God to the highest point it has ever attained by his fiercely contemptuous denunciation of the blood sacrifices, and his inspired and inspiring demand "What doth the Lord require of thee but to do justly, and to love mercy, and to walk humbly with thy God?" [Micah 6:8] Before this victory of the human spirit over crude superstition Noah's God and Job's God go down like skittles: there is an end to them. And yet our children are taught, not to exult in this great triumph of spiritual insight over mere animal terror of the Bogey Man, but to believe that Micah's God and Job's God and Noah's God are one and the same, and that every good child must revere the spirit of justice and mercy and humility equally with the appetite for burnt flesh and human sacrifice, such indiscriminate and nonsensical reverence being inculcated as religion.

Later on comes Jesus, who dares a further flight. He suggests that godhead is something which incorporates itself in man: in himself, for instance. He is immediately stoned by his horrified hearers, who can see nothing in the suggestion but a monstrous attempt on his part to impersonate Jehovah. This misunderstanding, typical of dirty water theology, was made an article of religion eighteen hundred years later by Emanuel Swedenborg. But the unadulterated suggestion of Jesus is an advance on the theology of Micah; for Man walking humbly before an external God is an ineffective creature compared to Man exploring as the instrument and embodiment of God with no other guide than the spark of divinity within him. It is certainly the greatest break in the Bible between the Old and the New Testament. Yet the dirty water still spoils it; for we find Paul holding up Christ to the Ephesians as "an offering and a sacrifice to God for a sweet smelling savour," [Ephesians 5:2] thereby dragging Christianity back and down to the level of Noah. None of the apostles rose above that level; and the result was that the great advances made by Micah and Jesus were cancelled; and historical Christianity was built up on the sacrificial altars of Jehovah, with Jesus as the sacrifice. What he and Micah would say if they could return and see their names and credit attached to the idolatries they abhorred can be imagined only by those who understand and sympathize with them.

Jesus could be reproached for having chosen his disciples very unwisely if we could believe that he had any real choice. There are moments when one is tempted to say that there was not one Christian among them, and that Judas was the only one who shewed any gleams of common sense. Because Jesus had mental powers and insight quite beyond their comprehension they worshipped him as a superhuman and indeed supernatural phenomenon, and made his memory the nucleus of their crude belief in magic, their Noahism, their sentimentality, their masochistic Puritanism, and their simple morality with its punitive sanctions, decent and honest and amiable enough, some of it, but never for a moment on the intellectual level of Jesus, and at worst pregnant with all the horrors of the later wars of religion, the Jew burnings of [Spanish Dominican friar and first Grand Inquisitor Tomás de] Torquemada [1420–98], and the atrocities of which all the pseudo-Christian Churches were guilty the moment they became powerful enough to persecute.

Most unfortunately the death of Jesus helped to vulgarize his reputation and obscure his doctrine. The Romans, though they executed their own political criminals by throwing them from [the eighty-foot cliff of the Capitoline Hill in Rome] the Tarpeian rock, punished slave revolts by crucifixion. They crucified six thousand of the followers of the revolutionary gladiator, Spartacus [(111–71 BCE), who led an army

of escaped slaves against the Roman Republic], a century before Jesus was denounced to them by the Jewish high priest
as an agitator of the same kidney. He was accordingly tortured and killed in this hideous manner, with the infinitely
more hideous result that the cross and the other instruments
of his torture were made the symbols of the faith legally established in his name three hundred years later. They are still
accepted as such throughout Christendom. The crucifixion
thus became to the Churches what the Chamber of Horrors
is to a waxwork: the irresistible attraction for children and for
the crudest adult worshippers. Christ's clean water of life is
befouled by the dirtiest of dirty water from the idolatries of
his savage forefather; and our prelates and proconsuls take
Caiaphas and Pontius Pilate for their models in the name of
their despised and rejected victim.

The case was further complicated by the pitiable fact that
Jesus himself, shaken by the despair which unsettled the reason of Swift and Ruskin and many others at the spectacle of
human cruelty, injustice, misery, folly, and apparently hopeless political incapacity, and perhaps also by the worship of
his disciples and of the multitude, had allowed Peter to persuade him that he was the Messiah, and that death could not
prevail against him nor prevent him returning to judge the
world and establish his reign on earth for ever and ever. As
this delusion came as easily within the mental range of his
disciples as his social doctrine had been far over their heads,
"Crosstianity" became established on the authority of Jesus
himself. Later on, in a curious record of the visions of a drug
addict which was absurdly admitted to the canon under the
title of Revelation, a thousand years were specified as the period that was to elapse before Jesus was to return as he had
promised. In 1000 A.D. the last possibility of the promised
advent expired; but by that time people were so used to the
delay that they readily substituted for the Second Advent a

Second Postponement. Pseudo-Christianity was, and always will be, fact proof.

The whole business is an amazing muddle, which has held out not only because the views of Jesus were above the heads of all but the best minds, but because his appearance was followed by the relapse in civilization which we call the Dark Ages, from which we are only just emerging sufficiently to pick up the thread of Christ's most advanced thought and rescue it from the mess the apostles and their successors made of it.

Six hundred years after Jesus, Mahomet founded Islam and made a colossal stride ahead from mere stock-and-stone idolatry to a very enlightened Unitarianism [in exhorting his followers to worship a single deity]; but though he died a conqueror, and therefore escaped being made the chief attraction in an Arabian Chamber of Horrors, he found it impossible to control his Arabs without enticing and intimidating them by promises of a delightful life for the faithful, and threats of an eternity of disgusting torment for the wicked, after their bodily death, and also, after some honest protests, by accepting the supernatural character thrust on him by the childish superstition of his followers; so that he, too, now needs to be rediscovered in his true nature before Islam can come back to earth as a living faith.

And now I think the adventures of the black girl as revealed to me need no longer puzzle anyone. They could hardly have happened to a white girl steeped from her birth in the pseudo-Christianity of the Churches. I take it that the missionary lifted her straight out of her native tribal fetishism into an unbiassed contemplation of the Bible with its series of gods marking stages in the development of the conception of God from the monster Bogey Man to the Father; then to the spirit without body, parts, nor passions; and finally to the definition of that spirit in the words God is Love. For the primitive two her knobkerry [a club with a knobbed head] suffices; but when she reaches the end she has to point out that Love is not enough (like Edith Cavell making the same discovery about Patriotism) and that it is wiser to take Voltaire's advice by cultivating her garden and bringing up her piccaninnies than to spend her life imagining that she can find a complete explanation of the universe by laying about her with a knobkerry.

Still, the knobkerry has to be used as far as the way is clear. Mere agnosticism leads nowhere. When the question of the existence of Noah's idol is raised on the point, vital to high civilization, whether our children shall continue to be brought up to worship it and compound for their sins by sacrificing to it, or, more cheaply, by sheltering themselves behind another's sacrifice to it, then whoever hesitates to bring down the knobkerry with might and main is ludicrously unfit to have any part in the government of a modern State. The importance of a message to that effect at the present world crisis is probably at the bottom of my curious and sudden inspiration to write this tale instead of cumbering theatrical literature with another stage comedy.

12. Letters to Dame Laurentia McLachlan, 1933 and 1935. [*Shaw on Religion*, pp. 201–07]

[Smith notes (p. 239) that these letters are taken from a tribute volume by the Benedictines of Stanbrook Abbey to their Mother Abbess, In a Great Tradition (Harper and Brothers, 1956), pp. 262–63 and 270–72. Shaw had met Scottish Benedictine nun Laurentia McLachlan (1866–1953) at Stanbrook Abbey, Worcester, in April 1924.]

The Malvern Hotel
Great Malvern
July 24, 1933

Sister Laurentia,

You are the most unreasonable woman I ever knew. You want me to go out and collect 100,000 sold copies of *The Black Girl*, which have all been read and the mischief, if any, done; and then you want me to announce publicly that my idea of God Almighty is the antivegetarian deity who, after trying to exterminate the human race by drowning it, was coaxed out of finishing the job by a gorgeous smell of roast meat. Laurentia: has it never occurred to you that I might possibly have a more exalted notion of divinity, and that I don't as a matter of fact believe that Noah's deity ever existed or ever could exist? How could it possibly comfort you if I declared that I believed in him? It would simply horrify you. I know much better than you what you really believe. You think you believe the eighth chapter of Genesis [recounting the end of the flood and Noah's sacrifice]; and I know you don't: if you did I would never speak to you again. You think you believe that Micah, when he wrote the eighth verse of his sixth chapter ["What doth the Lord require of thee, but to do justly, and to love mercy, and to walk humbly with thy God?"], was a liar and a blasphemer; but I know that you agree heartily with Micah, and that if you caught one of your nuns offering rams and calves and her first-born (if she had one) as a sacrifice to Jehovah you would have her out of the convent and into the nearest lunatic asylum before she could say [the opening words of the Catholic prayer to the Virgin Mary] Hail, Mary. You think you are a better Catholic than I; but my view of the Bible is the view of the Fathers of the Church; and yours is that of a Belfast Protestant to whom the Bible is a fetish and religion entirely irrational. You think you believe that God

did not know what he was about when he made me and inspired me to write *The Black Girl*. For what happened was
that when my wife was ill in Africa God came to me and said
"These women in Worcester plague me night and day with
their prayers for you. What are you good for, anyhow?" So
I said I could write a bit but was good for nothing else. God
said then "Take your pen and write what I shall put into your
silly head." When I had done so, I told you about it, thinking that you would be pleased, as it was the answer to your
prayers. But you were not pleased at all, and peremptorily for-
bade me to publish it. So I went to God and said "The Abbess
is displeased." And God said "I am God; and I will not be
trampled on by any Abbess that ever walked. Go and do as I
have ordered you." ... "Well" I said "I suppose I must publish
the book if you are determined that I shall; but it will get me
into trouble with the Abbess; for she is an obstinate unreasonable woman who will never let me take her out in my car;
and there is no use your going to have a talk with her; for you
might as well talk to the wall unless you let her have everything all her own way just as they taught it to her when she
was a child." So I leave you to settle it with God and his Son
as best you can; but you must go on praying for me, however
surprising the result may be.

Your incorrigible
G. Bernard Shaw

Union-Castle Line
M. V. Llangibby Castle
April 12, 1935

On the Equator. 82 in the shade. On the East coast of Africa.
Cara Sorella Laurentia,
   You are a puzzle to me with your unexpected rages. I ask
myself, since I know that one becomes eminent in the

Church through capacity for business more easily than by capacity for religion, "Can Laurentia be a completely irreligious (or areligious) managing woman who becomes boss in a convent exactly as she would become boss in a castle or in a laundry?"

McLachlan? That suggests a clan of Covenanters to whom the worship of the B. V. M. [Blessed Virgin Mary] is a damnable idolatry to be wiped out with claymore and faggot. Has Laurentia got that in her blood? If not, why in the name of all the saints does she fly out at me when I devoutly insist that the Godhead must contain the Mother as well as the Father?

Or is it merely personal? So many women hate their mothers (serve them right, mostly!) and see red when the cult of maternity arises.

You want me, as if it were a sort of penance, to say a lot of Hail Maries. But I am always saying Hail, Mary! on my travels. Of course I don't say it in that artificial form which means nothing. I say it in my own natural and sincere way when She turns up in the temples and tombs of Egypt and among the gods of Hindustan—Hallo, Mary! For you really cannot get away from Her. She has many names in the guide books, and many disguises. But She never takes me in. She favours Brother Bernardo with special revelations and smiles at his delighted "Hallo, Mary!" When I write a play like *The Simpleton* [*of the Unexpected Isles: A Vision of Judgement* (1934)] and have to deal with divinity in it She jogs my elbow at the right moment and whispers "Now Brother B. don't forget *me.*" And I don't.

But then you come along in a fury and cry, "How dare you? Cut all this stuff out, and say fifty Hail Maries."

Which am I to obey? Our Lady of Stanbrook or Our Lady of Everywhere?

When you are old, as I am, these things will clear up and become real to you. I wonder whether, if Raphael had lived to be old like [Italian artist] Michael Angelo, he would have given us something less absurd than the highly respectable Italian farmers' daughters he imposed so smugly on the world as visions of the B. V. M. Never have I stood before one of his Madonnas and exclaimed Hallo, Mary! Raphael made the adoration of the Mother impossible; but his view was so frankly and nicely human and fleshly and kindly that in the Dresden Madonna he produced for all time the ideal wet nurse, healthy, comely, and completely brainless.

On the other hand there is the giantess-goddess of [Florentine painter] Cimabue [(c. 1240–1302), who painted a number of large Madonna portraits] with her magnetic stare, a much deeper conception, but with just a little too much of the image and too little reality to be as approachable as the Egyptian goddess [perhaps Isis] of the great period.

In short, the Christian Maries are all failures. This suggests that [adherents of the non-violent Indian religion Jainism] the Jains [who reject the idea of a creator-deity and believe the universe to be eternal] were right in excluding God from their ritual as beyond human power to conceive or portray. At least that is their theory; but in practice they have in their shrines images of extraordinary beauty and purity of design who throw you into an ecstasy of prayer and a trance of peace when they look at you, as no Christian iconography can.

I said to the pundit who showed me round "Those images are surely gods, are they not?" "Not at all," he said, "they are statues of certain very wise men of the Jains." This was obvious nonsense; so I pointed out that a man kneeling in the shrine (having first washed himself from head to foot) was clearly praying to a god. "Pooh!" said the pundit with enormous contempt, "he is only a heathen idolator."

It is in these temples that you escape from the frightful parochiality of our little sects of Protestants and Catholics, and recognize the idea of God everywhere, and understand how the people who struggled hardest to establish the unity of God made the greatest number of fantastically different images of it, producing on us the effect of a crude polytheism. Then comes the effort to humanize these images. The archaic [Roman goddess of wisdom and the arts] Minerva becomes the very handsome and natural Venus of Milo [the famous Greek sculpture of the goddess of love and beauty]. The Cimabue colossus becomes the wet nurse. [Venetian painter Giovanni] Bellini's [c. 1430–1516] favourite model becomes as well known to us in her blue hood [representing the Virgin Mary] as any popular actress. [Renown Italian polymath] Leonardo [da Vinci (1452–1519)], Michael Angelo, [Italian painter] Correggio [1489–1534] (once, in the dome in Parma) lift these leading ladies, these stars of the studio, for a moment out of the hopelessly common; but on the whole, wisdom is with the Jains.

I have been getting into trouble by backing up a proposal to give Christ's Cathedral in Dublin to the Catholics, leaving St Patrick's to the Protestants. The two cathedrals are in a poor neighbourhood within a stone's throw of one another. St Patrick's was restored [1860–65] by [Sir Benjamin] Guinness [1798–1868] the brewer, Christ's [1871–78] by [Henry] Roe the distiller. The drunkenness of the poor Catholics paid for both: why should they not have at least one?

But my own individual opinion is that cathedrals should be for all men, and not for this or that sect.

By this time we have passed the equator, and it is time for me to stop blaspheming.

Bless you, dear Laurentia.

G. Bernard Shaw

13. "Religious Summary," *Everybody's Political What's What?* (London: Constable, 1944), pp. 357–63.

[*"I cannot agree that we should bury the Bible only," writes Shaw; "we should burn the Prayer Book also." Shaw goes on to denounce the church for "the horrible practice of earth burial" and its refusal to allow divorce, and thinks the Inquisition is "not now so-called, but always in active operation." His bitterness is understandable, as he is writing in the context of what he calls "the murderous mess in which [our civilization] is at present staggering" and has "lived to see modern Germany discard Hail, Mary! and substitute Heil, Hitler!"*]

It is time to tell our Fundamentalists bluntly that they are the worst enemies of religion today; that Jehovah is no god, but a barbarous tribal idol; that the English Bible, though a masterpiece of literary art in its readable parts, and, being the work of many highly gifted authors and translators, rich in notable poems, is yet a jumble of savage superstitions, obsolete cosmology, and a theology which, beginning with Calibanesque idolatry and propitiatory blood sacrifices (Genesis to Kings), recoils into sceptical disillusioned atheistical Pessimism (Ecclesiastes); revives in a transport of revolutionary ardor as the herald of divine justice and mercy and the repudiation of all sacrifices (Micah and the Prophets); relapses into sentimentality by conceiving God as an affectionate father (Jesus); reverts to blood sacrifice and takes refuge from politics in Other-Worldliness and Second Adventism (the Apostles); and finally explodes in a mystical opium dream of an impossible apocalypse (Revelation): every one of these phases being presented in such an unbalanced one-sided way, that the first Christian Catholic Church forbad the laity to read the Bible without special permission. When the Reformation [beginning in 1517, when Luther posted his Ninety-Five Theses on the door of All Saints' Church in Wittenberg, Germany] let it loose on Mr Everyman, it produced a series of wars of religion which have culminated today in the Hitlerized world war. In this the campaigns of Joshua for the conquest of his world have broken out again with the difference that the Germans and not the Jews are the Chosen Race (*Herrenvolk*) who are to conquer and inherit the earth; and the lands flowing with milk and honey which they are to invade and put to the sword are not only the patches of North Africa which used to be called the land of Canaan but virtually the whole of five continents. It is one of the paradoxes of the situation that Joshua Hitler, born in comparative poverty into the bitter strife of petty commerce in which the successful competition of the Jews is specially dreaded and resented, and for which he is himself unfitted by his gifts, hates the Jews, and yet is so saturated by his early schooling with the Judaism of the Bible that he now persecutes the Jews even to extermination just as the first Joshua persecuted the Canaanites, and is leading his country to ruin not through anti-Semitism, but through Bible Semitism with its head turned.

Yet from my reading aloud of all this writing on the wall, Mr Everyman, who never listens critically to the ritual of having the lessons read to him every Sunday in Church (when he goes to Church: a habit which he is dropping), gathers nothing but that I am a damnably irreligious man who will certainly go to hell when I die if there be any such place as hell, which Mr Everyman is beginning to doubt, because it has uncomforting possibilities for himself as well as certainty for me.

If we must canonize some collection of writings as evolutionarily inspired, which is what we have done with the budget of selected samples of ancient Hebrew literature we call the Book of Books, surely we had better canonize our own modern literature, as it is equally inspired evolutionarily, and much more up-to-date socially and scientifically. The Bible in its canonical aspect is not helping us: it is obscuring us and making us dangerously irreligious. Rousseau said in the eighteenth century, "Get rid of your miracles and the whole world will fall at the feet of Christ"; and this was seasonably said at the moment; but he was wrong: the whole world has become indifferent to the Bible miracles, and instead of falling at the feet of Christ has fallen at the feet of [French chemist Louis] Pasteur [1822–95] and [Russian physiologist Ivan] Pavlov [1849–1936], and set up a new canon of miracles which it calls miracles of Science.

Yet is has not discarded its old Fundamentalist superstitions and taboos and mental habits. No longer ago than the end of the nineteenth century [controversial Christian Socialist and Anglican priest] Stewart Headlam [1847–1924], a clergyman, got into trouble with his ecclesiastical superiors by saying that what the Church needs is to bury the Bible for a hundred years, and let it then be discovered for what it really is. I cannot agree that we should bury the Bible only: we should burn the Prayer Book also. It is saturated with blood sacrifice beyond all possible revision; and its constant reiteration of "through Jesus Christ our Lord" grows more and more unbearable by its essential falsehood as more and more people realize that what is true in the Prayer Book would be equally true if Jesus had never existed, and that his martyrdom does not relieve us of a jot of our responsibility for our sins. For instance, though a thief can redeem himself by becoming honest, until he does so he remains none the less a thief, and a damned one at that, though Jesus had died a thousand times. Jesus never said "Sin as much as you like: my blood will wash it all off": he said "Sin no more." The Prayer Book, by incessantly holding him up as a scapegoat, discredits him and undoes the civilizing value of the Church. In this way the Prayer Book is keeping Mr Everyman away from church, though he still thinks he perhaps ought to go when in fact he doesn't. He certainly often spends his Sunday in a much duller and more expensive way than he would in a church brought honestly up to date.

The Roman Church, more worldly wise than the Church of England, and served by trained and professionalized priests instead of by casual amateur British gentlemen wearing slightly unusual collars, is even more handicapped because it will not admit that it has ever made mistakes, and refuses to make experiments although modern science has made it impossible to believe in God at all unless with the admission that God has made experimental mistakes. The world is full of them; and it is our job to correct them or get rid of them. For a familiar practical instance, the Roman Catholic must "suffer his holy ones to see corruption" [Psalm 16:10 and Acts 2:27] by the horrible practice of earth burial because his Church began by committing itself to the childish notion that a buried body can be resuscitated but not a burnt one, reminding me of an uncle of mine who, believing that he was about to be taken up to heaven like Elijah in a celestial chariot, took off his boots to facilitate the operation. The Roman Catholic Church, if it is to compete successfully with rival Catholicism for the faith of men better instructed than my uncle must rise above his level and admit that the law of change is the law of God.

For another instance, its refusal to allow divorce has forced it to annul marriages, sometimes on grounds that would not pass in a Dakota divorce court [where divorces had been notoriously easy to obtain; Fargo, e.g., was known as the "divorce capital of the West"].

Quakers and saints can be religious without ritual, and compose their own prayers; but there are others who if they do not go to church will forget their religion and go to the devil, or worse, to war. And in the long run they will not go to church if what they hear there is incredible and unreasonable. Dogmatic Sanctions and Prohibitions must be kept up to date fast enough to avoid a disastrous clash between

Dogma and Pragma. But when I say these things, all that Mr Everyman gathers is that he had better lock up his spoons when people like me are about. Yet he would dislike me still more if he discovered that I am religious enough to have spent a great part of my life trying to clean up the heavily barnacled creeds, and make them credible, believing as I do that society cannot be held together without religion. An incredible religion is also an uncomfortable one: that is why Mr Everyman dislikes religion and religious people. I began in my early teens by maintaining that it was not the Bible and its Ten Commandments that made people good, but their sense of honor: a recent acquirement of my own which had cured me of childish lying and stealing. My numerous uncles thereupon concluded that I was an atheist, and that something ought to be done about it. But as nothing was done I accepted the epithet as due to my intellectual integrity, ranking me with [Dominican friar, philosopher and astrologer] Giordano Bruno [(1548–1600), burned at the stake as a heretic by the Roman Inquisition for denying a number of Catholic doctrines] and the noble army of martyrs whom Science placed above the glorious company of the apostles. I submit that when quite respectable young gentlemen like Shelley and myself boast of being heretics, and clubs of them are formed at the universities, Mr Everyman is right in concluding that there must be something very wrong somewhere; for as heretics are clearly traitors to civilization, they should be liquidated (not necessarily burnt) by The Inquisition, not now so-called, but always in active operation, were it only to extinguish the heresies of Thuggee and Voodoo. When The Inquisition is out-of-date, and the heretics up-to-date, there is the devil to pay.

But nowadays institutional religion and the habit of churchgoing have so lost their hold on Mr Everyman that my criticism of the creeds has never been resented as Shelley's was by the indignant Englishman who is said to have knocked him down at sight in a post office. [...]

Mr and Mrs Everyman never seem to doubt that if anyone disagrees with them in any matter upon which they feel strongly, they have the right to injure the dissenter to any extent within their power short of *heretico comburendo* ["the burning of heretics" (Latin), the 1401 law passed by Parliament under King Henry IV punishing heretics with burning at the stake]. It seems to them as natural a right as their right to inflict the most mischievous and prolonged torments on lawbreakers, or to cuff and flog their naughty children and share that right with the school teacher. If they pleaded in justification that their tempers are so explosive that they would wreck civilization without a safety valve one could argue with them; but they pretend instead that two blacks make a white, and that they are acting with judicial calm in the best interest of society. When I tell them that they have no right to punish anybody (except perhaps themselves); that when Jesus told them he was giving them sound practical advice; and that our treatment of criminals is diabolical, they dismiss me as a dreamy sentimentalist; but when I add that far from sympathizing with those who demand the abolition of capital punishment and the substitution of a penal servitude worse than death, I demand the liquidation, as kindly as possible, of all incorrigible living nuisances, I muddle and amaze them as much as when I profess myself a democrat and yet demand the disfranchisement and disqualification of political nincompoops from every political activity except that of ventilating their grievances and choosing between ruler and proved competence.

I was present once at the induction of a rector into a Church of England living. Although I knew beforehand that the bishop would have to ask the postulant a question to which the answer would be a deliberate lie, known to be such to both of them, and was prepared to admit that they were both doing this under duress, having to do it or have their vocations closed to them, it was none the less shocking to see and hear it actually done. The best brain among our Church dignitaries has given it to us in writing that if the Thirty-nine Articles (the subject of the lie) were taken seriously the Church would be staffed exclusively by fools, bigots, and liars. Until we have a Church and a Government righteous enough and strong enough to discard the Articles, rewrite the Prayer Book, and put the Bible in its proper place, we shall not get our civilization out of the murderous mess in which it is at present staggering. Science and religion at loggerheads are reflected politically in a suicidal world war. The popular notion that one of the two must be all right and the other all wrong is what I call Soot-or-Whitewash reasoning: it is not reasoning at all, but thoughtless unobservant jumping at conclusions. Both our science and our religion are gravely wrong; but they are not all wrong; and it is our urgent business to purge them of their errors and get them both as right as possible. If we could get them entirely right the contradictions between them would disappear: we should have a religious science and a scientific religion in a single synthesis. Meanwhile we must do the best we can instead of running away from the conflict as we are cowardly enough to do at present.

Anthropomorphic Deism will remain for long as a workable hypothesis not only for children but for many adults. Prayer consoles, heals, builds the soul in us; and to enact a Prohibition of Prayer, as some Secularists would if they had the power, would be as futile as it would be cruel. But there are all sorts of prayers, from mere beggars' petitions and magic incantations to contemplative soul building, and all sorts of divinities to pray to. A schoolboy who witnessed a performance of my play St Joan [1924] told his schoolmaster that he disliked Jesus and could not pray to him, but that he could pray to Joan. An Ulster Orange schoolmaster would probably have given him an exemplary thrashing to make a proper young Protestant of him; but this schoolmaster was wiser: he told the boy to pray to Joan by all means: it is the prayer and not the prayee that matters. To the Franciscan, Francis and not Jesus is the redeemer; and to countless Catholics and not a few Anglicans Our Lady is the intercessor. To the Jains God is Unknowable; but their temple in Bombay is full of images of all sorts of saints, from nameless images of extraordinary beatific peace to crude elephant-headed idols. As a Protestant child I was taught that my Roman Catholic fellow countrymen would all go to hell because they said Hail, Mary! At the same time my English contemporary [physician and author of the Sherlock Holmes detective stories] Arthur Conan Doyle [1859–1930] was being taught at [Roman Catholic (Jesuit)] Stonyhurst [College] that I should be damned for not saying it. I have lived to see modern Germany discard Hail, Mary! and substitute Heil, Hitler!; and for the life of me I cannot bring myself to regard he change as an improvement. It looks too like a revival of the worship of the ancient Egyptian [sun] god Ra, whose head was the head of a hawk. Still, I think the Church of England wrong in imposing Jesus, whom many people dislike as my schoolboy devotee of Joan did, as the sole form in which God can be prayed to. Every Church should be a Church of All Saints, and every cathedral a place for pure contemplation by the greatest minds of all races, creeds, and colors.

14. "The God of Bernard Shaw," *The Freethinker* 66 (30 June 1946), p. 241. [*Agitations*, pp. 338–39]

[Reply to a letter by barrister and journalist C. G. L. (Charles Garfield Lott) Du Cann (b. 1889), "The God of Bernard Shaw," in The Freethinker *(16 June 1946).]*

Sir,—I have to thank Mr. Du Cann and your good self for an astonishingly accurate account of my philosophy, such as it is.

When I described the heart of the despairing pessimist as sinking into a heap of sand I was not thinking of any experience of my own nor of any of the atheists, secularists, freethinkers, and other godless persons of my acquaintance. I never suffered the least inconvenience from my desertion of my old Nobodaddy [William Blake's punitive, absentee God], nor as far as I know did they. But the others did and do; and I had to take them into account in a rhetorical passage written for platform delivery.

My biology starts with the fact that there is no discovered chemical difference between a live body and a dead one. The same creature has ceased to breathe and pump its blood; and it presently disintegrates and rots, nobody knows why. Until we do know, the Life Force, as I call it, though visibly at work everywhere, is a miracle and a mystery; but we can say of it that it has evident purposes which transcend those of self-preservation and reproduction by visible operations. It has an evolutionary appetite for power and knowledge, in pursuit of which it will risk martyrdom and face the extremity of hardship and danger. The man who might be the prosperous churchwarden prefers to be the persecuted village freethinker. The squire abandons his comfortable country house, and undertakes "the worst journey in the world" [the title of Apsley Cherry-Garrard's 1922 chronicle of the ill-fated Robert Falcon Scott expedition to the Antarctic] to gather an egg or two of the Emperor Penguin because it is a missing link in genetic theory.

Rationalism, Materialism, Hedonism cannot account for this—it is just a hard fact of incalculable importance and promise. Freethinkers and Fundamentalists alike must face it, whatever arguments or legends they may decorate it with.

I am no more a Christian than I am a Confucian, a Moslem, or a Jain. The sentimental "Love one another" and "Our Father" of Jesus do not fit into a world of thinly veneered unlovable savages. To love them would be unnatural vice. The counsel of perfection is to be just and humane to those whom we rightly detest. Jesus was deeply right in urging us to discard revenge and punishment. Two blacks do not make a white. We must weed the garden, but not unkindly.

As a crude political agitator Jesus must be classed with [the leader of the 1601 rebellion against Elizabeth I, Robert Devereux, 2nd Earl of] Essex [1566–1601], [the leader of the 1803 Irish Rebellion, Robert] Emmet [1778–1803], and the many other novices who have attempted an insurrection without an army, and have been at once taken by the police and executed. And his advice to the rich young man will not hold water.

In short, "the god of Bernard Shaw" is very obviously not a god at all as the word goes. The Life Force is a metaphysical hypothesis deducted from undeniable facts, not the imaginary sitter painted by Michael Angelo, Raphael, and Blake. Mankind is an experiment in godhead, so far not a successful one. But the Life Force will no doubt try again.

Yours, &c.,

G. Bernard Shaw

15. "What Is My Religious Faith?" *Sixteen Self Sketches* (London: Constable, 1949), pp. 73–79.

[Published in Rationalist Annual for the Year 1945 *(London: C. A. Watts, 1945), pp. 3–7. According to Laurence (Bibliography I: 457), it was "extensively revised" for* Sixteen Self Sketches. *Shaw offers again his unique interpretation of certain religious beliefs before surveying, in the wake of Darwin, the role of science as "the new substitute for religion." What "the Churches call Providence"*

Shaw calls "the Life Force and the Evolutionary Appetite," which, "proceeds by trial and error and creates the problem of evil by its unsuccessful experiments and its mistakes."]

I am by infant baptism a member of the Protestant Episcopal Church of Ireland; but I cannot believe more than two tenets of its creed, and these (the Communion of Saints and the Life Everlasting) only in an entirely unconventional sense, nor in its Thirtynine Articles, which, compiled for the sake of political peace and quietness to face both ways between Roman Catholicism and Puritanism, are too self-contradictory to be accepted by anyone capable of consecutive thinking. Its other creed, the Athanasian, much objected to by the Broad Churchmen of my time because they thought its damnatory clause implied a belief in a brimstone hell, against which they were in full revolt, I endorse, because I interpret it as meaning that understanding and not faith is what the world most needs, and that people not subtle enough to accept its apparent paradoxes as valid statements of biological fact may be rhetorically described as intellectually damned.

Such scepticisms would make me chargeable with apostasy under what is called the Blasphemy Law if I had ever been confirmed; but as I was not, I shall plead, if indicated, that the charge lies against my godfathers and godmothers (they are all dead) and not against myself.

This leaves me open to the question "If you are not a Protestant Churchman, what are you?"

At first I used to reply that I was an Atheist. But this was no answer; for what sensible people need to know is what people believe, not what they don't believe. At that time, however, professed Atheists, unless also plutocrats, were being savagely persecuted. Bradlaugh was thrown out of the House of Commons with such violence that John Bright, who arrived just in time to see him dragged down the stairs by six policemen, was horrified. His successor as head of the National

Secular Society, G. W. Foote, was imprisoned for a year [in 1883] for publishing [in 1882] a picture of Samuel anointing Saul [1 Samuel 9–10] in modern clothes. It was a point of honor for their fellow-apostates to give them emphatic and unqualified support by professing themselves either Atheists or Agnostics. I preferred to call myself an Atheist because belief in God then meant belief in the old tribal idol called Jehovah; and I would not, by calling myself an Agnostic, pretend that I did not know whether it existed or not. I still, when I am dealing with oldfashioned Fundamentalists, tell them that as I do not believe in this idol of theirs they may as well write me off as for their purposes, an Atheist.

What, then, was I? When G. W. Foote became insolvent and his petition in bankruptcy raised the question of who was to succeed him if he had to resign his presidency of the National Secular Society, some of the members, headed by George Standring, placed me on a list of possibilities, and invited me to address the Society and be judged as to my eligibility. My subsequent career has proved that I should not have been their worst choice; but after my address to them on Progress in Freethought, their Fundamentalists (for there is as high a percentage of such in the National Secular Society as in the Salvation Army [founded 1865]) went white with rage, and made Standring aware that I had rather less chance of election than the Archbishop of Canterbury. My demonstration that the Trinity is not an arithmetical impossibility, but the commonplace union of father, son, and spirit in one person; that the doctrine of Immaculate Conception is an instalment of the sacred truth that all conceptions are immaculate; that the Roman Catholic worship of the Madonna is in effect a needed addition of The Mother to The Father in The Godhead; and that any clever Jesuit could convert an average Secularist to Roman Catholicism, froze the marrow in their bones. Mrs Besant's conversion to Theosophy had not then shocked and shaken them.

Charles Watts [1836–1906], one of the ablest Secularist leaders, called himself neither Atheist nor Agnostic, but Rationalist. This was a stronger position, being a positive one, than the Atheism of Bradlaugh, though Bradlaugh's heroic personality kept him in the centre of the stage until his victory over the House of Commons extinguished and finally killed him. But a profession of Rationalism implies the belief that reason is not only method, but motive; and I was too critical a reasoner to make this mistake. I knew that [architect of the so-called Reign of Terror (mass guillotining) during the French Revolution, Maximilien] Robespierre [1758–94], when he set up a Goddess of Reason [proclaimed on 10 November 1793], soon found out that reason is only a machinery of thought, and had to agree with Voltaire that if there were no God, it would be necessary to invent one. To govern men, practical rulers must reckon with honor, conscience, public spirit, social compunction, patriotism, self-sacrifice in pursuit of science and power over circumstances: in short, the apriorist virtues as well as their opposite vices: all inevitable but irrational. As I used to put it prosaically, reason can discover for you the best way—bus or tram, underground or taxi—to get from Piccadilly Circus to Putney, but cannot explain why you should want to go to Putney instead of staying in Piccadilly. Rationalism was also associated with Materialism; and I was and still am a Vitalist to whom vitality, though the hardest of all facts, is a complete mystery. I have to deal constantly in reason and with matter; but I am neither a Rationalist nor a Materialist.

At least, it may be said, I might have called myself an Evolutionist. But at that time it was generally assumed that Darwin invented Evolution. He had done just the opposite. He had shewn that many of the evolutionary developments ascribed to a divine creator could have been produced accidentally without purpose or even consciousness. This process he called Natural Selection. The anti-clerical anti-Bible reaction was then so strong among the skeptical intelligentsia that they swallowed Natural Selection hook, line, and sinker. Weismann, then the most prominent neo-Darwinian, insisted that all our gestures and actions are mere reflexes.

This was all very well as far as it went; but the farseeing Samuel Butler, after being carried away by the reaction for six weeks, suddenly realized that by banishing purpose from natural history Darwin had, as Butler put it, banished mind from the universe. It soon began to appear that he had banished morality also; for Science, with a capital S, the new substitute for religion, claimed exemption from all decent and humane considerations. It idolized half-witted monomaniacs like [surgeon and pioneer of antiseptic surgery Joseph] Lister [1827–1912] and Pavlov; established vivisection as the only avenue to biological science; flourished childish amateur statistics as recklessly as the Fundamentalists flourished what they called Christian evidence; declared that as there is no chemical difference between a live body and a dead one there is no scientific difference at all; rejected the harmless poetic rite of baptism as a barbarous superstition, and substituted fifty poisonous inoculations all warranted to make us immune from disease; prophesied the extinction of terrestrial life through the cooling of the sun; and generally plunged into an orgy of fanatical credulity and bigotry that at last provoked an outcry for a return to Christianity, or to any creed that has a place in it for Micah's postulate of justice, mercy, and humility before the enormity of our ignorance and the crudity of our mental processes. Darwinians who would have faced martyrdom sooner than deny their faith in Darwin or affirmed a belief in God, were sometimes, when women or money were concerned, conscienceless rascals.

What then am I, an artist-biologist, to call myself when asked to define my religion? I am a Catholic because I am a Communist (the two words mean the same) intelligent enough to perceive that our civilization, such as it is, could not exist for a week without its vast Communist basis of policed roads and bridges, water supplies and street lamps, courts of justice, schools, churches, legislatures, administrations, common and statutory law, armies, navies, air forces, etc. all staring in the faces of the ignorant majority of people to whom Communist is only a term of vulgar abuse, and Communism an epitome of everything evil and infamous. But if I call myself a Catholic I am taken to be a member of one or other of the established Christian Churches, all self-styled Catholic, whether Roman, Anglican, Greek, or what not, and all saturated with opiate fancies such as the Atonement, dear to the dishonest who, dreading the bugbear of a brimstone hell, dare not sin for six days without being washed clean in the blood of the Lamb on the seventh, and all clinging to a fiction of personal immortality, which anesthetizes the fear of death for the average man. "The average man is a coward" said Mark Twain.

As to the cardinal Christian precept "Love one another" I, contemplating humanity in the persons of a few rich ladies and gentlemen confronted by a multitude of poor working folk, glorying in warfare, and wallowing in superstition, not only do not love them but dislike them so much that they must be replaced by more sensible animals if civilization is to be saved. I really cannot love Hitlers and Pavlovs and their idolaters any more than I could have loved the saintly Torquemada or the esthetic Nero.

If I call myself a Vitalist I shall be classed as a Materialist by the scientists who admit the existence of a life force but conceive it as purely mechanical like steam or electricity.

If I call myself simply an Evolutionist I shall be listed as a Darwinian. Yet if I repudiate Darwin it will be assumed that I attach no importance to the part played in human destiny by Natural Selection and by Reason; for the popular imagination works only in extremes: soot or whitewash, Right or

Left, white or black. I am neither white nor black, but a classical grey, being very ignorant. All cats are grey in the dark.

I do not accept even the almost unquestioned sequence of Cause and Effect. It is the other way about with me. Bar pure accident, it is the aim, the purpose, the intended effect, that produces its so-called cause. If I shoot my neighbour it is not the fault of my gun and its trigger, nor is the rope the cause of my execution. Both are the effects of my intention to murder and the jury's sense of justice.

And so, as Bergson is the established philosopher of my sect, I set myself down as a Creative Evolutionist. And at that I should leave it, being too old a dog to pick up new tricks, were it not that I am asked where God comes into my religion. When I parry such questions by "Where does He come into yours?" the two replies come to the same. The Churches have to postulate a God Almighty who, obviously, is either not almighty or not benevolent; for the world is crowded with evil as much as with good to such an extent that many of its ablest thinkers, from Ecclesiastes to Shakespear, have been pessimists; and the optimists have had to postulate a devil as well as a god. Both have had to reckon with the operation of a natural agency which the Churches call Providence and the scientists Phlogiston [a fire-like element within combustible bodies postulated in 1667], Functional Adaptation, Natural Selection, *Vis Naturae Medicatrix*, the Necessary Myth, and Design in the Universe. I have called it the Life Force and the Evolutionary Appetite. Bergson called it the *Élan Vitale* [*sic*], Kant the Categorical Imperative, Shakespear the "divinity that shapes our ends, rough-hew them how we will." [*Hamlet* 5.ii] They all come to the same thing: a mysterious drive towards greater power over our circumstances and deeper understanding of Nature, in pursuit of which men and women will risk death as explorers or martyrs, and sacrifice their personal comfort and safety against all prejudice, all probability, all common sense.

As this unaccountable agency confronts every religion alike as a hard fact in spite of its many different names, it might as well be called Providence, which is the most expressive vernacular word for it. Thus much of the difference between the crudest Evangelism and Creative Evolution is found in administrative practice to be imaginary. Certainly the Bible Gods, of whom there are at least five, are all held on paper to be almighty, infallible, omnipotent and omniscient, whereas the Life Force, however benevolent, proceeds by trial and error and creates the problem of evil by its unsuccessful experiments and its mistakes. No practical administrative authority has ever been able to function on the assumption that almighty power, infallibility, and omniscience exist, or have ever existed or will exist in the world. When an atheist becomes a Plymouth Brother, or vice versa, the final comment is *plus ça change, plus c'est la même chose* [The more things change, the more they remain the same (French)]. The infallibility of God is a fiction that may be as necessary politically as the infallibility of the Pope or of the Judicial Committee of the House of Lords; but it is a fiction all the same.

It matters hardly at all what our denominations are; and I must disclaim any design to impose my denomination on others. I do not forget the warning of Jesus that if we try to clear established religions of their weeds we may pull up the wheat as well and leave the husbandmen without any religion. I detest the doctrine of the Atonement, holding that ladies and gentlemen cannot as such possibly allow anyone else to expiate their sins by suffering a cruel death. But I know as a hard fact that Methodism, which is saturated with this abhorrent superstition, changed our colliers and their wives and mothers from savages into comparatively civilized beings; and that any attempts to convert them to Creative Evolution would have made them more dangerous savages than ever, with no scruples, no personal god (the only sort of God they could believe in), and no fear of hell to restrain them.

To change a credulous peasantry to a sceptical one by inculcating a negative atheism plus a science beyond the reaches of their brains may make an end of civilization, not for the first time. It may even make an end of mankind, as it has already made an end of diplodocus and dinosaur, mammoth and mastodon. Creative Evolution can replace us; but meanwhile we must work for our survival and development as if we were Creation's last word. Defeatism is the wretchedest of policies.

16. "If I Were a Priest," *Atlantic Monthly* 185.5 (May 1950), pp. 70–72.

[Published as "A Tribute to a Great Churchman" in Church of England Newspaper *69 (13 January 1950) and reprinted in Brian Tyson, ed.,* Bernard Shaw's Book Reviews 1884 to 1950 *(University Park: Pennsylvania State University Press, 1966), pp. 536–45. This is Shaw's review of* Diary of a Dean: St. Paul's 1911–1934 *(1949) by W. R. Inge, who was also a eugenicist, a prolific author, and for twenty-five years a columnist for the* Evening Standard.*]*

It is puzzling to be born a Quaker, bred a Churchman, and made a Prelate. Dean Inge must often have said to himself, "For which among the rest was I ordained?" In his *Diary* he confesses to the Quaker; but I, now one of his few remaining contemporaries, being often challenged to denominate myself, and being much of the Dean's various opinions, have ceased to reply that my nearest to an established religion is the Society of Friends, and, while calling myself a Creative Evolutionist, might also call myself a Jainist Tirthankara [a "saint" who has attained *nirvana*] as of eight thousand years ago.

When the Dean and I were young the religious world was a battlefield of controversy and persecution. [American chemist and pioneer in photochemistry John William]

Draper's [(1811–82) A *History of the*] *Conflict between Religion and Science* [1874] was a text book. I preached Fabian Socialism in Victoria Park to my little crowd with a Christian Endeavour Apostle [the first Christian Endeavour society was founded in 1881 in Portland, Maine] preaching on my right and an atheist doing the same on my left: the one vociferating that all atheists had been in the dock at the police court or divorced for adultery, and the other calling the inn at Nazareth the Pig and Whistle, both of them convinced that they were uttering the profoundest religious doctrine and the most unquestionable scientific truth respectively.

All the controversies were in terms of what old photographers called Soot and Whitewash, and Ibsen's Brand All or Nothing. If the Nazareth inn had the sign of the Pig and Whistle, God did not exist. If the translators of the Authorized Version changed a negative into a positive to save the doctrine of the resurrection of the body, if the Ark was too small to hold all the earth's fauna in couples, if Joshua could not have stopped the sun in the Valley of Ajalon [in Joshua 10:12] without putting the whole universe out of action, if asses and serpents could not have conversed in human speech with [Old Testament prophet] Balaam and Eve, then the Bible was untrue in every word and sentence from beginning to end. If a Secularist lecturer had been convicted of having travelled by rail without a ticket or kept a mistress (or being kept by one), or advocated birth control, then all Secularists were thieves, fornicators, swindlers, rascals, and prostitutes: and only the ruthless exercise of the Blasphemy Acts could save us from moral chaos and material ruin. Association of ideas passed for logic.

Muscular parsons

Even within the Church of England itself there was controversy. There were muscular Christian rectors who, determined to show that they were no killjoy mealy-mouthed parsons, wore nothing clerical except jampot collars buttoned at the back, and were as assiduous at sports as in services. There were Anglo-Catholics who wore birettas and cassocks, called themselves priests, held up two fingers in blessing, and advertised their services as Masses. There were artist parsons who hung pictures of nudes all round their rooms to show that they had no sympathy with the zealots who held that sex is original sin.

There was the [influential Christian socialist] Reverend C[harles]. L[atimer]. Marson [1859–1914], who maintained that the first Article of the Church of England is, from the point of view of Jehovah's Witnesses [(founded 1870s) who deny the Trinity and believe Jesus is the archangel Michael] and the Plymouth Brethren, flat atheism. The vehicle in which he made his rounds was a donkey cart; and the donkey's name was [famed French stage actress] Sarah Bernhardt [1844–1923]. He collected folk songs, which his humbler parishioners classed as debauchery, as they did all fine art and merriment. There were the Christian Socialists, organized in [the high church association] the Guild of St. Matthew [1877–1909]: some of them in the Church and Stage Guild with ballet stars and Lions Comiques [music hall parodies of upper-class swells], notably [performer] Jolly John Nash [James Taylor (1830–1901)], who made his living by singing the praises of champagne, and was sincerely pious in private. And there were those who followed Herbert Spencer in holding that God is unknowable and unfathomable: in short, Neo-Jainists.

A precious rarity

Into this boiling cauldron of controversy Ralph Inge was born, foredoomed by heredity and environment to be a minister of the Church of England, and destined to be that unique phenomenon, a famous dean who refused a bishopric and became a famous journalist.

It is no part of my business to describe or explain the steps of this unusual development. I know only too well the annoyance and corruption of doctrine caused by people who write and read about noted authors instead of reading what the authors themselves have written, mostly much better. All a reviewer has any right to say of another man's book is "Read it" unless the verdict is "Don't read it," in which case he should give his reasons. But in the Dean's case, the word is so emphatically "You must read it" that I shall permit myself only a note or two.

Many years ago I received for review a book entitled *Outspoken Essays* [1919], and had hardly read three sentences before I smelt a very precious rarity, an original mind and a first-rate literary craftsman. As I was a bit in this line myself I was intensely interested, and reviewed it [in 1920] to that effect. My estimate has never changed. It led to a friendship which has made the kindly references to me and my late wife in the *Diary* so dear to me that any pretence of impartiality on my part would be ridiculous. But there was a difference. He had met many people I had met, and read many books I had read. But I had read Ruskin, Ibsen, and Marx; ...whereas in the index to the *Diary*, Ruskin, Ibsen, and Marx are not mentioned [...].

A turnip ghost

I divide sages into pre-Marx and post-Marx. The pre-Marxists, brought up on [historian and essayist Thomas Babington] Macaulay [1800–59] and [Liberal prime minister William Ewart] Gladstone [1809–98], regard and regret the nineteenth century as an age of prosperity increasing by leaps and bounds. To the post-Marxists it is a bottomless pit of hell from which Marx lifted the lid. In the *Diary* [economist and socialist] Sidney Webb [1859–1947] is referred to only once, and then in a quotation from a noodle who described him as a negligible nobody. And the Diarist records how, when we met, he found himself in unexpected agreement with me, but could not understand my obsession about Russia. Had he read Marx and discovered [the socialist organization (founded 1884) that promoted gradual, rather than revolutionary, change] the Fabian Society he would have understood. On this point he dates as does another famous friend of mine, [renowned Oxford classical scholar] Gilbert Murray [1866–1957]. He withdraws his description of Gilbert Chesterton's scriptures as the "elephantine capers of an obese mountebank," but does not define him as what he was: an extraordinarily gifted Peter Pan who never grew up.

Curiously enough, though he never mentions Ibsen, he was bothered, as Ibsen was when he wrote *Ghosts* [1881], by a Darwinian turnip ghost. For Ibsen, disease, especially syphilitic dementia, was inevitably inherited. For the Diarist it was the cooling of the sun, and the freezing to death of mankind on an ice-cap over the whole solar system. Science has since made hay of both these prospects; but they started the notion that Ibsen and Inge were pessimists.

Freedom or slavery?

Clerically, the Dean escaped the worst trial of a parson's intellectual conscience: that of having to countenance superstitions he does not share with his more primitive parishioners, yet finding it impossible to cure their souls on any other terms. Rousseau told the world two thundering lies, both of which the Churches swallowed with shut eyes and open mouth. Number one: Men are born free. Number two: Get rid of your miracles and the whole world will fall at the feet of Jesus.

Had Rousseau been born an employer he would have known that we are all born slaves to our necessities: bread and water, clothes and shelter, sleep and play and sanitation. Until these are satisfied there can be no freedom. Had he been a priest in a slum parish he would soon have learnt that if he got rid of the miracles his flock would go straight to the devil. An Irish Catholic statesman of my acquaintance was advised by a clever political lady to adopt a certain not quite straightforward stroke of diplomacy. He refused. She asked why. He replied, "Because I happen to believe that there is such as place as hell."

Jesus had to warn his missionaries that if they tried to weed the superstitions out of an established religion they would pull out the wheat as well as the tares. Mahomet, who when the Arabs were worshippers of sticks and stones made Unitarians [for whom God is a single being (in contrast to Trinitarians, for whom he is three beings in one)] of them at the risk of his life, found that he could not govern them without promising them a paradise of houris ["pure beings" (Arabic), female companions awaiting Muslim believers], threatening them with a loathsome hell, and claiming divine revelation for his oracles.

Expediencies

Were I an Irish priest and all my parishioners peasants I should say nothing of my own creed of Creative Evolution, which they could neither believe nor understand. I should educate the women in the cult of the Blessed Immaculate Virgin. I should bind and loose in the confessional. I should redeem the dead from purgatory for a cash consideration. I should elevate the Host as the real presence. Only so could I give them a religion they could revere.

All this would have been hard on Ralph Inge if his living had been in Hoxton or the Isle of Dogs. He would soon have been in trouble like [Bishop John William] Colenso [(1814–83), whose *Pentateuch and the Book of Joshua Critically Examined* (1862–79) was deemed heretical] or Bishop Barnes [whose *The Rise of Christianity* (1947) questioned the Virgin Birth and the Resurrection]. Happily he graduated clerically in Ennismore Gardens [in well-to-do Knightsbridge, London], where his parishioners [at the fashionable Church of All Saints, where Inge was vicar (1905–07)] were—how shall I put it?—up to snuff. Thereafter as Dean of St. Paul's in London City he had no slums to visit and could speak his mind, leaving unspoken the brimstone specialities of the Little Bethels [small chapels; perhaps Baptist ones]. Even I was invited to preach in the City Temple, and did so with complete acceptance more than once.

"No Faith in Democracy"

In the *Diary* the reason given for our getting on so well together is that we both had "no faith in Democracy." This must be interpreted as no faith in government and administration by parliaments of anybodies or nobodies elected by everybody. Administration is a highly skilled profession; and government is possible only for the five per cent or so born with the extra mental range it requires. Call them Mahatmas ["great souls" (Sanskrit)]. The Diarist, having that extra range, knows that the remaining ninety-five per cent do not possess it, and are a continual obstruction and a tyranny to those who do.

Young Mahatmas, unconscious of their scarcity, and supposing all their fellow creators to be as wise as themselves, are always puzzled at first by the stoppage of common minds at the point where the next step seems to the Mahatma to be glaringly obvious, and yet is inconceivable, invisible, and impossible to Monsieur *Tout le Monde* [Mr. Everybody (French)]. History soon convinces him that at best Monsieur elects Second Bests doing only what was done last time, and at worst Titus Oates [(1649–1705), fabricator of the 1678–81 Popish Plot (Catholic conspiracy) to assassinate Charles II], Lord George Gordon [(1751–93), instigator of the 1780 Gordon Riots, an anti-Catholic protest against the Papists Act of 1778 that had reduced official discrimination against British Catholics], favourite actors and soldiers ([renowned actor] Henry Irving

[1838–1905] and [distinguished Field Marshal Frederick Roberts] Lord Roberts [1832–1914], for instance, the backbone of law and order all the time being the [satirical] Vicars of Bray [who change their principles to retain ecclesiastical office] who obey any government that happens to be in power, and mind their own business "whatsoever king shall reign." [a line from the refrain of the early-eighteenth-century song "The Vicar of Bray"]

The real use of votes for everybody is to prevent us from being governed better than we can bear, as in the case of Prohibition of intoxicating drink in the U.S.A., which had to be repealed in spite of its proved betterment. The Welfare State is not possible with an Illfare constitution. Nobody knows this better than the exceptional thinkers.

A shy scholar

On the first page of the introduction to the *Diary* his friends will enjoy a laugh which the Diarist did not intend. He describes himself as a "shy scholar handicapped by a ridiculous inability to remember faces." In fact, there is nothing wrong with his memory. He cannot remember faces simply because he never looks at them. This habit may have begun when he was young and shy, as we all are if we are not congenitally impudent. But the Dean's hundreds of sermons must have cured him of that. When anyone looks at me candidly straight in the face when making an assertion, I know at once that he (or she) is lying. We are all taught that liars can never do so, though as a matter of fact they never do anything else. The Dean cannot do it. He never looks at you at all. I have known only one other man who had this trick. [Jurist] Sir Frederick Pollock [1845–1937], if he sat facing you, shifted round inch by inch, and left you addressing the nape of his neck. He was none the less a clever man and a wit.

The illustrations in the *Diary* really illustrate it, and are most interesting. The Dean, an extraordinarily handsome intellectual, with an enchanting smile, should have been depicted in his gaiters; for the full dress of a dean is more becoming than any other now in vogue, except its one rival, the evening dress of a Scottish chieftain.

Part III. Prefaces to the Plays

1. From the preface to *John Bull's Other Island*, 1906. [*The Bodley Head Bernard Shaw*, vol. 2, pp. 821–26]

[Shaw's "Preface for Politicians," marked as "(to the First Edition in 1906)," to John Bull's Other Island *(written and performed 1904) was first published in* John Bull's Other Island and Major Barbara *(New York: Brentano's, 1907). Using examples from his own upbringing, Shaw discusses the nature of Protestantism in Ireland.]*

Irish Protestantism Really Protestant

[...] First, let me tell you that in Ireland Protestantism is really Protestant. It is true that there is an Irish Protestant Church (disestablished some 35 years ago [on 1 January 1871]) in spite of the fact that a Protestant Church is, fundamentally, a contradiction in terms. But this means only that the Protestants use the word Church to denote their secular organization, without troubling themselves about the metaphysical sense of Christ's famous pun, "Upon this rock I will build my church." [Matthew 16:18] The Church of England, which is a reformed Anglican Catholic Anti-Protestant Church, is quite another affair. An Anglican is acutely conscious that he is not a Wesleyan; and many Anglican clergymen do not hesitate to teach that all Methodists incur damnation. In Ireland all that the member of the Irish Protestant Church knows is that he is not a Roman Catholic. The decorations of even the "lowest" English Church seem to him to be extravagantly Ritualistic and Popish. I myself entered the Irish Church by baptism, a ceremony performed by my uncle in "his own church." But I was sent, with many boys of my own denomination, to a Wesleyan school where the Wesleyan catechism was taught without the least protest on the part of the parents, although there was so little presumption in favor of any boy there being a Wesleyan that if all the Church boys had been withdrawn at any moment, the school would have become bankrupt. And this was by no means analogous to the case of those working class members of the Church of England in London, who send their daughters to Roman Catholic schools rather than to the public elementary schools. They do so for the definite reason that the nuns teach girls good manners and sweetness of speech, which have no place in the County Council curriculum. But in Ireland the Church parent sends his son to a Wesleyan school (if it is convenient and socially eligible) because he is indifferent to the form of Protestantism provided it is Protestantism. There is also in Ireland a characteristically Protestant refusal to take ceremonies and even sacraments very seriously except by way of strenuous objection to them when they are conducted with candles or incense. For example, I was never confirmed, although the ceremony was specially needed in my case as the failure of my appointed godfather to appear at my baptism had led to his responsibilities being assumed on the spot, at my uncle's order, by the sexton. And my case was a very common one, even among people quite untouched by modern scepticisms. Apart from the weekly churchgoing, which holds its own as a respectable habit, the initiations are perfunctory, the omissions regarded as negligible. The distinction between churchman and dissenter, which in England is a class distinction, a political distinction, and even occasionally a religious distinction, does not exist. Nobody is surprised in Ireland to find that the squire who is the local pillar of the formerly established Church is also a Plymouth Brother, and, except on certain special or fashionable occasions, attends the Methodist meetinghouse. The parson has no priestly character and no priestly influence: the High Church curate of course exists and has his vogue among religious epicures of the other sex; but the general attitude of his congregation towards him is that of [Baptist minister and influential Nonconformist] Dr [John] Clifford [1836–1923]. The clause in the Apostles' creed professing belief in a Catholic Church is a standing puzzle to Protestant children; and when they grow up they dismiss it from their minds more often than they solve it, because they really are not Catholics but Protestants to the extremest practical degree of individualism. It is true that they talk of church and chapel with all the Anglican contempt for chapel; but in Ireland the chapel means the Roman Catholic church, for which the Irish Protestant reserves all the class rancor, the political hostility, the religious bigotry, and the bad blood generally that in England separates the Establishment from the nonconforming Protestant organizations. When a vulgar Irish Protestant speaks of a "Papist" he feels exactly as a vulgar Anglican vicar does when he speaks of a Dissenter. And when the vicar is Anglican enough to call himself a Catholic priest, wear a cassock, and bless his flock with two fingers, he becomes horrifically incomprehensible to the Irish Protestant Churchman, who, on his part, puzzles the Anglican by regarding a Methodist as tolerantly as an Irishman who likes grog regards an Irishman who prefers punch.

2. From the preface to *Major Barbara*, 1906. [*The Bodley Head Bernard Shaw*, vol. 3, pp. 50–51, 56]

[*Shaw's preface (dated June 1906) to* Major Barbara *(written and performed 1905) was first published in* John Bull's Other Island *and* Major Barbara *(New York: Brentano's, 1907).*]

[...] Churches are suffered to exist only on condition that they preach submission to the State as at present capitalistically organized. The Church of England itself is compelled to add to the thirtysix articles in which it formulates its religious tenets, three more in which it apologetically protests that the moment any of these articles comes in conflict with the State it is to be entirely renounced, abjured, violated, abrogated and abhorred, the policeman being a much more important person than any of the Persons of the Trinity. And this is why no tolerated Church nor Salvation Army can ever win the entire confidence of the poor. It must be on the side of the police and the military, no matter what it believes or disbelieves; and as the police and the military are the instruments by which the rich rob and oppress the poor (on legal and moral principles made for the purpose), it is not possible to be on the side of the poor and of the police at the same time. Indeed the religious bodies, as the almoners of the rich, become a sort of auxiliary police, taking off the insurrectionary edge of poverty with coals and blankets, bread and treacle, and soothing and cheering the victims with hopes of immense and inexpensive happiness in another world when the process of working them to premature death in the service of the rich is complete in this. [...]

Christianity has two faces. Popular Christianity has for its emblem a gibbet, for its chief sensation a sanguinary execution after torture, for its central mystery an insane vengeance bought off by a trumpery expiation. But there is a nobler and profounder Christianity which affirms the sacred mystery of Equality, and forbids the glaring futility and folly of vengeance, often politely called punishment or justice. The gibbet part of Christianity is tolerated. The other is criminal felony. [...]

3. From the preface to *Getting Married: A Disquisitory Play*, 1911. [*The Bodley Head Bernard Shaw*, vol. 3, pp. 532–35]

[*Shaw's undated preface to* Getting Married (*written 1907–08, performed 1908*) *was first published in* The Doctor's Dilemma, Getting Married, & The Shewing-up of Blanco Posnet (*London: Constable and Company Ltd., 1911*). *Shaw concludes the section preceding "Christian Marriage" as follows (p. 531): "The crimes and diseases of marriage will force themselves on public attention by their own virulence. I mention them here only because they reveal certain habits of thought and feeling with regard to marriage of which we must rid ourselves if we are to act sensibly when we take the necessary reforms in hand." Shaw goes on here to survey the historical background of the Church's views on sex, marriage, and divorce.]*

Christian Marriage

First among these is the habit of allowing ourselves to be bound not only by the truths of the Christian religion but by the excesses and extravagances which the Christian movement acquired in its earlier days as a violent reaction against what it still calls paganism. By far the most dangerous of these, because it is a blasphemy against life, and, to put it in Christian terms, an accusation of indecency against God, is the notion that sex, with all its operations, is in itself absolutely an obscene thing, and that an immaculate conception is a miracle. So unwholesome an absurdity could only have gained ground under two conditions: one, a reaction against a society in which sensual luxury has been carried to revolting extremes, and, two, a belief that the world was coming to an end, and that therefore sex was no longer a necessity. Christianity, because it began under these conditions, made sexlessness and Communism the two main practical articles of its propaganda; and it has never quite lost its original bias in these directions. In spite of the putting off of the Second Coming from the lifetime of the apostles to the millennium, and of the great disappointment of the year 1000 A.D., in which multitudes of Christians seriously prepared for the end of the world, the prophet who announces that the end is at hand is still popular. Many of the people who ridicule his demonstrations that the fantastic monsters of the book of Revelation are among us in the persons of our own political contemporaries, and who proceed sanely in all their affairs on the assumption that the world is going to last, really do believe that there will be a Judgment Day, and that it *might* even be in their own time. A thunderstorm, an eclipse, or any very unusual weather will make them apprehensive and uncomfortable.

This explains why, for a long time, the Christian Church refused to have anything to do with marriage. The result was, not the abolition of sex, but its excommunication. And, of course, the consequences of persuading people that matrimony was an unholy state were so grossly carnal, that the Church had to execute a complete right-about-face, and try to make people understand that it was a holy state: so holy indeed that it could not be validly inaugurated without the blessing of the Church. And by this teaching it did something to atone for its earlier blasphemy. But the mischief of chopping and changing your doctrine to meet this or that practical emergency instead of keeping it adjusted to the whole scheme of life, is that you end by having half-a-dozen contradictory doctrines to suit half-a-dozen emergencies. The Church solemnized and sanctified marriage without ever giving up its original Pauline doctrine [see 1 Corinthians 7] on the subject. And it soon fell into another confusion. At the point at which it took up marriage and endeavored to make it holy, marriage was, and it still is, largely a survival of the custom of selling women to men. Now in all trades a marked difference is made in price between a new article and a second-hand one. The moment we meet with this difference in value between human beings, we may know that we are in the slave-market, where the conception of our relations to the persons sold is neither religious nor natural nor human nor superhuman, but simply commercial. The Church, when it finally gave its blessing to marriage, did not, in its innocence, fathom these commercial traditions. Consequently it tried to sanctify them too, with grotesque results. The slave-dealer having always asked more money for virginity, the Church, instead of detecting the money-changer and driving him out of the temple, took him for a sentimental and chivalrous lover, and, helped by its only half-discarded doctrine of celibacy, gave virginity a heavenly value to ennoble its commercial pretensions. In short, Mammon [the personification of greed and wealth; see Matthew 6:24], always mighty, put the Church in his pocket, where he keeps it to this day, in spite of the occasional saints and martyrs who contrive from time to time to get their heads and souls free to testify against him.

Divorce a Sacramental Duty

But Mammon overreached himself when he tried to impose his doctrine of inalienable property on the Church under the guise of indissoluble marriage. For the Church tried to shelter this inhuman doctrine and flat contradiction of the gospel by claiming, and rightly claiming, that marriage is a sacrament. So it is; but that is exactly what makes divorce a duty when marriage has lost the inward and spiritual grace of which the marriage ceremony is the outward and visible sign. In vain do bishops stoop to pick up the discarded arguments of the atheists of fifty years ago by pleading that the words of Jesus were in an obscure Aramaic dialect, and were probably misunderstood, as Jesus, they think, could not have said anything a bishop would disapprove of. Unless they are prepared to add that the statement that those who take the sacrament with their lips but not with their hearts eat and drink their own damnation is also a mistranslation from the Aramaic, they are most solemnly bound to shield marriage from profanation, not merely by permitting divorce, but by making it compulsory in certain cases as the Chinese do.

When spiritual revolt broke out in the sixteenth century, and the Church was reformed in several countries, the Reformation was so largely a rebellion against sacerdotalism that marriage was very nearly excommunicated again: our modern civil marriage, round which so many fierce controversies and political conflicts have raged, would have been thoroughly approved of by Calvin, and hailed with relief by Luther. But the instinctive doctrine that there is something holy and mystic in sex, a doctrine which many of us now easily dissociate from any priestly ceremony, but which in those days seemed to all who felt it to need a ritual affirmation, could not be thrown on the scrap-heap with the sale of Indulgences [payments to the Catholic Church for the remission of penances and forgiveness of sins, an abuse that prompted Luther to write his Theses] and the like; and so the Reformation left marriage where it was: a curious mixture of commercial sex slavery, early Christian sex abhorrence, and later Christian sex sanctification.

4. From "Parents and Children," the preface to *Misalliance*, 1914. [*The Bodley Head Bernard Shaw*, vol. 4, pp. 67–70, 74–76, 124–33]

[*Shaw's undated preface to* Misalliance (*written 1909, performed 1910) was first published in* Misalliance, The Dark Lady of the Sonnets, *and* Fanny's First Play (*London: Constable and Company Ltd., 1914*). *Shaw discusses his views on the teaching of religion to children. Rather than "birchings and terrifyings and threats of hell fire," children should be taught "that Allah is simply the name by which God is known to Turks and Arabs, who are just as eligible for salvation as any Christian." He goes on to consider the harm done by that "most horrible of all religions," Natural Selection, "which teaches us to regard ourselves as the helpless prey of a series of senseless accidents." The Bible itself is not sufficient, however, and the child also needs fine art, literature and music. "Every device of art should be brought to bear on the young."*]

The Sin of Athanasius

It seems hopeless. Anarchists are tempted to preach a violent and implacable resistance to all law as the only remedy; and the result of that speedily is that people welcome any tyranny that will rescue them from chaos. But there is really no need to choose between anarchy and tyranny. A quite reasonable state of things is practicable if we proceed on human assumptions and not on academic ones. If adults will frankly give up their claim to know better than children what the purposes of the Life Force are, and the child as an experiment like themselves, and possibly a more successful one, and at the same time relinquish their monstrous parental claims to personal private property in children, the rest may be left to common sense. It is our attitude, our religion, that is wrong. A good beginning might be made by enacting that any person dictating a piece of conduct to a child or to anyone else as the will of God, or as absolutely right, should be dealt with as a blasphemer: as, indeed, guilty of the unpardonable sin against the Holy Ghost. If the penalty were death, it would rid us at once of that scourge of humanity, the amateur Pope. As an Irish Protestant, I raise the cry of No Popery [the slogan of the Gordon Riot protesters] with hereditary zest. We are overrun with Popes. From curates and governesses, who may claim a sort of professional standing, to parents and uncles and nurserymaids and school teachers and wiseacres generally, there are scores of thousands of human insects groping through our darkness by the feeble phosphorescence of their own tails, yet ready at a moment's notice to reveal the will of God on every possible subject; to explain how and why the universe was made (in my youth they added the exact date) and the circumstances under which it will cease to exist; to lay down precise rules of right and wrong conduct; to discriminate infallibly between virtuous and vicious character; and this with such certainty that they are prepared to visit all the rigors of the law, and all the ruinous penalties of social ostracism on those, however harmless their actions may be, who venture to laugh at their monstrous conceit or to pay their assumptions the extravagant compliment of criticizing them. As to children, who shall say what canings and birchings and terrifyings and threats of hell fire and impositions and humiliations and petty imprisonings and sendings to bed and standing in corners and the like they have suffered because their parents and guardians and teachers knew everything so much better than [Greek philosopher] Socrates [c. 470–399 BCE] or [Greek lawmaker] Solon [c. 638–c. 558 BCE]?

It is ignorant uppishness that does the mischief. A stranger on the planet might expect that its grotesque absurdity would provoke enough ridicule to cure it; but unfortunately quite the contrary happens. Just as our ill health delivers us into the hands of medical quacks and creates a passionate demand for impudent pretences that doctors can cure the diseases they themselves die of daily, so our ignorance and helplessness set us clamoring for spiritual and moral quacks who pretend that they can save our souls from their own damnation. If a doctor were to say to his patients, "I am familiar with your symptoms, because I have seen other people in your condition; and I will bring the very little knowledge we have to your treatment; but except in that very shallow sense I don't know what is the matter with you; and I can't undertake to cure you" he would be a lost man professionally; and if a clergyman, on being called on to award a prize for good conduct in the village school, were to say, "I am afraid I cannot say who is the best-behaved child, because I really do not know what good conduct is; but I will gladly take the teacher's word as to which child has caused [the] least inconvenience" he would probably be unfrocked, if not excommunicated. And yet no honest and intellectually capable doctor or parson can say more. Clearly it would not be wise of the doctor to say it, because optimistic lies have such immense therapeutic value that a doctor who cannot tell them convincingly has mistaken his profession. And a clergyman who is not prepared to lay down the law dogmatically will not be of much use in a village school, though it behooves him all the more to be very careful what law he lays down. But unless both the clergyman and the doctor are in the attitude expressed by these speeches they are not fit for their work. The man who believes that he has more than a provisional hypothesis to go upon is a born fool. He may have to act vigorously on it. The world has no use for the Agnostic who won't believe anything because anything might be false, and won't deny anything because anything might be true. But there is a wide difference between saying, "I believe this; and I am going to act on it," or, "I don't believe it; and I won't act on it," and saying, "It is true; and it is my duty and yours to act on it," or, "It is false; and it is my duty and yours to refuse to act on it." The difference is as great as that between the Apostles' Creed and the Athanasian Creed. When you repeat the Apostles' Creed you affirm that you believe certain things. There you are clearly within your rights. When you repeat the Athanasian Creed, you affirm that certain things are so, and that anybody who doubts that they are so cannot be saved. And this is simply a piece of impudence on your part, as you know nothing about it except that as good men as you have never heard of your creed. The apostolic attitude is a desire to convert others to our beliefs for the sake of sympathy and light: the Athanasian attitude is a desire to murder people who don't agree with us. I am sufficient of an Athanasian to advocate a law for the speedy execution of all Athanasians, because they violate the fundamental proposition of my creed, which is, I repeat, that all living creatures are experiments. The precise formula for the Superman, ci-devant ["from an earlier time" (French)], The Just Man Made Perfect [Hebrews 12:23], has not yet been discovered. Until it is, every birth is an experiment in the Great Research which

is being conducted by the Life Force to discover that formula.
[...]

Antichrist

Among the worst effects of the unnatural segregation of
children in schools and the equally unnatural constant association of them with adults in the family is the utter defeat of
the vital element in Christianity. Christ stands in the world
for that intuition of the highest humanity that we, being
members one of another, must not complain, must not scold,
must not strike, nor revile nor persecute nor revenge nor
punish. Now family life and school life are, as far as the moral
training of children is concerned, nothing but the deliberate
inculcation of a routine of complaint, scolding, punishment,
persecution, and revenge as the natural and only possible
way of dealing with evil or inconvenience. "Ain't nobody to
be whopped for this here?" exclaimed Sam Weller [in *The
Pickwick Papers* (1837) by Charles Dickens] when he saw his
employer's name written up on a stage coach, and conceived
the phenomenon as an insult which reflected on himself.
This exclamation of Sam Weller is at once the negation of
Christianity and the beginning and the end of current morality; and so it will remain as long as the family and the school
persist as we know them: that is, as long as the rights of
children are so utterly denied that nobody will even take
the trouble to ascertain what they are, and coming of age is
like the turning of a convict into the streets after twenty-one
years penal servitude. Indeed it is worse; for the convict, having learnt before his conviction how to live at large, may remember how to set about it, however lamed his power of ini-
tiative may have become through disuse; but the child knows
no other way of life than the slave's way. Born free, as
Rousseau says, he has been laid hands on by slaves from the
moment of his birth and brought up as a slave. How is he,
when he is at last set free, to be anything else than the slave

he actually is, clamoring for war, for the lash, for police, pris-
ons, and scaffolds in a wild panic of delusion that without
these things he is lost. The grown-up Englishman is to the
end of his days a badly brought-up child, beyond belief quar-
relsome, petulant, selfish, destructive, and cowardly: afraid
that the Germans will come and enslave him; that the bur-
glar will come and rob him; that the bicycle or motor car will
run over him; that the smallpox will attack him; and that the
devil will run away with him and empty him out like a sack
of coals on a blazing fire unless his nurse or his parents or
his schoolmaster or his bishop or his judge or his army or
his navy will do something to frighten these bad things away.
And the Englishman, without the moral courage of a louse,
will risk his neck for fun fifty times every winter in the hunting field, and at Badajos [Spain] sieges [notably in 1811 and
1812] and the like will ram his head into a hole bristling with
sword blades rather than be beaten in the one department in
which he has been brought up to consult his own honor. As
a Sportsman (and war is fundamentally the sport of hunting
and fighting the most dangerous of the beasts of prey) he feels
free. He will tell you himself that the true sportsman is never
a snob, a coward, a duffer, a cheat, a thief, or a liar. Curious,
is it not, that he has not the same confidence in other sorts of
man?

And even sport is losing its freedom. Soon everybody will
be schooled, mentally and physically, from the cradle to the
end of the term of adult compulsory military service, and
finally of compulsory civil service lasting until the age of su-
perannuation. Always more schooling, more compulsion.
We are to be cured by an excess of the dose that has poisoned
us. Satan is to cast out Satan. [...]

The Impossibility of Secular Education

Now children must be taught some sort of religion. Secular
education is an impossibility. Secular education comes to

this: that the only reason for ceasing to do evil and learning to do well is that if you do not you will be caned. This is worse than being taught in a church school that if you become a dissenter you will go to hell; for hell is presented as the instrument of something eternal, divine, and inevitable: you cannot evade it at the moment the schoolmaster's back is turned. What confuses this issue and leads even highly intelligent religious persons to advocate secular education as a means of rescuing children from the strife of rival proselytizers is the failure to distinguish between the child's personal subjective need for a religion and its right to an impartially communicated historical objective knowledge of all the creeds and Churches. Just as a child, no matter what its race and color may be, should know that there are black men and brown men and yellow men, and, no matter what its political convictions may be, that there are Monarchists and Republicans and Positivists, Socialists and Unsocialists, so it should know that there are Christians and Mahometans and Buddhists and Shintoists and so forth, and that they are on the average just as honest and well-behaved as its own father. For example, it should not be told that Allah is a false god set up by the Turks and Arabs, who will all be damned for taking that liberty; but it should be told that many English people think so, and that many Turks and Arabs think the converse about English people. It should be taught that Allah is simply the name by which God is known to Turks and Arabs, who are just as eligible for salvation as any Christian. Further, that the practical reason why a Turkish child should pray in a mosque and an English child in a church is that as worship is organized in Turkey in mosques in the name of Mahomet and in England in churches in the name of Christ, a Turkish child joining the Church of England or an English child following Mahomet will find that it has no place for its worship and no organization of its religion within its reach. Any other teaching of the history and present facts of religion is false teaching, and is politically extremely dangerous in an empire in which a huge majority of the fellow-subjects of the governing island do not profess the religion of that island.

But this objectivity, though intellectually honest, tells the child only what other people believe. What it should itself believe is quite another matter. The sort of Rationalism which says to a child "You must suspend your judgment until you are old enough to choose your religion" is Rationalism gone mad. The child must have a conscience and a code of honor (which is the essence of religion) even if it be only a provisional one, to be revised at its confirmation. For confirmation is meant to signalize a spiritual coming of age, and may be a repudiation. Really active souls have many confirmations and repudiations as their life deepens and their knowledge widens. But what is to guide the child before its first confirmation? Not more orders, because orders must have a sanction of some sort or why should the child obey them? If, as a Secularist, you refuse to teach any sanctions, you must say "You will be punished if you disobey." "Yes," says the child to itself, "if I am found out; but wait until your back is turned and I will do as I like, and lie about it." There can be no more objective punishment for successful fraud; and as no espionage can cover the whole range of a child's conduct, the upshot is that the child becomes a liar and a schemer with an atrophied conscience. And a good many of the orders given to it are not obeyed after all. Thus the Secularist who is not a fool is forced to appeal to the child's vital impulse towards perfection, to the divine spark; and no resolution not to call this impulse an impulse of loyalty to the Fellowship of the Holy Ghost, or obedience to the Will of God, or any other standard theological term, can alter the fact that the Secularist has stepped outside Secularism and is educating the child religiously, even if he insists on repudiating that pious adverb and substituting the word metaphysically.

Natural Selection as a Religion

We must make up our minds to it therefore that whatever measures we may be forced to take to prevent the recruiting sergeants of the Churches, free or established, from obtaining an exclusive right of entry to schools, we shall not be able to exclude religion from them. The most horrible of all religions: that which teaches us to regard ourselves as the helpless prey of a series of senseless accidents called Natural Selection, is allowed and even welcomed in so-called secular schools because it is, in a sense, the negation of all religion; but for school purposes a religion is a belief which affects conduct: and no belief affects conduct more radically and often so disastrously as the belief that the universe is a product of Natural Selection. What is more, the theory of Natural Selection cannot be kept out of schools, because many of the natural facts that present the most plausible appearance of design can be accounted for by Natural Selection; and it would be as absurd to keep a child in delusive ignorance of so potent a factor in evolution as to keep it in ignorance of radiation or capillary attraction. Even if you make a religion of Natural Selection and teach the child to regard itself as the irresponsible prey of its circumstances and appetites (or its heredity as you will perhaps call them), you will none the less find that its appetites are stimulated by your encouragement and daunted by your discouragement; that one of its appetites is an appetite for perfection; that if you discourage this appetite and encourage the cruder acquisitive appetites the child will steal and lie and be a nuisance to you; and that if you encourage its appetite for perfection and teach it to attach a peculiar sacredness to it and place it before the other appetites, it will be a much nicer child and you will have a much easier job, at which point you will, in spite of your pseudo-scientific jargon, find yourself back in the old-fashioned religious teaching as deep as [theologian and prolific hymn writer] Dr [Isaac] Watts [(1674–1748), Doctor of Divinity 1728] and in fact fathoms deeper.

Moral Instruction Leagues

And now the voices of our Moral Instruction Leagues [founded 1897, they opposed religious instruction in schools] will be lifted, asking whether there is any reason why the appetite for perfection should not be cultivated in rationally scientific terms instead of being associated with the story of Jonah and the great fish and the thousand other tales that grow up round religions. Yes: there are many reasons; and one of them is that children like the story of Jonah and the whale (they insist on its being a whale in spite of demonstrations by Bible smashers without any sense of humor that Jonah would not have fitted into a whale's gullet—as if the story would be credible of a whale with an enlarged throat) and that no child on earth can stand moral instruction books or catechisms or any other statement of the case for religion in abstract terms. The object of a moral instruction book is not to be rational, scientific, exact proof against controversy, nor even credible: its object is to make children good. If it makes them sick instead its place is the wastepaper basket. And if it is to be read it must be readable.

Take for an illustration the story of Elisha and the bears. To the authors of the moral instruction books it is in the last degree reprehensible. It is obviously not true as a record of fact; and the picture it gives us of the temper of God (which is what interests an adult reader) is shocking and blasphemous. But it is a capital story for a child. It interests a child because it is about bears; and it leaves the child with an impression that children who poke fun at old gentlemen and make rude remarks about bald heads are not nice children, which is a highly desirable impression, and just as much as a child is capable of receiving from the story. When a story is about God and a child, children take God for granted and criticize the child. Adults do the opposite, and are thereby often led to talk great nonsense about the bad effect of Bible stories on infants.

But let no one think that a child or anyone else can learn religion from a teacher or a book or by any academic process whatever. It is only by an unfettered access to the whole body of Fine Art: that is, to the whole body of inspired revelation, that we can build up that conception of divinity to which all virtue is an aspiration. And to hope to find this body of art purified from all that is obsolete or dangerous or fierce or lusty, or to pick and choose what will be good for any particular child, much less for all children, is the shallowest of vanities. Such schoolmasterly selection is neither possible nor desirable. Ignorance of evil is not virtue but imbecility: admiring it is like giving a prize for honesty to a man who has not stolen your watch because he did not know you had one. Virtue chooses good from evil; and without knowledge there can be no choice. And even this is a dangerous simplification of what actually occurs. We are not choosing: we are growing. Were you to cut all of what you call the evil out of a child, it would drop dead. If you try to stretch it to full human stature when it is ten years old, you will simply pull it into two pieces and be hanged. And when you try to do this morally, which is what parents and schoolmasters are doing every day, you ought to be hanged; and some day, when we take a sensible view of the matter, you will be; and serve you right. The child does not stand between a good and a bad angel: what it has to deal with is a middling angel who, in normal healthy cases, wants to be a good angel as fast as it can without killing itself in the process, which is a dangerous one.

Therefore there is no question of providing the child with a carefully regulated access to good art. There is no good art, any more than there is good anything else in the absolute sense. Art that is too good for the child will either teach it nothing or drive it mad, as the Bible has driven many people mad who might have kept their sanity had they been allowed to read much lower forms of literature. The practical moral is that we must read whatever stories, see whatever pictures, hear whatever songs and symphonies, go to whatever plays we like. We shall not like those which have nothing to say to us; and though everyone has a right to bias our choice, no one has a right to deprive us of it by keeping us from any work of art or any work of art from us.

I may now say without danger of being misunderstood that the popular English compromise called Cowper-Templeton (unsectarian Bible education) is not so silly as it looks. It is true that the Bible inculcates half a dozen: some of them barbarous; some cynical and pessimistic; some amoristic and romantic; some skeptical and challenging; some kindly, simple, and intuitional; some sophistical and intellectual; none suited to the character and conditions of western civilization unless it be the Christianity which was finally suppressed by the Crucifixion, and has never been put into practice by any State before or since. But the Bible contains the ancient literature of a very remarkable Oriental race; and the imposition of this literature, on whatever false pretenses, on our children left them more literate than if they knew no literature at all, which was the practical alternative. And as our Authorized Version is a great work of art as well, to know it was better than knowing no art, which also was the practical alternative. It is at least not a school book; and it is not a bad story book, horrible as some of the stories are. Therefore as between the Bible and the blank represented by secular education in its most matter-of-fact sense, the choice is with the Bible.

The Bible

But the Bible is not sufficient. The real Bible of modern Europe is the whole body of great literature in which the inspiration and revelation of Hebrew Scripture has been continued to the present day. Nietzsche's [novel] *Thus Spake Zoroaster* [1883–91] is less comforting to the ill and unhappy than the Psalms; but it is much truer, subtler, and more edifying. The pleasure we get from the rhetoric of the book of Job and its tragic picture of a bewildered soul cannot disguise the ignoble irrelevance of the retort of God with which it closes [Job 42:7–8], nor supply the need for such modern revelations as Shelley's [lyrical drama] *Prometheus* [*Unbound* (1820)] or [the epic four-opera cycle] *The Niblung's Ring* [1848–74] of [German composer] Richard Wagner [1813–83]. There is nothing in the Bible greater in inspiration than Beethoven's ninth symphony [1824]; and the power of modern music to convey that inspiration to a modern man is far greater than that of Elizabethan English, which is, except for people steeped in the Bible from childhood like [historical novelist] Sir Walter Scott [1771–1832] and Ruskin, a dead language.

Besides, many who have no ear for literature or for music are accessible to architecture, to pictures, to statues, to dresses, and to the arts of the stage. Every device of art should be brought to bear on the young; so that they may discover some form of it that delights them naturally; for there will come to all of them that period between dawning adolescence and full maturity when the pleasures and emotions of art will have to satisfy cravings which, if starved or insulted, may become morbid and seek disgraceful satisfactions, and, if prematurely gratified otherwise than poetically, may destroy the stamina of the race. And it must be borne in mind that the most dangerous art for this necessary purpose is the art that presents itself as religious ecstasy. Young people are ripe for love long before they are ripe for religion. Only a very foolish person would substitute the Imitation of Christ [the popular devotional book by Thomas à Kempis (c. 1380–1471)] for [the 1883 adventure novel] Treasure Island [by Robert Louis Stevenson (1850–94)] as a present for a boy or girl, or for [poet George Gordon, Lord] Byron's [(1788–1824) unfinished epic verse satire] Don Juan [1819–24] as a present for a swain or lass. Pickwick is the safest saint for us in our nonage. [French realist novelist Gustave] Flaubert's [1821–80] Temptation of St Anthony [1874] is an excellent book for a man of fifty, perhaps the best within reach as a healthy study of visionary ecstasy; but for the purposes of a boy of fifteen [Walter Scott's novels] Ivanhoe [1820] and the Templar [most likely *The Talisman* (1825), which deals with the Knights Templar] make a much better saint and devil. And the boy of fifteen will find this out for himself if he is allowed to wander in a well-stocked literary garden, and hear bands and see pictures and spend his pennies on cinematograph shows. His choice may often be rather disgusting to his elders when they want him to choose the best before he is ready for it. The greatest Protestant Manifesto ever written, as far as I know, is [English-born German author] Houston Chamberlain's [1855–1927] Foundations of the Nineteenth Century [1899]: everybody capable of it should read it. Probably the History of Maria Monk [*Awful Disclosures of Maria Monk, or, The Hidden Secrets of a Nun's Life in a Convent Exposed* (1836)] by Monk [1816–49] is at the opposite extreme of merit (this is a guess: I have never read it); but it is certain that a boy let loose in a library would go for Maria Monk and have no use whatsoever for Mr Chamberlain. I should probably have read Maria Monk myself if I had not had the Arabian Nights and their like to occupy me better. In art, children, like adults, will find their level if they are left free to find it, and not restricted to what adults think good for them. Just at present our young people are going mad over ragtimes, apparently because syncopated rhythms are new to them. If they had learnt what can be done with syncopation from Beethoven's third Leonora overture, they would enjoy the ragtimes all the more; but they would put them in their proper place as amusing vulgarities.

5. From "Preface on the Prospects of Christianity," the preface to *Androcles and the Lion: A Fable Play*, 1915. [*The Bodley Head Bernard Shaw*, vol. 4, pp. 463–64, 479–72, 486–87, 562–63, 567–70]

[*Shaw's preface (dated December 1915) to* Androcles and the Lion: A Fable Play (*written 1912, performed 1913*) *was first published in* Androcles and the Lion, Overruled, Pygmalion (*New York: Brentano's, 1916). Shaw discusses the trial of Jesus ("not falsely accused, nor denied full opportunities of defending himself"), the doctrine of Atonement ("Nothing easier, nothing cheaper"), miracles ("Jesus's teaching has nothing to do with miracles"), belief in immortality and the teaching of Christianity to children.*]

Was Jesus a Martyr?

It is important therefore that we should clear our minds of the notion that Jesus died, as some are in the habit of declaring, for his social and political opinions. There have been many martyrs to those opinions; but he was not one of them, nor, as his words shew, did he see any more sense in martyrdom than Galileo did. He was executed by the Jews for the blasphemy of claiming to be a God; and Pilate, to whom this was a mere piece of superstitious nonsense, let them execute him as the cheapest way of keeping them quiet, on the formal plea that he had committed treason against Rome by saying that he was the King of the Jews. He was not falsely accused, nor denied full opportunities of defending himself. The proceedings were quite straightforward and regular; and Pilate, to whom the appeal lay, favored him and despised his judges, and was evidently willing enough to be conciliated. But instead of denying the charge, Jesus repeated the offence. He knew what he was doing: he had alienated numbers of his own disciples and been stoned in the streets for doing it before. He was not lying: he believed literally what he said. The horror of the High Priest was perfectly natural: he was a Primate confronted with a heterodox street preacher uttering what seemed to him an appalling and impudent blasphemy. The fact that the blasphemy was to Jesus a simple statement of fact, and that it has since been accepted as such by all western nations, does not invalidate the proceedings, nor give us the right to regard Annas and Caiaphas as worse men than the Archbishop of Canterbury and the Head Master of Eton. If Jesus had been indicted in a modern court, he would have been examined by two doctors; found to be obsessed by a delusion; declared incapable of pleading; and sent to an asylum: that is the whole difference. [...] Just so, the claim to divinity made by Jesus was to the High Priest, who looked forward to the coming of a Messiah, one that might conceivably have been true, and might therefore have misled the people in a very dangerous way. That was why he treated Jesus as an impostor and a blasphemer where we should have treated him as a madman.

The Difference Between Atonement and Punishment

The primitive idea of justice is partly legalized revenge and partly expiation by sacrifice. It works out from both sides in the notion that two blacks make a white, and that when a wrong has been done, it should be paid for by an equivalent suffering. It seems to the Philistine majority a matter of course that this compensating suffering should be inflicted on the wrongdoer for the sake of its deterrent effect on other would-be wrongdoers; but a moment's reflection will show that this utilitarian application corrupts the whole transaction. For example, the shedding of innocent blood cannot be balanced by the shedding of guilty blood. Sacrificing a criminal to propitiate God for the murder of one of his righteous servants is like sacrificing a mangy sheep or an ox with the [infectious viral cattle disease] rinderpest: it calls down divine wrath instead of appeasing it. In doing it we offer God as a sacrifice the gratification of our own revenge and the protection of our own lives without cost to ourselves; and cost to ourselves is the essence of sacrifice and expiation. However much the Philistines have succeeded in confusing these things in practice, they are to the Salvationist sense distinct and even contrary. [...]

The point is a cardinal one, because until we grasp it not only does historical Christianity remain unintelligible to us, but those who do not care a rap about historical Christianity may be led into the mistake of supposing that if we discard revenge, and treat murderers exactly as God treated Cain [who was declared cursed for killing his brother Abel; see Genesis 4:11–16]: that is, exempt them from punishment by putting a brand on them as unworthy to be sacrificed, and let them face the world as best they can with that brand on them, we should get rid both of punishment and sacrifice. It would not at all follow: on the contrary, the feeling that there must be an expiation of the murder might quite possibly lead to our putting some innocent person—the more innocent the better—to a cruel death to balance the account with divine justice.

Salvation at First a Class Privilege; and the Remedy

Thus, even when the poor decide that the method of purchasing salvation by offering rams and goats or bringing gold to the altar must be wrong because they cannot afford it, we still do not feel "saved" without a sacrifice and a victim. In vain do we try to substitute mystical rites that cost nothing, such as circumcision, or, as a substitute for that, baptism. Our sense of justice still demands an expiation, a sacrifice, a sufferer for our sins. And this leaves the poor man still in his old difficulty; for if it was impossible for him to procure rams and goats and shekels, how much more impossible is it for him to find a neighbor who will voluntarily suffer for his sins: one who will say cheerfully "You have committed a murder.

Well, never mind: I am willing to be hanged for it in your stead"?

Our imagination must come to our rescue. Why not, instead of driving ourselves to despair by insisting on a separate atonement by a separate redeemer for every sin, have one great atonement and one great redeemer to compound for the sins of the world once for all? Nothing easier, nothing cheaper. The yoke is easy, the burden light. All you have to do when the redeemer is once found (or invented by the imagination) is to believe in the efficacy of the transaction, and you are saved. The rams and goats cease to bleed; the altars which ask for expensive gifts and continually renewed sacrifices are torn down; and the Church of the single redeemer and the single atonement rises on the ruins of the old temples, and becomes a single Church of the Christ.

The Miracles

[...] But the deepest annoyance arising from the miracles would be the irrelevance of the issue raised by them. Jesus's teaching has nothing to do with miracles. If his mission had been simply to demonstrate a new method of restoring lost eyesight, the miracle of curing the blind would have been entirely relevant. But to say "You should love your enemies; and to convince you of this I will now proceed to cure this gentleman of cataract" would have been, to a man of Jesus's intelligence, the proposition of an idiot. If it could be proved today that not one of the miracles of Jesus actually occurred, that proof would not invalidate a single one of his didactic utterances; and conversely, if it could be proved that not only did the miracles actually occur, but that he had wrought a thousand other miracles a thousand times more wonderful, not a jot of weight would be added to his doctrine. And yet the intellectual energy of sceptics and divines has been wasted for generations in arguing about the miracles on the assumption that Christianity is at stake in the controversy as to whether the stories of Matthew are false or true. According to Matthew himself, Jesus must have known this only too well; for wherever he went he was assailed with a clamor for miracles, though his doctrine created bewilderment. [...]

Belief in Personal Immortality no Criterion

Nor is belief in individual immortality any criterion. Theosophists, rejecting vicarious atonement so sternly that they insist that the smallest of our sins brings its [consequential] Karma [action or deed (Sanskrit)], also insist on individual immortality and metempsychosis [the transmigration of the soul in reincarnation after death] in order to provide an unlimited field for Karma to be worked out by the unredeemed sinner. The belief in the prolongation of individual life beyond the grave is far more real and vivid among table-rapping Spiritualists [who believe that the spirits of the dead can communicate with the living] than among conventional Christians. The notion that those who reject the Christian (or any other) scheme of salvation by atonement must reject also belief in personal immortality and in miracles is as baseless as the notion that if a man is an atheist he will steal your watch. [...]

The Importance of Hell in the Salvation Scheme

The seriousness of throwing over hell whilst still clinging to the Atonement is obvious. If there is no punishment for sin there can be no self-forgiveness for it. If Christ paid our score, and if there is no hell and therefore no chance of our getting into trouble by forgetting the obligation, then we can be as wicked as we like with impunity inside the secular law, even from self-reproach, which becomes mere ingratitude to the Savior. On the other hand, if Christ did not pay our score, it still stands against us; and such debts make us extremely uncomfortable. The drive of evolution, which we call conscience and honor, seizes on such slips, and shames us to the dust for being so low in the scale as to be capable of them. The "saved" thief experiences an ecstatic happiness which can never come to the honest atheist: he is tempted to steal again to repeat the glorious sensation. But if the atheist steals he has no such happiness. He is a thief and knows that he is a thief. Nothing can rub that off him. He may try to sooth his shame by some sort of restitution or equivalent act of benevolence; but that does not alter the fact that he did steal; and his conscience will not be easy until he has conquered his will to steal and changed himself into an honest man by developing that divine spark within him which Jesus insisted on as the everyday reality of what the atheist denies. [...]

The Right to Refuse Atonement

Consequently, even if it were mentally possible for all of us to believe in the Atonement, we should have to cry off it, as we evidently have a right to do. Every man to whom salvation is offered has an inalienable natural right to say "No, thank you: I prefer to retain my full moral responsibility: it is not good for me to be able to load a scapegoat with my sins: I should be less careful how I committed them if I knew they would cost me nothing." Then, too, there is the attitude of Ibsen: that iron moralist to whom the whole scheme of salvation was only an ignoble attempt to cheat God; to get into heaven without paying the price. To be let off, to beg for and accept eternal life as a present instead of earning it, would be mean enough even if we accepted the contempt of the Power on whose pity we were trading; but to bargain for a crown of glory as well! that was too much for Ibsen: it provoked him to exclaim, "Your God is an old man whom you cheat," and to lash the deadened conscience of the nineteenth century back to life with a whip of scorpions.

The Teaching of Christianity

[...] If children are to be delivered from the proselytizing atheist on the one hand, and the proselytizing nun in the convent school on the other, with all the other proselytizers that lie between them, they must not be burdened with idle controversies as to whether there ever was such a person as Jesus or not. [...] We must cut the controversy short by declaring that there is the same evidence for the existence of Jesus as for that of any other person of his time; and the fact that you may not believe everything Matthew tells you no more disproves the existence of Jesus than the fact that you do not believe everything Macaulay tells you disproves the existence of William III. [...]

The teacher of Christianity has then to make known to the child, first the song of John Barleycorn, with the fields and seasons as witness to its eternal truth. Then, as the child's mind matures, it can learn, as historical and psychological phenomena, the tradition of the scapegoat, the Redeemer, the Atonement, the Resurrection, the Second Coming, and how, in a world saturated with this tradition, Jesus has been largely accepted as the long expected and often prophesied Redeemer, the Messiah, *the* Christ. It is open to the child also to accept him. [...]

6. From the preface to *Saint Joan: A Chronicle Play in Six Scenes and an Epilogue*, 1924. [*The Bodley Head Bernard Shaw*, vol. 6, pp. 54–56]

[Shaw's preface (dated May 1924) to Saint Joan: A Chronicle Play in Six Scenes and an Epilogue *(written and performed 1923) was first published in* Saint Joan: A Chronicle Play in Six Scenes and an Epilogue *(London: Constable and Company Ltd., 1924). The play dramatizes the famous trial of French heroine and Roman Catholic saint Jeanne d'Arc (c. 1412–1431) and is considered*

by many to be Shaw's masterpiece. (He was awarded the 1925 Nobel Prize in Literature.)]

Catholicism not yet Catholic Enough

And so, if we admit, as we must, that the burning of Joan was a mistake, we must broaden Catholicism sufficiently to include her in its charter. Our Churches must admit that no official organization of mortal men whose vocation does not carry with it extraordinary mental powers (and this is all that any Church Militant [living Christians who struggle against sin] can in the face of fact and history pretend to be), can keep pace with the private judgment of persons of genius except when, by a very rare accident, the genius happens to be Pope, and not even then unless he is an exceedingly overbearing Pope. The Churches must learn humility as well as teach it. The Apostolic Succession [the Catholic belief in the continuous succession of spiritual authority from the apostles through successive bishops] cannot be secured or confined by the laying on of hands: the tongues of fire have descended on heathens and outcasts too often for that, leaving anointed Churchmen to scandalize History as worldly rascals. When the Church Militant behaves as if it were already the Church Triumphant [those in Heaven], it makes these appalling blunders about Joan and Bruno and Galileo and the rest which make it so difficult for a Freethinker to join it; and a Church which has no place for Freethinkers: nay, which does not inculcate and encourage freethinking with a complete belief that thought, when really free, must by its own law take the path that leads to The Church's bosom, not only has no future in modern culture, but obviously has no faith in the valid science of its own tenets, and is guilty of the heresy that theology and science are two different and opposite impulses, rivals for human allegiance.

I have before me the letter of a Catholic priest. "In your play," he writes, "I see the dramatic presentation of the conflict of the Regal, sacerdotal, and Prophetical powers, in which Joan was crushed. To me it is not the victory of any one of them over the others that will bring peace and the Reign of the Saints in the Kingdom of God, but their fruitful interaction in a costly but noble state of tension." The Pope himself could not put it better; nor can I. We must accept the tension, and maintain it nobly without letting ourselves be tempted to relieve it by burning the thread. This is Joan's lesson to The Church; and its formulation by the hand of a priest emboldens me to claim that her canonization was a magnificently Catholic gesture as the canonization of a Protestant saint by the Church of Rome. But its special value and virtue cannot be apparent until it is known and understood as such. If any simple priest for whom this is too hard a saying tells me that it was not so intended, I shall remind him that the Church is in the hands of God, and not, as simple priests imagine, God in the hands of the Church; so if he answers too confidently for God's intentions he may be asked "Hast thou entered into the springs of the sea? or hast thou walked in the recesses of the deep?" And Joan's own answer is also the answer of old: "Though He slay me, yet will I trust in Him; *but I will maintain my own ways before Him.*" [Job 13:15]

7. From the preface to *Too True to Be Good: A Political Extravaganza*, 1933. [*The Bodley Head Bernard Shaw*, vol. 6, pp. 414–16, 418–20]

[Shaw's preface (dated 1933) to Too True to Be Good *(written 1931, performed 1932) was first published in* Too True to Be Good, Village Wooing & On the Rocks. Three Plays *(London: Constable and Company Ltd., and New York: Dodd, Mead & Co., 1934). Shaw briefly surveys the origins of early Church organization ("self-elected... without the smallest reference to the opinions of the uncalled and unordained") and the ensuing failure of "the Chris-*

tian system," whereby "Catholics and Protestants set to work to exterminate one another with rack and stake, fire, sword, and gunpowder."]

The Catholic Solution

To begin with, the Church, being catholic, was necessarily democratic to the extent that its aim was to save the souls of all persons without regard to their age, sex, nationality, class, or color. The nobleman who felt that God would not lightly damn a man of his quality received no countenance from the Church in that conviction. Within its fold all souls were equal before God.

But the Church did not draw the ridiculous conclusion that all men and women are equally qualified or equally desirous to legislate, to govern, to administer, to make decisions, to manage public affairs or even their own private affairs. It faced the fact that only about five per cent. of the population are capable of exercising these powers, and are certain to be corrupted by them unless they have an irresistible religious vocation for public work and a faith in its beneficence which will induce them to take vows to abstain from any profit that is not shared by all the rest, and from all indulgences which might blunt their consciences or subject them to the family influences so bitterly deprecated by Jesus.

The natural "called" minority was never elected in the scandalous way we call democratic. Its members were in the first instance self-elected: that is, they voluntarily lived holy lives and devoted themselves to the public welfare in obedience to the impulse of the Holy ghost within them. This impulse was their vocation. They were called from above, not chosen by the uncalled. To protect themselves and obtain the necessary power, they organized themselves, and called their organization The Church. After that, the genuineness and sufficiency of the vocation of the new recruits were judged by The Church. If the judgment was favorable, and the candidates took certain vows, they were admitted to the official priesthood and set to govern as priests in the parish and spiritual directors of the family, all of them being eligible, if they had the requisite ability, for promotion to the work of governing the Church itself as bishops or cardinals, or to the supreme rank of Pope or Vicar of Christ on earth. And all this without the smallest reference to the opinions of the uncalled and unordained. [...]

Why the Christian System Failed

The answer is that the Christian system failed, not because it was wrong in its psychology, its fundamental postulate of equality, or its anticipation of Lenin's principle that the rulers must be as poor as the ruled so that they can raise themselves only by raising their people, but because the old priests' ignorance of economics and political science blinded them to the mischief latent in the selfishness of private property in the physical earth. Before the Church knew where it was (it has not quite located itself yet) it found itself so prodigiously rich that the Pope was a secular Italian prince with armies and frontiers, enjoying not only the rent of Church lands, but selling salvation on such a scale that when Torquemada began burning Jews instead of allowing them to ransom their bodies by payments to the Roman treasury, and leaving their souls to God, a first-rate quarrel between the Church and the Spanish Inquisition was the result.

But the riches of the Church were nothing compared to the riches of the Church's great rival, the Empire. And the poverty of the priest was opulence compared to the poverty of the proletarian. Whilst the Church was being so corrupted by its own property, and by the influence on it of the lay proprietors, that it lost all its moral prestige, the warriors and robbers of the Empire had been learning from experience that a pirate ship needs a hierarchy of officers and an iron discipline even more than police boats, and that the work of

robbing the poor all the time involves a very elaborate system of government to ensure that the poor shall, like bees,
continue to produce not only their own subsistence but the
surplus that can be robbed from them without bringing on
them the doom of the goose that lays the golden eggs. Naked
coercion is so expensive that it became necessary to practise
on the imaginations of the poor to the extent of making them
believe that it is a pious duty to be robbed, and that their moment of life in this world is only a prelude to an eternity in
which the poor will be blest and happy, and the rich horribly
tortured.

Matters at last reached a point at which there was more law
and order in the Empire than in The Church. Emperor Philip
[II] of Spain [1527–98] was enormously more respectable and
pious, if less amiable, than Pope Alexander [VI] Borgia
[1431–1503]. The Empire gained moral prestige as The Church
lost it until the Empire, virtuously indignant, took it on itself
to reform The Church, all the more ready as the restoration
of priestly poverty was a first-rate excuse for plundering it.

Now The Church could not with any decency allow itself
to be reformed by a plutocracy of pirate kings, robber barons,
commercial adventurers, moneylenders, and deserters from
its own ranks. It reformed itself from within by its own saints
and the Orders they founded, and thus "dished" the Reformation; whilst the Reformers set up national Churches and
free Churches of their own under the general definition of
Protestants, and thereby found themselves committed to a
curious adulteration of their doctrine of Individualism, or
the right of private judgment, with most of the ecclesiastical
corruptions against which they had protested. And as neither Church nor Empire would share the government of
mankind with the other nor allow the common people any
say in the matter, the Catholics and Protestants set to work to
exterminate one another with rack and stake, fire, sword, and
gunpowder, aided by the poison gas of scurrilous calumny,

until the very name of religion began to stink in the nostrils of all really charitable and faithful people.

8. From the preface to *On the Rocks: A Political Comedy*, 1933. [*The Bodley Head Bernard Shaw*, vol. 6, pp. 586–89]

[*The preface (dated 22 October 1933) to* On the Rocks (*written and performed 1933) was first published in* Too True to Be Good, Village Wooing & On the Rocks. Three Plays (*London: Constable and Company Ltd., and New York: Dodd, Mead & Co., 1934). Shaw examines the case for "the extermination of Jesus Christ" and its aftermath ("The chief instrument of torture is the subject of a special Adoration").*]

Leading Case of Jesus Christ

I dislike cruelty, even cruelty to other people, and should therefore like to see all cruel people exterminated. But I should recoil with horror from a proposal to punish them. Let me illustrate my attitude by a very famous, indeed far too famous, example of the popular conception of criminal law as a means of delivering up victims to the normal popular lust for cruelty which has been mortified by the restraint imposed on it by civilization. Take the case of the extermination of Jesus Christ. No doubt there was a strong case for it. Jesus was from the point of view of the High Priest a heretic and an impostor. From the point of view of the merchants he was a rioter and a Communist. From the Roman Imperialist point of view he was a traitor. From the commonsense point of view he was a dangerous madman. From the snobbish point of view, always a very influential one, he was a penniless vagrant. From the police point of view he was an obstructor of thoroughfares, a beggar, an associate of prostitutes, an apologist of sinners, and a disparager of judges; and his daily companions were tramps whom he had seduced into vagabondage from their regular trades. From the point of view of the pious he was a Sabbath breaker, a denier of the efficacy of circumcision and the advocate of a strange rite of baptism, a gluttonous man and a winebibber. He was abhorrent to the medical profession as an unqualified practitioner who healed people by quackery and charged nothing for the treatment. He was not anti-Christ: nobody had heard of such a power of darkness then; but he was startlingly anti-Moses. He was against the priests, against the judiciary, against the military, against the city (he declared that it was impossible for a rich man to enter the kingdom of heaven), against all the interests, classes, principalities and powers, inviting everybody to abandon all these and follow him. By every argument, legal, political, religious, customary, and polite, he was the most complete enemy of the society of his time ever brought to the bar. He was guilty on every count of the indictment, and on many more that his accusers had not the wit to frame. If he was innocent then the whole world was guilty. To acquit him was to throw over civilization and all its institutions. History has borne out the case against him; for no State has ever constituted itself on his principles or made it possible to live according to his commandments: those States who have taken his name have taken it as an alias to enable them to persecute his followers more plausibly.

It is not surprising that under these circumstances, and in the absence of any defence, the Jerusalem community and the Roman government decided to exterminate Jesus. They had just as much right to do so as to exterminate the two thieves who perished with him. He was entitled to the painless death of Socrates. We may charitably suppose that if the death could have been arranged privately between Pilate and Caiaphas Jesus would have been dispatched as quickly and suddenly as John the Baptist [who preached the practice of baptism for the forgiveness of sins (Mark 1:4) and who baptized Jesus (Matthew 3:13–16)]. But the mob wanted the horrible fun of seeing somebody crucified: an abominably cruel method of execution. Pilate only made matters worse by trying to appease them by having Jesus flogged. The soldiers, too, had to have their bit of sport, to crown him with thorns and, when they buffeted him, challenge him ironically to guess which of them had struck the blow.

"Crosstianity"

All this was cruelty for its own sake, for the pleasure of it. And the fun did not stop there. Such was and is the attraction of these atrocities that the spectacle of them has been reproduced in pictures and waxworks and exhibited in churches ever since as an aid to piety. The chief instrument of torture is the subject of a special Adoration. Little models of it in gold and ivory are worn as personal ornaments; and big reproductions in wood and marble are set up in sacred places and on graves. Contrasting the case with that of Socrates, one is forced to the conclusion that if Jesus had been humanely exterminated his memory would have lost ninetynine per cent of its attraction for posterity. Those who were specially susceptible to his morbid attraction were not satisfied with symbolic crosses which hurt nobody. They soon got busy with "acts of faith" which consisted of great public shows at which Jews and Protestants or Catholics, and anyone else who could be caught out on a point of doctrine, were burnt alive. Cruelty is so infectious that the very compassion it rouses is infuriated to take revenge by still viler cruelties.

The tragedy of this—or, if you will, the comedy—is that it was his clearness of vision on this very point that set Jesus so high above his persecutors. He taught that two blacks do not make a white; that evil should not be countered by worse evil but by good; that revenge and punishment only duplicate wrong; that we should conceive God, not as an irascible and vindictive tyrant but as an affectionate father. No doubt many private amiabilities have been inspired by this teaching;

but politically it has received no more quarter than Pilate gave it. To all Governments it has remained paradoxical and impracticable. A typical acknowledgement of it was the hanging of a crucifix above the seat of the judge who was sentencing evildoers to be broken on the wheel.

9. From "The Infidel Half Century," the preface to *Back to Methuselah: A Metabiological Pentateuch*, 1921. [*The Bodley Head Bernard Shaw*, vol. 5, pp. 325–31]

[*The preface (dated "1921 Revised, 1944") to* Back to Methuselah (*written 1918–20, performed 1922) was first published in* Back to Methuselah: A Metabiological Pentateuch *(New York: Brentano's, 1921). According to Laurence (Bibliography I: 149), "In 1944 Shaw extensively revised both the preface and the play... for the World's Classics series published by the Oxford University Press" in 1946. Shaw maintains that the Bible cannot be used as "an accurate historical chronicle, and a complete guide to conduct," as it is a compendium of "grotesque perversions of natural truths and poetic metaphors," but cautions against throwing away "legend and parable and drama: they are the natural vehicles of dogma."*]

Religion and Romance
It is the adulteration of religion by the romance of miracles and paradises and torture chambers that makes it reel at the impact of every advance in science, instead of being clarified by it. If you take an English village lad, and teach him that religion means believing that the stories of Noah's Ark and the Garden of Eden are literally true on the authority of God himself, and if that boy becomes an artisan and goes into the town among the sceptical city proletariat, then, when the jibes of his mates set him thinking, and he sees that these stories cannot be literally true, and learns that no candid prelate now pretends to believe them, he does not make any fine

distinction: he declares at once that religion is a fraud, and persons and teachers hypocrites and liars. He becomes indifferent to religion if he has little intellectual conscience, and indignantly hostile to it if he has a good deal.

The same revolt against wantonly false teaching is happening daily in the professional classes whose recreation is reading and whose intellectual sport is controversy. They banish the Bible from their houses, and sometimes put into the hands of their unfortunate children Ethical and Rationalist tracts of the deadliest dullness, compelling these wretched infants to sit out the discourses of Secularist lecturers (I have delivered some of them myself), who wearied them at a length now abandoned in the Church of England. Our minds have reacted so violently towards provable logical theorems and demonstrable mechanical or chemical facts that we have become incapable of metaphysical truth, and try to cast out our incredible and silly lies by credible and clever ones, calling in Satan to cast out Satan, and getting more into his clutches than ever in the process. Thus the world is kept sane less by the saints than by the vast mass of the indifferent, who neither act nor react in the matter. Butler's preaching of the gospel of Laodicea was a piece of common sense founded on his observation of this.

But indifference will not guide nations through civilization to the establishment of the perfect city of God. An indifferent statesman is a contradiction in terms; and a statesman who is indifferent on principle, a Laisser-faire or Muddle-Through doctrinaire, plays the deuce with us in the long run. Our statesmen must get a religion by hook or by crook; and while we are ruled by Adult Suffrage it must be a religion capable of vulgarization. The thought first put into words by the Mills when they said "There is no God; but this is a family secret," and long held unspoken by aristocratic statesmen and diplomatists, will not serve now; for the revival of civilization after the war cannot be effected by artificial breathing: the driving force of undeluded consent is indispensable, and will be impossible until the statesmen can appeal to the vital instincts of the people in terms of a common religion.

The Danger of Reaction

And here arises the danger that when we realize this we shall run back in terror to our old superstitions. We jumped out of the frying-pan into the fire; and we are just as likely to jump back again, now that we feel hotter than ever. History records very little in the way of mental activity on the part of the mass of mankind except a series of stampedes from affirmative errors into negative ones and back again. It must therefore be said very precisely and clearly that the bankruptcy of Darwinism does not mean that Nobodaddy was Somebodaddy *with* "body, parts, and passions" after all; that the world was made in the year 4004 B.C.; that damnation means an eternity of blazing brimstone; that the Immaculate Conception means that sex is sinful and that Christ was parthenogenetically [without fertilization] brought forth by a virgin descended in like manner from a line of virgins right back to Eve; that the Trinity is an anthropomorphic monster with three heads which are yet only one head; that in Rome the bread and wine on the altar become flesh and blood, and in England, in a still more mystical manner, they do and they do not; that the Bible is an infallible scientific manual, an accurate historical chronicle, and a complete guide to conduct; that we may lie and cheat and murder and then wash ourselves innocent in the blood of the Lamb on Sunday at the cost of a *credo* ["I believe" (Latin), the title and first word of the Apostles' Creed] and a penny in the [Church collection] plate; and so on and so forth. Civilization cannot be saved by people not only crude enough to believe these things, but irreligious enough to believe that such belief constitutes a religion. The education of children cannot safely be left in their hands. If dwindling sects like the Church of England, the Church of Rome, the Greek Church, and the rest, persist in trying to cramp the human mind within the limits of these grotesque perversions of natural truths and poetic metaphors, then they must be ruthlessly banished from the schools to free the soul that is hidden in every dogma. The real Class War will be a war of intellectual classes; and its conquest will be the souls of children.

A Touchstone for Dogma

The test of a dogma is its universality. Any doctrine that the British churchgoer, the Brahman, the Jainist, the Buddhist, the Mussulman cannot hold in common, however varied their rituals, is an obstruction to the fellowship of the Holy Ghost. The only frontier to the currency of a sound dogma as such is the frontier of capacity for understanding it.

This does not mean that we should throw away legend and parable and drama: they are the natural vehicles of dogma; but woe to the Churches and rulers who substitute the legend for the dogma, the parable for the history, the drama for the religion! Better by far declare the throne of God empty than set a liar and a fool on it. What are called wars of religion are always wars to destroy religion by affirming the historical truth or material substantiality of some legend, and killing those who refuse to accept it as historical or substantial. But who has ever refused to accept a good legend with delight *as* a legend? The legends, the parables, the dramas, are among the choicest treasures of mankind. No one is ever tired of stories of miracles. In vain did Mahomet repudiate the miracles ascribed to him: in vain did Christ furiously scold those who asked him to give them an exhibition as a conjurer: in vain did the saints declare that God chose them not for their powers but for their weaknesses; that the humble might be exalted, and the proud rebuked. People will have their miracles, their stories, their heroes and heroines and saints and martyrs and divinities to exercise their gifts of affection, admiration, wonder, and worship, and their Judases and devils to enable them to be angry and yet feel that they do well to be angry. Every one of these legends is the common heritage of the human race; and there is only one inexorable condition attached to their healthy enjoyment, which is that no one shall believe them literally. The reading of stories and delighting in them made Don Quixote a gentleman: the believing them literally made him a madman who slew lambs instead of feeding them. In England today good books of Eastern religious legends are read eagerly; and Protestants and Atheists read legends of the saints with pleasure. Sceptical Freethinkers read the Bible: indeed they seem to be its only readers now except the parsons at the Church lecterns. This is because the imposition of the legends as literal truths at once changes them from legends into falsehoods. The feeling against the Bible has become so strong at last that educated people will not tolerate even the chronicles of King David, which may be historical, and are certainly more candid than the official biographies of our contemporary monarchs.

What to do With the Legends

What we should do, then, is to pool our legends and make a delightful stock of religious folk-lore on an honest basis for all children. [...] All the sweetness of religion is conveyed to children by the hands of storytellers and image-makers. Without their fictions the truths of religion would for the multitude be neither intelligible nor even apprehensible; and the prophets would prophesy and the philosophers cerebrate in vain. And nothing stands between the people and the fictions except the silly falsehood that the fictions are literal truths, and that there is nothing in religion but fiction.

10. From the preface to *Farfetched Fables*, 1948–49. [*The Bodley Head Bernard Shaw*, vol. 7, pp. 385–87, 389–401]

[Shaw's preface (dated 1948–49) to Farfetched Fables *(written 1948, performed 1950) was first published in* Buoyant Billions, Farfetched Fables, & Shakes versus Shav *(London: Constable and Company Ltd., 1951). Shaw, "writing by what is called inspiration," presents himself "as an instrument of the Life Force." He goes on to discuss such topics as miracles, the Thirty-Nine Articles, and the fragmentation of Christianity into countless sects and persuasions.]*

Divine Providence

Providence, which I call The Life Force, when not defeated by the imperfection of its moral instruments, always takes care that the necessary functionaries are born specialized for their job. When no specialization beyond that of common ability is needed, millions of "hands" (correctly so called industrially) are born. But as they are helpless without skilled craftsmen and mechanics, without directors and deciders, without legislators and thinkers, these also are provided in the required numbers. [Geoffrey] Chaucer [c. 1343–1400] and Shakespear, Dante and Michael Angelo, Goethe and Ibsen, Newton and Einstein, [moral philosopher and political economist] Adam Smith [1723–90] and Karl Marx arrive only once at intervals of hundreds of years, whilst carpenters and tailors, stockbrokers and parsons, industrialist and traders are all forthcoming in thousands as fast as they are needed.

I present myself therefore as an instrument of the Life Force, writing by what is called inspiration; but as the Life Force proceeds experimentally by Trial-and-Error, and never achieves a 100 per cent success, I may be one of its complete failures, and certainly fall very short not only of perfection but of the Force's former highest achievements. For instance I am much less mentally gifted than, say, [German mathematician and philosopher Gottfried Wilhelm von] Leibnitz [1646–1716], and can only have been needed because, as he was so gifted as to be unintelligible to the mob, it remained for some simpler soul like myself to translate his monads and his universal substance, as he called the Life Force, into fables which, however farfetched, can at least interest, amuse, and perhaps enlighten those capable of such entertainment, but baffled by Leibnitz's algebraic symbols and his philosophic jargon.

Here I must warn you that you can make no greater mistake in your social thinking than to assume, as too many do, that persons with the rarest mental gifts or specific talents are in other respects superior beings. The Life Force, when it gives some needed extraordinary quality to some individual, does not bother about his or her morals. It may even, when some feat is required which a human being can perform only after drinking a pint of brandy, make him a dipsomaniac, like [Shakespearean actor] Edmund Kean [1787–1833], [comic actor Frederick] Robson [1821–64], and Dickens on his last American tour. Or, needing a woman capable of bearing first rate children, it may endow her with enchanting sexual attraction yet leave her destitute of the qualities that make married life with her bearable. Apparently its aim is always the attainment of power over circumstances and matter through science, and is to this extent benevolent; but outside this bias it is quite unscrupulous, and lets its agents be equally so. Geniuses are often spendthrifts, drunkards, libertines, liars, dishonest in money matters, backsliders of all sorts, whilst many simple credulous souls are models of integrity and piety, high in the calendar of saints. [...]

Satanic Solution of the Problem of Evil

A difficulty was raised by the fact that evil was in the world as well as good, and often triumphed over the good. Consequently there must be a devil as well as a divinity. Poochlihoochli as well as Hoochlipoochli, [the Zoroastrian deities] Ahriman [darkness] as well as Ormuzd [light], Lucifer, Beelzebub [two of the seven princes of Hell, according to Christian demonology] and [the demonic] Apollyon [whom Christian combats and overcomes in *Pilgrim's Progress*] as well as the Holy Trinity, the Scarlet Woman [in Revelation 17] as well as Our Lady: in short as many demons as saints.

At first, however, this setting up against God of a rival deity with a contrary ideology was resented as a Manichean heresy, because plague, pestilence and famine, battle, murder and sudden death, were not regarded with horror as the work of Shelley's Almighty Fiend, but with Awe as evidence of the terrible greatness of God, the fear of him being placed to his credit as the beginning of wisdom. The invention of Satan is a heroic advance on Jahvism. It is an attempt to solve the Problem of Evil, and at least faces the fact that evil is evil.

Thus the world, as we imagine it, is crowded with anthropomorphic supernatural beings of whose existence there is no scientific proof. None the less, without such belief the human race cannot be civilized and governed, though the ten per cent or so of persons mentally capable of civilizing and governing are mostly too clever to be imposed on by fairy tales, and in any case have to deal with hard facts as well as fancies and fictions.

Mendacity Compulsory in Kingcraft and Priestcraft

This lands them in the quaintest moral dilemmas. It drives them to falsehoods, hypocrisies, and forgeries most distressing to their intellectual consciences. When the people demand miracles, worship relics, and will not obey any authority that does not supply them, the priest must create and nourish their faith by liquefying the blood of [martyred Bishop of Naples] Saint Januarius [d. 305], and saying Mass over a jawbone labeled as that of [Portuguese Franciscan] Saint Anthony of Padua [1195–1231]. When the people believe that the earth is flat, immovable, and the centre of the universe, and Copernicus and Leonardo convince both Galileo the scientist and the Vatican that the earth is a planet of the sun, the Pope and the cardinals have to make Galileo recant and pretend that he believes what the people believe, because, if the Church admits that it has ever been mistaken, its whole authority will collapse, and civilization perish in anarchy. If Joshua could not make the sun stand still, there is a blunder in the Bible. When the Protestants blew the gaff to discredit the Vatican, and the secret could no longer be kept by forbidding Catholics to read the Bible, the people were not logical enough to draw subversive inferences. They swallowed the contradiction cheerfully.

Meanwhile the people had to be threatened with a posthumous eternity in a brimstone hell if they behaved in an uncivilized way. As burning brimstone could not hurt a spirit, they had to be assured that their bodies would be resurrected on a great Day of Judgment. But the official translators of the Bible in England were presently staggered by a passage in the Book of Job, in which that prophet declared that as worms would destroy his body, in the flesh he should not see God. Such a heresy, if published, would knock the keystone out of the arch of British civilization. There was nothing for it but to alter the word of God, making Job say that though worms would destroy his body yet in his flesh he should see God. The facts made this forgery necessary; but it was a forgery all the same.

A later difficulty was more easily got over. The apostles were Communists so Red that St Peter actually struck a man and his wife dead for keeping back money from the common stock. The translators could not pretend that St Peter was a disciple of the unborn Adam Smith rather than of Jesus; so they let the narrative stand, but taught that Ananias and Sapphira were executed for telling a lie and not for any economic misdemeanor. This view was impressed on me in my childhood. I now regard it as a much graver lie than that of Ananias.

"The lie" said [German jurist and political activist] Ferdinand Lassalle [1825–64] "is a European Power." He might, however, have added that it is none the worse when it does a necessary job; for I myself have been a faker of miracles. Let me tell one of my old stories over again.

G. B. S. Miracle Faker

When I was a vestryman I had to check the accounts of the Public Health Committee. It was a simple process: I examined one in every ten or so of the receipted accounts and passed it whilst my fellow members did the same; and so enough of the accounts got checked to make their falsification too risky.

As it happened, one which I examined was for sulphur candles to disinfect houses in which cases of fever had occurred. I knew that experiments had proved that the fumes of burning sulphur had no such effect. Pathogenic bacilli like them and multiply on them.

I put the case to the Medical Officer of Health, and asked why the money of the ratepayers should be spent on a useless fumigant. He replied that the sulphur was not useless: it was necessary. But, I urged, the houses are not being disinfected at all. "Oh yes they are" he said. "How?" I persisted. "Soap and water and sunshine" he explained. "Then why sulphur?" "Because the strippers and cleaners will not venture into an infected house unless we make a horrible stink in it with burning sulphur."

I passed the account. It was presently equivalent to liquefying the blood of Saint Januarius.

Some twenty years later I wrote a play called *Saint Joan* in which I made the archbishop explain that a miracle is an event that creates faith, even if it is faked for that end. Had I not been a vulgar vestryman as well as a famous playwright I should not have thought of that. All playwrights should know that had I not suspended my artistic activity to write political treatises and work on political committees long enough to have written twenty plays, the Shavian idiosyncrasy which fascinates some of them (or used to) and disgusts the Art for Art's Sake faction [who believe that art should serve no didactic or moral function], would have missed half its value, such as it is.

Parental Dilemmas

The first and most intimate of the moral dilemmas that arise from differences in mental ability are not between classes and Churches, but in the daily work of bringing up children. The difference between Einstein and an average ploughman is less troublesome than the difference between children at five, at ten, and at fifteen. At five the Church catechism is only a paradigm: I learnt it at that age and still remember its phrases; but it had no effect on my conduct. I got no farther with it critically than to wonder why it obliged me, when asked what my name was, to reply that it was N or M, which was not true.

What did affect my conduct was my nurse's threat that if I was naughty or dirty the cock would come down the chimney. I confidently recommend this formula to all parents, nurses, and kindergarten teachers, as it effects its purpose and then dies a natural death, fading from the mind as the child grows out of it without leaving any psychic complexes.

But the same cannot be said for more complicated schemes of infant civilization. If they begin with [Anglican priest William] Law's [1686–1761] Serious Call [to a Devout and Holy Life (1728)], as many pious parents think they should, they may be worse than no scheme at all. I knew a man whose youth was made miserable by a dread of hell sedulously inculcated from his infancy. His reaction against it carried him into Socialism, whereupon he founded a Labor Church in which all the meetings began by calling on the speakers to pray: a demand which so took aback my Fabian colleagues that one of them began with "Heavenly Father: unaccustomed as I have been many years to address you, I *etc. etc.*" The Labor Church did not last; but the reaction did; and the last I heard of its founder was that he was helping the movement against Victorian prudery in a very practical way as a Nudist photographer, the basis of that prudery being the fact that the clothing, or rather upholstering, of Victorian women was much more aphrodisiac than their unadorned bodies.

As to the Socialist orator who parodied "Unaccustomed as I am to public speaking," he died in the bosom of the Roman Catholic Church.

I tell these anecdotes because they give an impression, better than any abstract argument could, of the way in which highly intelligent children of pious families, or of irreligious ones capable of nothing more intellectual than sport and sex, reacted against their bringing-up. One day, at a rehearsal of one of my plays, an actress who was a Roman Catholic consulted me in some distress because her adolescent son had become an atheist. I advised her not to worry; for as family religions have to be cast off as thoughtless habits before they can be replaced by genuine religious convictions, she might safely leave her son's case to God.

[British novelist] Edmund Gosse [1849–1928] was the son of a Plymouth Brother, and was baptized by total immersion, of which he wrote a highly entertaining description in his book called *Father and Son* [1907]. The immersion had washed all the father's pious credulity out of the son. [British novelist] George Eliot [1819–80], also piously brought up, began her reaction by translating [in 1846] Emil [*sic*] [German liberal Protestant theologian David Friedrich] Strauss's [1808–74] [*The*] *Life of Jesus* [*Critically Examined* (1835)], which divested the worshipped Redeemer of supernatural attributes, and even questioned the sanity of his pretension to them.

The All or Nothing Complex

In those days we were all what I called Soot or Whitewash merchants, pilloried as All or Nothings in Ibsen's *Brand*. When one link in our mental chain snapped we did not pick up the sound links and join them, we threw the chain away as if all its links had snapped. If the story of Noah's Ark was a fable, if Joshua could not have delayed the sunset in the Valley of Ajalon, if the big fish could not have swallowed Jonah nor he survive in its belly, then nothing in the Bible was true. If Jehovah was a barbarous tribal idol, irreconcilable with the God of Micah, then there was no God at all, and the heavens were empty. On the other hand if Galileo, the man of science, knew better than Joshua, and [Swedish botanist, zoologist and physician Carl] Linn[a]eus [1707–78] and Darwin better than Moses, then everything that scientists said was true. Thus the credulity that believed in the Garden of Eden with its talking serpent, and in the speeches of Balaam's ass, was not cured. It was simply transferred to Herbert Spencer and John Stuart Mill. The transfer was often for the worse, as when baptism by water and the spirit, consecrating the baptized as a soldier and a servant of the Highest, was replaced by the poisonous rite of vaccination on evidence that could not have imposed on any competent statistician, and was picked up by Jenner from a dairy farmer and his milkmaids.

Catholicism Impracticable

The lesson of this is that a totally Catholic Church or Communist State is an impossible simplification of social organization. It is contrary to natural history. No Church can reconcile and associate in common worship a Jehovah's Witness with William Blake, who called Jehovah Old Nobodaddy. [French Emperor] Napoleon [Bonaparte (1769–1821)], who pointed to the starry sky and asked "Who made all that?" did not kneel beside those who replied that it made itself, or retorted "We don't know: and neither do you." I, as a Creative Evolutionist, postulate a creative Life Force or Evolutionary Appetite seeing power over circumstances and mental development by the method of Trial and Error, making mistake after mistake, but still winning its finally irresistible way. Where in the world is there a Church that will receive me on such terms, or into which I could honestly consent to be received? There are Shaw Societies; but they are not Catholic Churches in pretence, much less in reality. And this is exactly as it should be, because, as human mental capacity varies from grade to grade, those who cannot find a creed which fits their grade have no established creed at all, and are ungovernable unless they are naturally amiable Vicars of Bray supporting any government that is for the moment established. There are hosts of such creedless voters, acting strongly as a conservative force, and usefully stabilizing government as such. But they make reforms very difficult sometimes.

The Tares and the Wheat

I therefore appreciate the wisdom of Jesus's warning to his missionaries that if they tore up the weeds they would tear up the wheat as well, meaning that if they tried to substitute his gospel for that of Moses instead of pouring the new wine into the old bottles (forgive the Biblical change of metaphor) nothing would be left of either Jesus or Moses. As I put it, the conversion of savagery to Christianity is the conversion of Christianity to savagery.

This is as true as ever. Not only are the immediate black converts of our missionaries inferior in character both to the unconverted and the born converted, but all the established religions in the world are deeply corrupted by the necessity for adapting their original inspired philosophic creeds to the narrow intelligences of illiterate peasants and of children. Eight thousand years ago religion was carried to the utmost reach of the human mind by the Indian Jainists, who renounced idolatry and blood sacrifice long before Micah, and repudiated every pretence to know the will of God, forbidding even the mention of his name in the magnificent temples they built for their faith.

But go into a Jainist temple today: what do you find? Idols everywhere. Not even anthropomorphic idols but horse idols, cat idols, elephant idols and what not? The statues of the Jainist sages and saints, far from being contemplated as great seers, are worshipped as gods.

The Thirtynine Articles

For such examples it is not necessary to travel to Bombay. The articles of the Church of England begin with the fundamental truth that God has neither body, parts, nor passions, yet presently enjoin the acceptance as divine revelation of a document alleging that God exhibited his hind quarters to one of the prophets, and when he had resolved to destroy the human race as one of his mistakes, was induced to make an exception in the case of Noah and his family by a bribe of roast meat. Later articles instruct us to love our fellow-creatures, yet to obey an injunction to hold accursed all who do good works otherwise than in the name of Christ, such works being sinful. In one article it is at first assumed that the swallowing of a consecrated wafer is only the heathen rite of eating the god (transubstantiation) and as such abominable, and then that it is holy as a memorial of the last recorded supper of Jesus. No man can be ordained a minister of the Church of England unless he swears without any mental reservation that he believes these contradictions. I once held lightly that candidates of irresistible vocation might swear this blamelessly because they were under duress. But one day I was present at the induction of a rector. When the bishop asked the postulant to tell a flat lie which both of them knew to be a lie, and he told it without a blush, the impression made on me was so shocking that I have felt ever since that the Church of England must revise its articles at all hazards if it is to be credited with the intellectual honesty necessary to its influence and authority. Shake that authority, and church-going will be nothing more than parading in our best clothes every Sunday.

A Hundred Religions and Only One Sauce

As it is, Christianity has split into sects, persuasions, and Nonconformities in all directions. The Statesman's Year-Book [first published in 1864 and listing political and social data on the countries of the world] has given up trying to list them. They range from Pillars of Fire, Jehovah's Witnesses, Plymouth Brothers, and [the Christian sect founded c. 1730 in Scotland by John Glas (1695–1773), the] Glasites, to Presbyterians, Methodists, Congregationalists [who govern their own independent, ecclesiastically sovereign congregations], Baptists [who preach salvation through Scripture alone], Friends (Quakers), and Unitarians. Within the Established Church itself there are Ritualists, Anglo-Catholics who call their services Masses and never mention the Reformation, Laodicean Broad Churchmen, and Low Church Protestants. The Friends abhor ritual and dictated prayers, and repudiate cathedral services and Masses as playacting, whilst the Anglo-Catholics cannot think religiously without them. Presbyterians and Congregationalists differ from the clergy of the Established Church on the political issue of episcopal or lay Church government. The Unitarians reject the Trinity and deny deity to Jesus. Calvinists deny universal atonement, preached by our missionaries, who are practically all independents.

Common to these irreconcilable faiths is the pretension that each is the true Catholic Church, and should hand over all whom it cannot convert to the State (the Secular Arm) to be exterminated for the crime of heresy by the cruelest possible methods, even to burning alive. This does not mean that all rulers who order such extermination are horribly cruel. "Bloody Mary" [Queen Mary I (1516–1558), so called because of her execution of numerous Protestants] believed that heretics must be liquidated; but she was not responsible for the political circumstance that the secular criminal law was atrociously cruel, and that no other agency could effect the liquidation. Calvin agreed that [Spanish theologian and physician Michael] Servetus [c. 1509–53] must be killed [as a heretic for denying the dogma of the Trinity]; but he objected humanely to his being burned [which he was]. [King] Charles II [1630–85], humane (indeed, as some think, too humane in his kindness to his dozen dogs and half dozen mistresses), could not question the necessity for punishing the Regicides with death; but he loathed the butchering of them in the hideous manner ordained centuries earlier for the punishment [by Edward I of England] of [Scottish knight Sir] William Wallace [who was hanged, drawn, and quartered for high treason in 1305], and stopped it as soon as he dared. It was still unrepealed during my own lifetime; and has only just (1948) been repealed in Scotland.

So far I have not been imprisoned, as poorer men have been in my time, for blasphemy or apostasy. I am not technically an apostate, as I have never been confirmed; and my godparents are dead. But having torn some of the Thirtynine Articles to rags, I should have been pilloried and had my ears cropped had I lived in the days of the British Inquisition called the Star Chamber [the court of law (late 1500s–c. 1641) which sat at the Palace of Westminster, where witnesses and defendants were examined in secret]. Nowadays Nonconformity and Agnosticism are far too powerful electorally for such persecution. But the Blasphemy Laws are still available and in use against obscure sceptics, whilst I suffer nothing worse than incessant attempts to convert me. All the religions and their sects, Christian or Moslem, Buddhist or Shinto, Jain or Jew, call me to repentance, and ask me for subscriptions. I am not so bigoted as to dismiss their experience as the inventions of liars and the fancies of noodles. They are evidence like any other human evidence; and they force me to the conclusion that every grade of human intelligence can be civilized by providing it with a frame of reference peculiar to its mental capacity, and called a religion.

Sources and Further Reading

[For comprehensive and up-to-date bibliographies and other important research aids for work on Bernard Shaw in electronic and print forms, see the Research Aids section on the website of the International Shaw Society: www.shawsociety.org. The selection here focuses on Shaw's religious interests and activities.]

Bibiliography

Carpenter, Charles A. "Shaw and Religion/Philosophy: A Working Bibliography." In Charles A. Berst, ed., *SHAW: The Annual of Bernard Shaw Studies. Volume 1. Shaw and Religion.* University Park and London: Pennsylvania State University Press, 1981, 225–46.

Autobiography

An Autobiography. Selected From His Writings by Stanley Weintraub. 2 vols. New York: Weybright and Talley, 1970.

The Diaries 1885–1897. Ed. Stanley Weintraub. 2 vols. University Park: Pennsylvania State University Press, 1986.

Sixteen Self Sketches. London: Constable, 1949.

Biography

Gibbs, A. M. *Bernard Shaw: A Life.* Gainesville: University Press of Florida, 2005.

———. *A Bernard Shaw Chronology.* Basingstoke: Palgrave, 2001.

Holroyd, Michael. *Bernard Shaw.* 5 vols. London: Chatto & Windus, 1988–92.

Letters

Agitations. Letters to the Press 1875–1950. Eds. Dan H. Laurence and James Rambeau. New York: Frederick Ungar, 1985.

Bernard Shaw: Collected Letters. Ed. Dan H. Laurence. 4 vols. New York: Viking Penguin, 1965–88.

Selected Correspondence of Bernard Shaw. Series Editors J. Percy Smith and L. W. Conolly. Toronto: University of Toronto Press, 1995– [ongoing]. *Bernard Shaw Theatrics*, ed. Dan H. Laurence, 1995; *Bernard Shaw and H. G. Wells*, ed. J. Percy Smith, 1995; *Bernard Shaw and Gabriel Pascal*, ed. Bernard F. Dukore, 1996; *Bernard Shaw and Barry Jackson*, ed. L. W. Conolly, 2002; *Bernard Shaw and the Webbs*, eds. Alex C. Michalos and Deborah C. Poff, 2002; *Bernard Shaw and Nancy Astor*, ed. J. P. Wearing, 2005; *Bernard Shaw and His Publishers*, ed. Michel W. Pharand, 2009; *Bernard Shaw and Gilbert Murray*, ed. Charles A. Carpenter, 2014.

Plays And Prefaces

The Bodley Head Bernard Shaw. Collected Plays With their Prefaces. Under the editorial supervision of Dan H. Laurence. 7 vols. London: Max Reinhardt, the Bodley Head, 1970–74.

Collected Religious Essays

Smith, Warren Sylvester, ed. *The Religious Speeches of Bernard Shaw.* University Park: Pennsylvania State University Press, 1963.

— — —, ed. *Shaw on Religion.* London: Constable, 1967.

Criticism

Abbott, Anthony S. *Shaw and Christianity.* New York: Seabury, 1965.

Adam, Ruth. "About God." *What Shaw Really Said.* London: Macdonald, 1966, 21–36.

Appasamy, S. P. "God, Mammon and Bernard Shaw." *Commonwealth Quarterly* 2.7 (1978): 98–112.

Baker, Stuart E. *Bernard Shaw's Remarkable Religion: A Faith That Fits the Facts*. Gainesville: University Press of Florida, 2002.

Barr, Alan P. *Victorian Stage Pulpiteer: Bernard Shaw's Crusade*. Athens: University of Georgia Press, 1973.

Bentley, Eric. "The Fool in Christ." *Bernard Shaw 1856–1950*. 1947. Rev. ed. New York: New Directions, 1957, 183–219.

Berst, Charles A. "Androcles and the Lion: Christianity in Parable." *Bernard Shaw and the Art of Drama*. Urbana: University of Illinois Press, 1973, 175–95.

———, ed. *SHAW: The Annual of Bernard Shaw Studies. Volume 1. Shaw and Religion*. University Park and London: Pennsylvania State University Press, 1981.

Braybrooke, Patrick. "Bernard Shaw and Christianity." *The Subtlety of George Bernard Shaw*. London: Cecil Palmer, 1930, 135–60.

Brown, G. E. "The Religious Plays." *George Bernard Shaw*. London: Evans Brothers, 1970, 66–92.

Brown, Ivor. "Things Believed." *Shaw in His Time*. London: Nelson, 1965, 165–81.

Carpenter, Charles A. "Shaw's Ethical Aims." *Bernard Shaw & the Art of Destroying Ideals: The Early Plays*. Madison: University of Wisconsin Press, 1969, 9–13.

Chesterton, G. K. "The Puritan." *George Bernard Shaw*. London: Bodley Head, 1909, 24–43.

Collis, John S. "Divination: God: The Divinity that Shapes Our Ends: Shaw's Message to Normal Man." *Shaw*. London: Jonathan Cape, 1925, 41–49.

Corrigan, Felicitas. *The Nun, the Infidel, and the Superman: The Remarkable Friendships of Dame Laurentia McLachlan with Sydney Cockerell, Bernard Shaw and Others*. Chicago: University of Chicago Press, 1985.

Deane, Barbara. "Shaw and Gnosticism." *Shaw Review* 16 (1973): 104–22.

Demaray, John G. "Bernard Shaw and C. E. M. Joad: The Adventures of Two Puritans in Their Search for God." *PMLA* 78 (1963): 262–70.

Donaghy, Henry J. "Chesterton on Shaw's Views of Catholicism." *Shaw Review* 10 (1967): 108–16.

Duffin, Henry C. "Religious Matters." *The Quintessence of Bernard Shaw*. London: Allen & Unwin, 1920, 148–74. (See also "Immorality and Heresy," 35–61.)

Dunkel, Wilbur Dwight. "Bernard Shaw's Religious Faith." *Theology Today* 6 (1949): 369–76.

Ervine, St. John. "The Shavian Belief." *Yale Review* 18 (1928): 290–301.

Frank, Joseph. "*Major Barbara*: Shaw's 'Divine Comedy.'" *PMLA* 71 (1956): 61–74.

Ganter, Annika. "Shavian Religion in *Captain Brassbound's Conversion* and *St Joan*." *The Shavian* 10.7 (2008): 2–13.

Hackett, J. P. *Shaw: George Versus Bernard*. London: Sheed & Ward, 1937. (Especially 27–45 and 136–66; Roman Catholic point of view.)

Hugo, Leon H. *Bernard Shaw's "The Black Girl in Search of God": The Story Behind the Story*. Gainesville: University Press of Florida, 2003.

Inge, William R. "Shaw as a Theologian." In Stephen Winsten, ed., *G. B. S. 90: Aspects of Bernard Shaw's Life and Work*. London: Hutchinson, 1946, 110–21.

Leary, Daniel J., and Richard Foster. "Adam and Eve: Evolving Archetypes in *Back to Methuselah*." *Shaw Review* 4.2 (1961): 12–23, 25.

Lindblad, Ishrat. "George Bernard Shaw." *Catholic World* 102 (1916): 768–80.

McKinley, R. D. "George Bernard Shaw and the Atonement." *Dalhousie Review* 46 (1966): 112–19.

Meisel, Martin. "Christian Melodrama and Christmas Pantomime." *Shaw and the Nineteenth-Century Theatre*. Princeton: Princeton University Press, 1963, 324–48.

Minney, R. J. "Shaw and Religion." *Recollections of George Bernard Shaw*. Englewood Cliffs, NJ: Prentice-Hall, 1969, 81–93.

Nathan, Rhoda B. "Bernard Shaw and the Inner Light." *Shaw Review* 14 (1971): 107–19.

Nelson, Raymond S. "The Church, the Stage, and Shaw." *Midwest Quarterly* 11 (1970): 293–308.

— — —. "Blanco Posnet—Adversary of God." *Modern Drama* 13 (1970): 1–9.

— — —. "*Back to Methuselah*: Shaw's Modern Bible." *Costerus* 5 (1972): 117–23.

— — —. "Shaw's Heaven, Hell, and Redemption." *Costerus* 6 (1972): 99–108.

— — —. "Shaw's Heaven and Hell." *Contemporary Review* 226 (1975): 132–36.

Oatridge, Norman C. *Bernard Shaw's God: An Anglican Looks at the Religion of GBS*. Haywards Heath: P. Smith, Boltro Press, 1967.

O'Donnell, Norbert. "Shaw, Bunyan, and Puritanism." *PMLA* 72 (1957): 520–33.

Rodríguez Martín, Gustavo A. "Shaw's Subversions of Biblical Language." In Marc Dipaolo, ed., *Godly Heretics: Essays on Alternative Christianity in Literature and Popular Culture*. Jefferson, NC: McFarland, 2013, 114–32.

Smith, Warren Sylvester. "Bernard Shaw and the Quakers." *Bulletin of the Friends Historical Association* 45 (1956): 106–18.

— — —. *Bishop of Everywhere: Bernard Shaw and the Life Force*. University Park and London: Pennsylvania State University Press, 1982.

Stone, Susan C. "Biblical Myth Shavianized." *Modern Drama* 18 (1975): 153–63.

Stoppel, Hans. "Shaw and Sainthood." *English Studies* 36 (1955): 49–63.

Turco, Alfred, Jr. *Shaw's Moral Vision: The Self and Salvation.* Ithaca, NY: Cornell University Press, 1976.

Wagenknecht, Edward. "Bernard Shaw's Religion." *A Guide to Bernard Shaw.* New York: Appleton, 1929, 69–85.

Watson, Barbara B. "Sainthood for Millionaires: *Major Barbara.*" *Modern Drama* 11 (1968): 227–44.

Weintraub, Rodelle. "Shaw's Jesus and Judas." *Shaw Review* 15 (1972), 81–83.

Weintraub, Stanley. "Shaw's Jesus and Judas: Passion Without 'Passion.'" *Who's Afraid of Bernard Shaw? Some Personalities in Shaw's Plays.* Gainesville: University Press of Florida, 2011, 1–16.

Whitehead, George. *Bernard Shaw Explained: A Critical Exposition of the Shavian Religion.* London: Watts, 1925.

Whitman, Robert F. *Shaw and the Play of Ideas.* Ithaca, NY: Cornell University Press, 1977.

Wood, Herbert G. "G. Bernard Shaw and Religion." *Contemporary Review* 123 (1923): 623–28.

Yorks, Samuel. "Shaw and Religion." *The Evolution of Bernard Shaw.* Washington: University Press of America, 1981, 127–53.

CPSIA information can be obtained
at www.ICGtesting.com
Printed in the USA
LVHW030011220520
656258LV00004B/1022